The NIRVANA Companion

The NIRVANA *Companion*

Two
Decades of
Commentary

A Chronicle of
the End of Punk

Edited by
JOHN ROCCO

Assistant Editor
BRIAN ROCCO

Foreword by
EVERETT TRUE

SCHIRMER BOOKS
An Imprint of
Simon & Schuster Macmillan
New York

Prentice Hall International
London Mexico City New Delhi Singapore Sydney
Toronto

Schirmer Books
An Imprint of Simon & Schuster Macmillan
1633 Broadway
New York, New York 10019

Library of Congress Catalog Number: 98-16171
Printed in the United States of America

Printing number
1 2 3 4 5 6 7 8 9 10

Library of Congress Cataloging-in-Publication Data

The Nirvana companion : two decades of commentary / edited by John Rocco ; assistant editor , Brian Rocco.
     p. cm.
    Discography : p.
    Includes bibliographical references (p.   ) and index.
    ISBN 0-02-864930-3
1. Nirvana (Musical group) 2. Rock musicians—United States—Biography. 3. Grunge music—United States—History and criticism. I. Rocco, John (John M.) II. Rocco, Brian.
ML421.N57N5 1998
782.42166'092'2
[B]—dc21   98-16171
                                               CIP
                                             MN

for Mary Clancy
I carry the sun in a golden cup,
The moon is a silver bag.

He could have shouted and could not.
                    —Samuel Beckett, "Assumption"

Nous vivons en enfants perdus nos aventures incompletes.
    —the last line of Guy Debord's *Hurlements en faveur de Sade*

Contents

Acknowledgments

My first thanks go to Richard Carlin for listening to me when I proposed this book; he was consistently supportive and patient. I also owe thanks to Sandra Sousa, Melanie Carroll, Andrew Libby, and everyone else at Schirmer Books who helped get the book into print.

Despite the fact that the Atlantic roared in silence between us, the music of Everett True's writing on Nirvana inspired every stage of this book. Without his work, this book would have been impossible. Without his writing, we would have understood much less about a band that has been consistently misunderstood.

David Fricke helped me get in touch with Everett, whose essay on the *Unplugged* performance demonstrates the critical sensitivity and intelligence that has made him one of our finest rock writers. Gillian G. Gaar not only let me reprint her spectacular article on Nirvana's recording history, but also hooked me up with Dawn Anderson. Dawn let me include her wonderful and groundbreaking words, and filled me in on the meaning of "fish beer," and she also sent me cool originals of *Backlash*.

My brother, Brian Rocco, gave me my first Nirvana album, and he helped me in every stage of this book. He did more than just assisting—he pushed and provoked and energized.

My sister, Mary Bridget Rocco, helped with everything and we owe her a big thanks filled with love.

As always, I owe Dana more than I can describe, so I steal: "Life's life and strikes my your our blossoming sphere."

Brian and I have dedicated this book to Mary Clancy because she has given us everything.

And one last thanks: thank you Nirvana.

Foreword

There's a photo—one photo—of Kurt that I really fucking hate. You must've seen it. Taken by an English photographer called Martyn Goodacre, it just shows Kurt up close, staring moodily into the camera, black eyeliner on, hair all scrawny—lighting perfect, make-up mussed up perfect, the whole tormented "rock star" schtick perfect. I can't fucking recognise him. It looks nothing like the Kurt Cobain I knew, presents such a one-dimensional, distorted picture of him . . . and it seems to've been everywhere since his death. Posters, T-shirts, calendars, tribute books. Everywhere. Each time I see it, I catch myself looking at it and thinking, "Is this the only way people remember Nirvana, as the backing band for a tormented moody fuck-up of an artist? Is this the only way people recognise Kurt Cobain—as the Axl Rose who never made it?"

I have nothing against Martyn Goodacre.

It's the lack of context I can't handle.

—Everett True

Introduction:
Nirvana at the End of History

What wonder, then, that the world goes from bad to worse, and that its evils increase more and more, as boredom increases, and boredom is the root of all evil.

The history of this can be traced from the beginning of the world. The gods were bored, and so they created man. Adam was bored because he was alone, and so Eve was created. Thus boredom entered the world, and increased in proportion to the increase of population. Adam was bored alone; then Adam and Eve were bored together; then Adam and Eve and Cain and Abel were bored *en famille*; then the population of the world increased, and the peoples were bored *en masse*. To divert themselves they conceived the idea of constructing a tower high enough to reach the heavens. This idea is itself as boring as the tower was high, and constitutes a terrible proof of how boredom gained the upper hand.

—Søren Kierkegaard, *Either/Or: A Fragment of Life* (translated by David F. Swenson, Lillian Marvin Swenson, and Walter Lowie)

History, Stephen said, is a nightmare from which I am trying to awake.

—James Joyce, *Ulysses*

The blood-dimmed tide is loosed and everywhere history ends with bangs and whimpers. Big bangs, really BIG bangs, and this is our story. To keep from being bored, we invented big bangs called music. To keep from getting bored of music, we invented rock 'n' roll. To keep from getting bored of rock 'n' roll, we invented punk. To keep from getting bored of punk, we ended history. The last battle of the bands takes place to keep away the boredom, and everywhere the ceremony of innocence is drowned in noise. (As the lake of fire covers Arizona, the Meat Puppets sing "We Don't Exist.") The worst are full of money while the best lack bottle openers. Brimstone and beer. Plague. The Pixies are taken away by flaming, screaming spaceships. Apocalypse. Earthquakes. Zombies. (Remember Roger's fate in *Dawn of the Dead*—don't lose it and get bitten.) The end of millions. Kill millions. Frances Farmer comes back as fire, rips the Space Needle from the earth, and beats the shit out of Seattle with it. The West has declined. Declined to answer. Declined to exist. The end.

History—the big stories, the master narratives—is over. Now we live in the soft afterglow of MTV transmitting the same images and the same sounds over and over and over again. The repetition soothes us, moves us toward sleep. But before sleep we have a moment in the half-light, half-quiet to think of that other world we once knew. This is postmodernism—post, after, beyond—what came before. Things are only references of other things; songs are other songs; paintings are no more. In this afterworld we have this time to read these pages and remember one of the endings of history. It woke us up for some time and kept the images and the sounds unsteady, almost as if they were about to crack open and reveal the Wizard behind the machine. A denial.

The beginning of this end began in a place where nothing has ever happened. But the small town of Aberdeen, Washington, is not unique in this regard—nothing has happened all over America. But something did happen in Aberdeen, and it wasn't just the death of many trees and the firing of guns in broad nightlight, or the donning of flannel, or the emptying of beer pitchers. Kurt Cobain and Krist Novoselic happened to Aberdeen. (The Melvins also happened to Aberdeen, but more on them later.) Native sons—Krist's family moved there in 1979, so he's not quite native but close enough—they lived and grew surrounded by depression, stumps, and rednecks. Native sons, they left Aberdeen for the world but, like the trees that had grown all around them, their roots lie there, deep and silent. Well, maybe not silent: maybe loud, maybe in a cassette tape containing noise Kurt made with Dale Crover of the Melvins. As Krist told Everett True, he heard the tape and "I thought it was really cool, so I said to start this band." Krist heard Kurt's tape in 1986; Kurt was nineteen, Krist was twenty-one, and America was 210. Dave Grohl, who then lived on the other coast, was seventeen.) Napoleon once said that the only way to know a man is to know what the world was like when he was twenty years old. Above-ground America in 1986 was a place where Ronald Reagan ruled, the Cold War raged on, and bands like Warrant, Whitesnake, and Van Halen packed stadiums, the airwaves, and MTV, which was just five years old back then. However, as Berlin had its twilight world of thieves and beggars in Fritz Lang's M, America had an underground where something dark, vital, and unsafe endured and prospered in the 1980s.

The history of underground music in America is an uneven chronicle of eruptions and lulls, of stunning creation and deafening absence. To approach it we must go where it lives—deep underground, as deep as Hell. In Dante's *Inferno,* Hell is depicted as the exact opposite of the perfection of Heaven. Thus, in contrast to the omnipotence of Dante's God, Dante's Satan is an impotent, three-faced idiot forever crying and chewing on the heads of the world's most infamous traitors. In contrast to the warmth of divine Heaven, the lowest circle of Hell is a lake of ice (which we "won't see again until the fourth of July"). Thus, the underground during Reagan's reign existed in exact and corresponding opposition to the mainstream—an inversion of the corporate Heaven where hits and bands were manufactured by record companies. It is no historical accident that MTV was born in 1981—it was the ultimate extension of corporate control over music because it created a new market and a new realm for mainstream music. In contrast to the monolithic Heaven of Reagan's America and its mainstream music, the 1980s music underground was diverse and fecund. In contrast to the seamless products of corporate rock and its new magic lantern called MTV, the underground fostered subgenres like hardcore (Black Flag, the Germs, the Dead Kennedys, X, Saccharine Trust, the Circle Jerks), melodic post-punk (the Minutemen, Hüsker Dü, the Pixies), and post–No-Wave, art rock (Sonic Youth, Einstürzende Neubauten, Pussy Galore). The contrast is the thing in which we can catch the conscience of the scene.

The underground in the 1980s had its own music, its own audience, and its own distribution system through independent labels like SST and Alternative Tentacles. After the initial rampages of American and British punk, the underground dug in and set itself in opposition to the mainstream world of art and politics. In 1979 Jello Biafra ran for mayor of the city that had given birth to the Summer of Love. He lost. In 1980 John Lennon was shot to death in New York. We lost. In 1980 Ronald Reagan became the president of the United States. He won.

In 1986 Reagan ruled and Krist listened to Kurt's tape. But Kurt's tape would not have existed without another tape that Buzz Osborne of the Melvins had made for Kurt two years earlier. As Kurt later recalled, this tape was his first exposure to punk rock. It featured Black Flag and Flipper, and it was a revelation for him. This revelation was combined with that other thing that happened to Aberdeen: the Melvins. To continue our Dante parallel, the Melvins were the dark, broke, wacko, unpopular, fallen angels of the 1980s. They took their name from a guy named Melvin who got caught stealing Christmas trees. They took their music from the 1970s: Kiss, Black Sabbath, Alice Cooper, and Ted Nugent. But they added punk intelligence, humor, and blatant energy to the music they took. They also added their own Aberdeen insanity. (In Dante's *Inferno*, sinners are punished according to the sins they committed while alive. In the Hell of Aberdeen, the Melvins whipped themselves with the thick chords and sludgy tempos of 1970s metal.) The Melvins' combination of metal, punk, and hardcore produced what is now called grunge. Kurt Cobain was fascinated by the Melvins: they opened a door in the wall of music for him. He once auditioned to be a member of the band (he didn't cut it) and was a long-suffering and happy roadie for them.

In 1986 Reagan reigned and Kurt and Krist started to play music together. The early names for the band were Fecal Matter, Ted Ed Fred, Bliss, Skid Row, Throat Oyster, and Pen Cap Chew. In 1988 they record-ed a demo at Reciprocal Studios with Dale Crover on drums. They were incredibly lucky to have Jack Endino in charge of the recording. Endino would later become known as the "godfather of grunge" for his role in recording the seminal bands of the area and for producing the first grunge compilation, *Deep Six*, in 1985. Endino was so impressed with the demo—which cost $152.44 to make—that he passed along a copy to Jonathan Poneman (or was it Bruce Pavitt?) of Sub Pop. Sub Pop was the independent label that promoted and packaged the music we have come to call grunge.

The last year of Reagan in the White House was 1988. As the French philosopher Jean Baudrillard describes it, Reagan's reign was a rule of illusion:

> In the image of Reagan, the whole of America has become Californian. Ex-actor and ex-governor of California that he is, he has worked up his euphoric, cinematic, extroverted, advertising vision of the artificial paradis-es of the West to all-American dimensions. He has introduced a system where the easy life exerts a kind of blackmail, reviving the original American pact of an achieved utopia. . . . This too is entirely Californian, for in reality it is not always sunny in California. You often get fog with the sun, or smog in Los Angeles. And yet you retain a sun-filled memory of the place, a sunny screen memory. This is what the Reagan mirage is like.[1]

It is the heavenly illusion of the 1980s that the underground pushed against, and it was Nirvana who finally broke through the mirrors and smoke. This break coincided with a TV war.

---

1. Jean Baudrillard, *America*, trans. Chris Turner (London and New York: Verso, 1988).

Men make their own history, but they do not make it just as they please; they do not make it under circumstances chosen by themselves, but under circumstances directly found, given and transmitted from the past. The tradition of all the dead generations weighs like a nightmare on the brain of the living.

—Karl Marx, *The Eighteenth Brumarie of Louis Bonaparte*

It's the end of the world!

—the drunk guy in Alfred Hitchcock's *The Birds*

In 1991 Nirvana left Sub Pop and signed with a major label, Geffen/DGC. They recorded and released *Nevermind* and went on tour throughout Europe with Sonic Youth. This tour was chronicled in the film *1991: The Year That Punk Broke,* a title Thurston Moore of Sonic Youth thought of to describe the growing and ambiguous force of punk in the mainstream (punk "broke" upon the world or "broke" apart). Something else broke in 1991: war. As Douglas Kellner puts it in *The Persian Gulf TV War,* it was no coincidence that the Gulf War began at 6:40 on January 16, 1991: "Because the Persian Gulf War was perhaps the first war ever orchestrated for television, it was appropriate that it broke out during the primetime television news." The bombs started to drop during prime time and they continued to be dropped on television until February 27, when Bush announced that the greatest air bombardment since World War II was over. So was the Gulf War. The dominating images from the TV were the images from the "smart" bombs hitting their targets. This recurring image—this hyperspace technowar—was the symbol of the war that was created by the Bush administration and propagated by the mass media. It was also, as Kellner describes it, a huge deception:

The illusion was projected that only machines and not people were involved in the new high-tech warfare, which was bloodless and antiseptic. The targets of the released footage were always ugly buildings, usually serving military functions. The austere buildings were seemingly always deserted, devoid of humans, so the bombing was coded as a positive surgical operation that was removing methodically the instruments of Iraqi war—medical discourse and imagery of clean surgery removing evil disease. This image proved to be quite untrue, yet the constant replaying of these tapes, and their power to produce images of a clean and precise technowar, created the impression that the military desired. Only after the war were figures released showing that most of the bombs dropped were not "smart" computer and laser guided bombs. Instead, most of the bombs missed their targets altogether and even the so-called smart bombs often produced a lot of dumb "collateral" destruction.[2]

A year later, another war raged on television, but not on CNN. This war was fought on MTV. The video for "Smells Like Teen Spirit" was played around the clock.

To this day nobody knows how it happened. At the beginning of 1992 *Nevermind* became the number one album on the *Billboard* charts. It did this by doing the impossible: a punk record climbed over U2, Guns N' Roses, Garth Brooks, and, in the most unlikely move of all, toppled Michael Jackson from the number-one spot. Thurston Moore summed up this event laconically: "Things led up to them being in the right place at the right time with the right record." *Nevermind*—a *punk* record—went on to sell over thirteen million copies. The underground was no longer underground. The underground was on Top-40 radio, on *Saturday Night Live*, and all over MTV. The dark, inverted, perverted image of Reagan-Bush America became the accepted image of mainstream America. Nothing like this had ever happened before. Punk had never been a mass market product before—it had never been consumed on this scale. This was astounding because punk, by its very nature, was always the opposite of the mainstream: a shout in the wilderness of pop culture. However, as Greil Marcus defines it, punk embodies a power to change not only music, but the world it is directed against:

> Punk was a new music, a new social critique, but most of all it was a new kind of free speech. It inaugurated a moment—a long moment, which still persists—when suddenly countless odd voices, voices no reasonable person could have expected to hear in public, were being heard all over the place: sometimes as monstrous shouts in the marketplace, sometimes as whispers from an alleyway. There was an absolute denial of self-censorship in the Sex Pistols' songs that gave people who heard them permission to speak as freely. If an ugly, hunched-over twenty-year-old could stand up, name himself an antichrist, and make you wonder if it wasn't true, then anything was possible.[3]

2. Douglas Kellner, *The Persian Gulf TV War* (Boulder and Oxford: Westview Press, 1992).

3. Greil Marcus, *Ranters and Crowd Pleasers: Punk in Pop Music, 1977–1992* (New York: Doubleday, 1993).

And this is what punk reached with the music of Nirvana. It reached a level where it represented, for a time at least, the *only* "monstrous shouts in the marketplace." Nirvana reached the impossible.

Nirvana broke open the gates of Heaven and admitted the underground into the mainstream. The band was as shocked as anybody by their success—Geffen/DGC was even more shocked at the fifty million dollars they eventually made from *Nevermind*. At first Nirvana seemed to see nothing constructive in their sudden and gargantuan success. All they saw ahead were bigger and bigger shows, arenas piled on top of arenas, and mounds of frat boys moshing on mounds of frat boys. They had become the thing they hated—successful corporate rock stars. But even when all their popularity seemed to be out of control and when the band itself was threatened by internal problems, Nirvana always saw itself as a kind of frontier scout in the alien territory of pop culture. They realized that they had the power to create openings for other underground bands. From their earliest interviews to their last public appearances, Nirvana ceaselessly supported the work of bands as popular as the Meat Puppets— Nirvana shared their *MTV Unplugged* session with Curt and Cris Kirkwood—and as obscure as Flipper, Bikini Kill, and the band who started it all, the Melvins. Nirvana's advocacy of these bands exposed kids whose normal musical tastes centered on corporate giants like Guns N' Roses and Bryan Adams to underground sounds. In this regard, Nirvana made the world safe for the rebellion of underground music—commercial rock was revealed as the constructed and manipulated commodity that it is. Through their conquering of the charts, Nirvana injected something of real artistic value into the mainstream, changed the market, and challenged our conceptions of popular music.

Nirvana's success had its price, which is one of the stories told in the pages of this book. The "smart" bombs that fell on Baghdad only seemed to fall on buildings that were empty of people; the video bombs of MTV also seemed to fall on an empty building—the quintessential spoiled rock band. But there were people inside Nirvana.

The sudden fame was electrifyingly bizarre for the members of Nirvana, primarily because they saw themselves trapped in a strange position. As cultural giants, they wielded immense commercial power and constantly had the attention of the mass media. But at the exact same time that they ruled the charts, minds, and emotions of America, they were cabined, cribbed, confined by the same force that made them popular. Every move was scrutinized by the press. And this all happened with stunning quickness.

By the time the *MTV Video Music Awards* came around in 1992, Nirvana was the biggest band in the world. But this did not mean that they had any choice about whether or not to perform on the awards show. They were compelled to perform because MTV threatened to boycott all bands under Gold Mountain, Nirvana's management company. This would have hurt the people who had supported Nirvana since they left Sub Pop. And when they finally agreed to play, they decided to perform "Rape Me," from their forthcoming album *In Utero*. MTV did not appreciate this choice—primarily because of the title—and they demanded that Nirvana perform one of the popular numbers from *Nevermind*. The biggest band in the world was bullied into playing "Lithium," but they scared the programming people by opening with the beginning of "Rape Me" before segueing into "Lithium." At the end of the song Krist threw his bass into the air and missed catching it—it landed on his head and knocked him to the stage. He had to crawl off.

When they won the award for Best Alternative Video, Nirvana sent a Michael Jackson impersonator up to the podium to accept it. The impersonator called himself the "King of Grunge" and delivered a rambling speech to an audience who watched in silent puzzlement. They did not get the joke. Kurt later explained, "I wanted it to be used as a reminder that I'm dealing with the same thing." The "thing" was uncontrollable fame. But no one got it that night because the fame machine is too powerful for one little punk prank to bring it down. The medium is the message.

Nirvana's use of a Michael Jackson impersonator to accept their award was an attempt to turn back the gaze of MTV onto itself; it was a joke but it was also an attempt to make a serious statement. Punk has always turned ideas and forms back upon themselves—the "peace and love" of the 1960s turned against itself to become the anger and energy of early punk (The Stooges' "I Wanna Be Your Dog" is a *love* song); the business of rock turned into the Sex Pistols signing a huge record contract in front of Buckingham Palace. As Greil Marcus points out, punk follows in a tradition of "intellectual terrorism" that derived one of its motivations from Guy Debord and the Situationist International, a group of anti-artists who attempted to turn established cultural forms against themselves. They did this through a process they called *détournement,* or what Debord described as "the *reversal* of established relationships between concepts and by the diversion . . . of all the attainments of earlier critical efforts."[4] In other words, they turned things on their heads.

---

4. Guy Debord, *The Society of the Spectacle*, trans. Donald Nicholson-Smith (New York: Zone Books, 1994).

(Debord once had one of his books published with a sandpaper cover—
it was an "anti-book" that would destroy any other books it came into
contact with.) This idea of reversal was a punk weapon—the Ramones
used it when they pointed their restricted lyrics ("Gabba Gabba Hey!")
against the bloated sentimentality of mainstream rock; the Sex Pistols did
it with the art work of Jamie Reid and the embrace of the Great Rock 'n'
Roll Swindle; and Sonic Youth did it when they renamed themselves
Ciccone Youth to cover Madonna and Robert Palmer's "Addicted to
Love" on a record called *The Whitey Album*. The entire Riot Grrrl movement is a turning back of male-centered rock upon itself, upon its own
energy and preoccupations.

Détournement is used effectively—and faithfully with respect to
Debord's conception of the term—by the artist Raymond Pettibone.
Pettibone was associated with SST and he drew many of the album covers
issued by the independent label. His work is indicative of the overall reac-
tion/critique of the mainstream given by the underground in the 1980s. As
Kim Gordon of Sonic Youth describes it, Pettibone feeds off images of the
mainstream in order to deconstruct them and send them back as ideolog-
ical time bombs to those who created them:

> Wandering outside the realm of the art world and attached to a music
> subculture, Pettibone can depict a wider range of subject matter than is
> considered appropriate or even possible within the avant-garde of the art
> world, because of the inhibiting values that prevail in that system. . . . The
> drawings feed off the simplistic morals of made-for-TV movies, which
> center around "contemporary" questions. Pettibone doesn't feel that the
> themes of the drawings are his inventions. They are meant to be clichés,
> unconscious scenes or situations which have appeared before.[5]

Pettibone did the cover for Sonic Youth's major-label debut, *Goo*. It featured a beatnik couple in a car wearing sunglasses with the caption: "I
stole my sister's boyfriend. It was all whirlwind, heat, and flash. Within a
week we killed my parents and hit the road.")

But the turning back of the MTV spectacle that Nirvana attempted at
the *Video Music Awards* in 1992 was not powerful enough to have much
effect. They could not turn against the mainstream because they *were* the
mainstream. To understand how Nirvana got into the position of being
the most famous punk band in the world—and of being trapped in their

---

5. Kim Gordon, "American Prayers," *Artforum* 23, no. 8 (April 1985): 73–77.

own fame—we must become unstuck in time, like Vonnegut's Billy Pilgrim, and leave 1992. We must become unstuck and leave MTV to watch another Television and another Hell.

> Television is abstract. It's a joke. History is a joke. Television and history are the centers of nothing. They are auras, like hair, available for styling twenty-four hours a day.
>
> —Richard Hell, *The Voidoid*

> The '60s manufactured an illusion of "here and now"; in the '80s truth passes into fiction and out again, history is recycled into the present without a context, and the present has become a leap of faith, as we sit back and enjoy the ultrafast life of MTV.
>
> —Kim Gordon, "American Prayers"

When the 1960s were ending two kids ended their normal lives and ran away from school. Their names were Tom Miller and Richard Meyer. They changed their names to Tom Verlaine and Richard Hell (reflecting Tom's interest in poetry and Richard's interest in Hell). These newly named entities then proceeded—in fits, returns to school, starts, menial jobs, stops, starts, pogoings, crashes, and more fits—to set the day on fire. Iggy Pop was the only one before them, but then everybody was after Iggy. In 1997 the Eagles and Fleetwood Mac were voted into the Rock 'n' Roll Hall of Fame, while Iggy and the Stooges remained outside. (Artaud was right: "It is idiotic to reproach the masses for having no sense of the sublime, when the sublime is confused with one or another of its formal manifestations, which are moreover always defunct manifestations."[6]) Their first band was called the Neon Boys, but then, continuing the movement into the electric light, they called themselves Television. They played their first show at CBGB's in New York City on March 13, 1974, around the same time that Patti Smith was drawn to the club. She had been performing her poetry with guitar accompaniment for several years. And it began: crazy people in love with words plug in guitars and beat the hell out of themselves, the stage, and the audience. And the Ramones came from Queens.

Let's follow the line. At the same time Television, the Ramones, and Patti Smith were playing CBGB's, Malcolm McLaren was managing the New York Dolls—actually trying to keep them together and, as a sec-

---

6. Antonin Artaud, *The Theater and Its Double*, trans. Mary Caroline Richards (New York: Grove Weidenfeld, 1958).

ondary consideration, attempting to keep them alive. But the Dolls had finished being the Dolls, and McLaren was struck by the intensity and energy of Smith and Television. Hell particularly fascinated McLaren because Hell reminded him of what rock had lost: the passion and energy of early 1950s rockers. But Hell had something else—with chopped hair, ripped clothes (the famous "Please Kill Me" T-shirt), and a basic fucked-up take on everything, he single-handedly made himself into the first punk. He based his appearance on an attempt to look like Arthur Rimbaud. (Interestingly, Lester Bangs thought he was a little too fucked up: "Did Dostoyevskey sit around mewling about I, I, I? . . . In spite of being one of the greatest rock 'n' rollers I have ever heard, you are full of shit."[7])

McLaren tried to lure Hell back to England. Hell stayed in America but left Television. He formed the Heartbreakers with ex-Dolls Jerry Nolan and Johnny Thunders, the Dean Martin of heroin. (This is the Nancy Spungen connection—from the New York Dolls to England to the Sex Pistols to Sid to back to New York to the Chelsea.) McLaren went back to the white cliffs of Dover and attempted to manufacture his own Hell. He chose kids who hung around his shop—discreetly called "Sex"—and outfitted them with the image he had seen in New York combined with the anti-art of the Situationist International. McLaren had the incredible good/bad luck of encountering a particularly unpleasant youth who had bad teeth, a Pink Floyd shirt with "I HATE" scrawled across it, weird staring eyes, bad manners, and bad everything. They called him Johnny Rotten. The band was called the Sex Pistols and all of their equipment was stolen. They became a household curse after appearing on television: Steve Jones said "fuck" on the air and the pillars of British society quickly proclaimed the end of civilization.

The Pistols were called fascists by the left and communists by the right. They were attacked in the streets. And it seemed that everyone in Britain who saw them started a band: the Clash, the Damned, the Buzzcocks, Siouxsie and the Banshees, the Slits, the Raincoats. Everybody hated them and everybody was changed by them.

The Sex Pistols performed their last show on January 14, 1978, at Winterland in San Francisco. That show has gone down in rock history as one of the worst performances of all time (it was also one of the only guitar-drum combos in music history—there was a bass on stage but you

---

7. Lester Bangs, "In Which Another Pompous Blowhard Purports to Possess the True Meaning of Punk Rock," in *The Penguin Book of Rock 'n' Roll Writing*, ed. Clinton Heylin (New York: Penguin, 1992).

know who was there). At the end of the show, Rotten asked the audience, "Ever get the feeling you've been cheated?" Jello Biafra was in the audience, and he had a feeling. Soon after the show Biafra started the Dead Kennedys and others followed—the Avengers, the Mutants, and what would eventually turn out to be Flipper. The Minutemen came out of San Pedro in 1980. But before the last Sex Pistols show, the earliest incarnation of Black Flag, X, and the Germs already existed. This is where Pat Smear makes his entrance—his maddening staccato guitar would later appear in the last line up of Nirvana.

On one of the seminal punk albums of the period, Flipper's *Album: Generic Flipper*, the question is asked again: "Ever feel that you've been had?" In Aberdeen, Buzz Osborne liked the question; he made a tape and gave it to Kurt Cobain.

If this line of descent from 1974 to *Bleach* sounds a little too neat, that's because it is. What about the Beatles and the Velvet Underground and the Vaselines and Black Sabbath and Scratch Acid and the Pixies and Soundgarden? There is no accounting for history when you live through it. There is no reason behind Nirvana becoming the biggest band in the world. No reason except for the music. In many respects, Nirvana was the summation of rock history and the end of pop music. Kurt Cobain was acutely aware of this, and he said so in the liner notes to *Incesticide*: "I don't feel the least bit guilty for commercially exploiting a completely exhausted Rock youth Culture because, at this point in rock history, Punk Rock (while still sacred to some) is, to me, dead and gone." Rock history was finished with *Nevermind*. Never mind what came before and what comes after because the show is over. And at the end of all great events there is always a bunch of dazed people standing around looking for free drinks and telling their stories.

This book tells stories about Nirvana, about the history we lived through. This is the first book to collect writing on Nirvana from a variety of sources—from fanzines, mainstream magazines, newspapers, and books. It is the end of history, and we need operating instructions. We needed Nirvana to end it all for us; Kant:

> But why do people expect the end of the world at all? And if this is granted to them, why precisely a terrifying end (which is the case for the majority of the human race)? The basis for the first belief seems to be that reason tells them the duration of the world has a value only to the extent that rational creatures in it are commensurate with the ultimate purpose of existence; but if this was not meant to be achieved, creation itself appears

to be pointless to them, like a drama that is totally without issue and has no rational design.[8]

By taking us out of history Nirvana has given a meaning to popular culture that goes beyond the old art form we call rock 'n' roll. Nirvana has given meaning to the drama. In one of Kurt Cobain's favorite books, the way to read Nirvana, the way to read the end of history, the way to read this book is given. This book calls itself a "How-To" Book. This book is William Bourough's *Naked Lunch,* and these are the instructions for us at the end of the music: "The Way OUT is the way IN."

---

8. Immanuel Kant, *On History*, trans. Lewis White Beck, Robert E. Anchor, and Emile L. Fackenheim (Indianapolis: Bobbs Merill, 1963).

PART ONE

This Is Outta My Range

All in all, we sound like the Knack and the Bay City Rollers being molested by Black Flag and Black Sabbath.

—Kurt Cobain on the music of Nirvana

Nirvana T-shirt, 1989: "Fudge-packin' crack-smokin' Satan-worshippin' motherfuckers." *Nirvana T-shirt, 1992:* "Flower-sniffin' kitty-pettin' baby-kissin' corporate rock whores."

—Clark Humphrey, *Loser: The Real Seattle Music Story*

Like the universe, Nirvana began with a bang. And like the universe's bang, Nirvana's bang took its time to reach throughout the cosmos. It was first heard in Aberdeen, Washington, then Olympia, then all of Seattle, then your bedroom. Dawn Anderson was one of the first people to hear the early bang—she was at the first Nirvana show and this was her motivation for being there: "I went with some friends who were casually acquainted with him as a fellow Melvins fan and they all thought it was real cute that little Kurt had a band."[1] Anderson has the first piece in this book because it is *the first thing ever published about Nirvana*. The year was 1988. She wrote it for *Backlash,* a 'zine she edited that covered the music scene (you can see her talking about the music of Seattle in the film *Hype!*). She explains how the writing came about in a preface to her piece that she wrote for this book.

---

1.   Dawn Anderson, in Clark Humphrey, *Loser: The Real Seattle Music Story* (Portland: Feral House, 1995).

Anderson's second article is a farewell to the band, who had just signed with Geffen/DGC. It is also one of the first published pieces to mention the name Dave Grohl.

Music critic Everett True contributes the most to this anthology because he contributed the most to the literature about Nirvana during their early performances, their rise to fame, and their last days. Sub Pop arranged for True to travel to Seattle to check out the bands they were recording and promoting. True was the first rock writer to break the grunge scene to the outside world—in a 1989 piece in *Melody Maker* he described what he saw in Seattle as "the most vibrant, kicking music scene encompassed in one city for at least 10 years." But this was only the beginning of his contact with the music that came out of the Pacific Northwest. As an acute cultural critic, True read the signs. And all the signs pointed toward Nirvana.

True met the members of Nirvana in 1989, just after the release of *Bleach*. (Chad Channing was the drummer for the band at this point.) "Nirvana: Bleached Wails," reprinted below, is the first article True wrote on the band, and you can just feel the future trying to rip apart his words. He was one of the first writers in a commercial publication to perceive the power of Nirvana; the future brought him into a close relationship with the band members that is evident throughout his writing on their music.

The second True piece in this section describes Nirvana—with Dave Grohl in the band—right after the release of *Nevermind* in 1991. It was a year of touring that culminated with a run through Europe with Sonic Youth. Nirvana was still having fun at this point, and you can see it in *1991: The Year That Punk Broke*. But this was before *Nevermind* reached number one on the charts.

True's close relationship with the band provided for some of the best writing produced on Nirvana, writing fueled by the energy and passion of their music. True became a particularly close confidant of Kurt Cobain and Courtney Love (see his interview with them in the third section of this book). It was thus fitting that True was the guy who pushed Cobain's wheelchair onto the stage at the Reading Festival in 1992. It was a mocking gesture to those who believed the rumors of Nirvana's demise: a member of the media pushed the rock star on stage to contradict the media's image of the rock star. (This footage is included on the video *Live! Tonight! Sold Out!*, and a picture of Cobain in the wheelchair appears on the inside cover of *In Utero*). The rumors of Nirvana's demise were much exaggerated, and the band killed the audience with a blistering set.

The remaining articles in this section focus on the beginnings of Nirvana. The excerpt from Gina Arnold's *Route 666: The Road to Nirvana*—an indispensable chronicle of American underground music—begins with her listening to songs that were intended to appear on *Nevermind*. Patrick MacDonald goes back to Aberdeen to find out where *Nevermind* came from, and he ends up talking to Krist Novoselic's mom. And Joe Gore's interview with Sonic Youth gives us a portrait of one of Nirvana's aesthetic inspirations (and also gives you guitarheads something to think about).

Note that Kurt Cobain spelled his name in various ways early on in his career. "Kurdt Kobain" is the most common variation. The name appears this way on *Bleach*, and Kurdt Kobain is credited with the "Monkey Photo" on *Nevermind*. The early articles in this collection feature his name in this early spelling.

Krist Novoselic changed the spelling of his first name from "Chris" somewhat later to reflect his Croatian heritage. The spelling "Krist" appears for the first time on *In Utero*.

Dave Grohl's name always seems to have stayed the same.

Nirvana goes beyond the process of perception, not only because of the inherent absence of form in our real nature but also because of its experience of the Totality-That-Is-One in its complete homogeneity.

—Robert Linssen, *Living Zen*

There was other good stuff in there too—a twelve pack of Bud kings, Fritos, some chips, and some kotexes probably for the guy's wife which naturally caused Russ to make a couple of cruder jokes but I didn't mind because of the moment at least we were free, free to just be ourselves, driving fast with the windows down and the heater blasting, smoking cigarettes and eating junk food and drinking beer and crankin' with Nirvana's "Serve the Servants" on WIZN screaming from the speakers.

—Russell Banks, *Rule of the Bone*

Being in the capitalistic music industry, I've learned one thing. You are either on the bottom or you are on the top. You're either scrounging around for scraps or you're on the top as a popular toy—Ken and Barbie syndrome—and being made a fool of, a laughing stock. You are either them or you are . . . sorry.

—Iggy Pop, *I Need More*

DAWN ANDERSON

IT MAY BE THE DEVIL AND IT MAY BE THE LORD . . . BUT IT SURE AS HELL AIN'T HUMAN

Backlash, August–September 1988

This was the first article ever published on Nirvana, appearing in my 'zine, Backlash, *in August 1988. I certainly would've put more time and thought into it had I known it would take on historical significance, but as it happened, I dashed this off about an hour before we went to press. I wrote the article the exact length to fit around the ads on the page, cut the drummer out of the picture (Dave Foster had left the band a few days before), called my roommate to ask her how to spell "Bodhisattva," and rushed the thing to the printers.*

My "better than the Melvins" line has already been quoted in at least two Nirvana books that I know of. At the time, this was considered an audacious comment, on par with saying Badfinger was as good as the Beatles. The folks I hung around with worshiped the Melvins, and so did the members of Nirvana.

Incidentally, "fish beer" refers to Schmidt, a bargain beer marketed to Northwest sportsmen with pictures of deer, ducks, and fish on the cans. It became popular among the rock crowd, mainly because of its price. The cans with the fishes were considered by far the coolest, for reasons nobody remembers.—DA

Ah, Aberdeen—a town where there's nothing to do but drink fish-beer and worship Satan. The Melvins were from Aberdeen. Remember? Now the Melvins' fan club is cranking out some pretty heavy riffs on their own. They call themselves Nirvana, a name that signifies both everything and nothing. If you don't understand this you can either take a course in world religion or you can witness Nirvana incarnate next time they perform in the big city.

Nirvana's head guru Kurdt Kobain lives in Olympia now, but he first began crunching out Melvins/Soundgarden style riffs in the town that time forgot, learning everything he knows by watching the Melvins practice. Endlessly.

"I've seen hundreds of Melvins practices," Kurdt recalls. "I drove their van on tour. Everybody hated them, by the way. And me and Matt [the Melvins' old bassist] even used the same calling card; it's almost like we were married."

Nirvana, consisting of Kurdt on guitar and vocals, Chris Novoselic on bass and Chad Channing on drums, is still a young band, but they're fast on their way to becoming Buddhas, or at least Bodhisattvas, of the Northwest pain-rock circuit.

Since some people seem to think *Backlash* is a consumer guide (what a novel idea!), it's probably only fair to inform you that if you didn't like the Melvins, or if you did like the Melvins but think leadbelly music has run its course, you won't like Nirvana. But it's also important to stress that this is not a clone band. The group's already way ahead of most mortals in the songwriting department and, at the risk of sounding blasphemous, I honestly believe that with enough practice, Nirvana could become . . . *better than the Melvins*!

"Our biggest fear at the beginning was that people might think we were a Melvins rip-off," Kurdt admits. Yet the association has probably also worked to the band's advantage. Nirvana recorded an ear-splitting demo tape which immediately had every noise addict in town flapping his lips over the next great white hope of grunge . . . and it probably didn't hurt that Melvin Dale was sitting in on drums (this was before Chad joined).

The band played its first gig as Nirvana at a Sub Pop Sunday at the Vogue. They weren't ready.

"We were uptight," recalls Kurdt. "It just didn't seem like a real show. We felt like we were being judged; it was like everyone should've had score cards. Plus, I was sick. I puked that day. That's a good excuse."

"We already had songs on the radio," adds Chris (KCMU has been playing "Paper Cuts"). "Everyone was already talking about us. There was a lot of pressure."

Unfortunately, Kurdt's nervousness was apparent on stage that night, but I've seen them twice since and they've gotten tighter each time. They're becoming the kind of band that can turn an entire audience into zombie pod people by their sheer heaviness (this is a compliment).

My only complaint is that Kurdt still can't seem to work up as much vocal finesse as he does on tape, since he's gotta play lead guitar and scream at the same time. But he'll work it out. In the meantime, look for the band's upcoming Sub Pop single, featuring one original and a cover of Shocking Blue's "Love Buzz."

And keep your ears tuned to Aberdeen, because idle towns are the Devil's workshop.

EVERETT TRUE
NIRVANA: BLEACHED WAILS

Melody Maker, October 21, 1989

Feel the noise. Everywhere you go, everywhere you look, Britain is being swamped in a deluge of long hair, hoary old Black Sabbath licks and American upstarts from Seattle. Rich and poor kids with nothing better to do with their time, now create devastating slabs of rock 'n' roll (some call it hard rock) and blow us away with their applied use of the wah-wah and suffocating powerchords. It's music which seems to have no real sense of purpose except to say, "Hi, we're here and aren't we having fun?" Soon it will be time to sweep the whole sorry mess under our carpets and wish to god Jimi Hendrix had never set his guitar on fire, but until then, I'd like you to welcome in the very best of the new breed on the block, hot on the footsteps of Mudhoney, Nirvana.

Nirvana are very much a band who would like to say, "Hi, this is us and we're having fun, too!," but the band are also a little bit *weird*. They're a little bit gross and a little bit awesome. And a bit too determined to be content with *just* messing around. What else could you be if you grew up in the backwoods redneck helltown of Aberdeen, a zillion miles away from the isolated capital of the Northwest, Seattle?

Their bassist, Chris Novoselic, takes up the story.

"See, Kurdt had this tape, right?" he explains. "And we're living in Aberdeen and he made it with Dale, the drummer from the Melvins [a band Matt from Mudhoney originally started in]. That was in '86, maybe. I heard it and I thought it was really cool, so I said to start this band so we started a band and we went through three drummers and we're here today, talking to you."

Chris is over six feet tall, friendly and *wired*. A competitive treeclimber, he was born and raised in Yugoslavia and looks forward to rockin' the Iron Curtain on Nirvana's forthcoming tour of Europe with Tad. Born to the outdoors, he worked as a commercial fisherman in Alaska for three years, painted bridges and has Elvis sideburns.

Kurdt Kobain is the vocalist, guitarist and main songwriter behind the trio, who turned into a quartet for the album *Bleach,* but turned into a trio again after extraneous guitarist Jason Everman upped plectrums and joined Soundgarden as bassist in July.[1] He's your archetypal small guy—wiry, defiantly working class and fiery. His provincial and witty lyrics bring to mind an American Mark E. Smith. He has a small goatee and his pet rat once bit Bruce Pavitt, Sub Pop records supremo.

Chris: "We were branded Satan worshippers back home. Fuck, this girl came knocking on our door looking for a wallet and she goes, 'You know what all the other kids told me in the neighborhood? Don't go in there, they worship the Devil.' That's why nobody ever bothered us in redneck country. We would neither confirm or deny Satanic affiliations."

"Maybe it was those desecrated cemetery pieces buried in our front yard," Kurdt wonders. "But you didn't have to do anything to be considered extreme back there. Just take a lot of acid."

Chad Channing, the drummer, is the quietest of the trio, if any of this thundering trio can be said to be noiseless. On stage he's a visual blur. He'd be a cook if it wasn't for this. He looks permanently stoned.

"I was offered the choice once between a guitar and a bicycle for my birthday," he recalls. "So I took the bicycle. Why did I start playing music? Boredom, I guess. I wanted to be able to play the drums. I still do."

At this point in the conversation, a guy stops by on a bicycle, hawking tapes. Kurdt asks him how much they are. "One dollar," comes the reply. "Shit," says Kurdt, "a dollar for a Van Morrison cassette? There are pawn shops all over here which'll give you 20 bucks for them." The guy disappears after trying to sell the band some hash.

"We set that one up, actually," Chris boasts. "To give you a taste of weird Americana. He's the fifth member of Nirvana."

So who do Nirvana listen to? The usual: Aerosmith, Tuxedomoon, NWA, Herman and the Hermits, Leadbelly, hard rock, punk rock, power pop, hip hop, Sub Pop—the sensibilities of the late Seventies mixed with

---

1. Jason Everman did not play on *Bleach,* although he is featured on the cover playing with the band. He lent Nirvana $600 to record the album.—*Ed.*

the raw power of the late Sixties. Are they aware of any kind of "Sub Pop movement?"

Kurdt: "Sort of, but we didn't start playing this stuff to join in, it just happened that way. Sure we're heavy, but a little bit diverse maybe. The album has a couple of beautiful pop tunes on it."

Chris: "We're definitely not groundbreaking. If there was no Sub Pop sound we'd still be doing this. If there's anything we're really close to, it's the Stooges—the momentum and the energy."

Where Nirvana differs from most of their contemporaries is in the strength of Kurdt's songwriting. Among those in the know, Nirvana are said to be the cream of the crop (*if* they can get their live act together). Listen to the wickedly named *Bleach* Sub Pop LP and you can hear those roots showing—far from being a melting potpourri of every loud noise imaginable, Nirvana crafts their songs with a diligence not seen this side of Creation. "Blew," "About a Girl," "Big Cheese" (the first mind-fuck of a single), "Sifting"; all these songs are crafted round a firm base of tune, chorus, harmony.

Okay, so they might smother them a little with licks that'd do prime-time Sabbath proud, but what the heck? Every boy's gotta have a *vocation*.

Jonathan Poneman from Sub Pop appears. A cat walks by on a leash. I have a five-minute coughing fit and nearly asphyxiate. Nirvana was suitably shocked. So I ask them what their name means to them.

"Big amplifiers," Chris replies, incisively. "Not giving a shit and having fun. Dreaming. Being free from distraction and not being uptight. Jamming, having lots of good shows, being polite, respecting our moms and dads."

Nirvana were once called too complex for their own good by our own Simon Reynolds—precisely the opposite to how I would describe them.

Kurdt: "Well, the track he was describing [off the *Sub Pop 200* box set] was pretty much the most complex thing we've ever done. We're moving towards simplicity and better songwriting all the time. There are songs on the album which only have two parts to them. That one has three. Fuck that guy, what does he know? He was probably in a bad mood or something! He doesn't like Robert Fripp, that's for sure. He probably doesn't listen to Eno, either, which is stupid! Eno's great!"

Chris: "We just want to make people happy. We just want to ROCK! Ninety-nine per cent of music out there is bullshit. There are way too many bands out there and they just get in the way. So quit! Give it up! Turn in your guitars for shovels! You guys suck!"

Kurdt: "The Pixies are a pretty good band though."

Chad: "Yeah, all the bands should have shovels or chainsaws, so they can get out there and *work* the stage!"

Where would you be if you weren't playing music?

"On the streets!"

"Living in Yugoslavia."

"I'd be one depressed muthafucker."

"I'd be one burly moustached guy."

"I'd be in a bowling league."

"I'd be eating chili dogs and drinking Budweisers."

"I'd have to resort to playing the game and marry a rich heiress and shack up with . . ."

"Let's start again. My name's Chris Novoselic, I play bass and I'm in this great new band called Nirvana and we're releasing this album on Sub Pop called *Bleach* full of hard rock riffs and beautiful songs and . . ."

Nirvana shortly have a limited edition 12-inch coming out on Tupelo featuring "Blew" from *Bleach*, "Love Buzz" from the first single and two new, Steve Fisk produced, tracks. It's great! They're gonna be over here any day now, touring with Tad. Don't, for Hendrix's sake, miss them.

DAWN ANDERSON

NIRVANA: SIGNIN' ON THE DOTTED LINE AND OTHER TALES OF TERROR

Backlash, March 1991

This was the cover story in the last issue of Backlash, *published in March 1991. At the time Nirvana had just signed to Geffen, Dave Grohl had just joined the band, and the three had not yet begun recording* Nevermind.

When photographer James Bush and I showed up at Kurt's house at about 2:00 in the afternoon, Chris had to rouse Kurt from bed, where he was sound asleep with his clothes on. James suggested we give him some time to wake up before he snapped the pictures, but Kurt insisted there was no problem. All musicians pretend they don't care about how they look; Kurt really didn't.

We drank fish beer and talked of things to come.—DA

I bummed a dollar from Kurt Cobain a couple of years ago, and, in return, he made me promise to put his band on the cover of *Backlash*.

Despite rumors to the contrary, I don't usually work that way, but Nirvana deserved it, with or without a dollar. They'd been one of my fave bands ever since I heard their incredible first demo (I hear it's a bootleg now), the one that got them "discovered" by Sub Pop. But sometimes it takes me a while (a *long* while, if you must know) to live up to my promises. First of all, *Backlash* had already done a feature on the band before they were really known as anybody but friends of the Melvins and I wanted to let enough time pass to warrant another story. Then when I was finally ready to put 'em on the cover, I found out *The Rocket* was planning to put them on *their* cover and my revulsion at the idea of duplicating the other 'zines is so extreme, I'm always pulling cover stories at the last minute to avoid it (and *that's* the reason for Slam Suzzanne, since so many of you asked).

And now so much has happened since that initial interview over two years ago that I wasn't even sure the guys would want to talk to me anymore. Nobody was surprised they "got signed"—by Geffen's DGC, no less, the same label that recently jumped the Posies. Nirvana is a grunge band even normal people like. To most ears they're the epitome of the lead-bottom Sub Pop sound, but their brilliant "Sliver" single and some of the songs on their *Bleach* LP reveal their ability to write hooks that'll jerk your head around. Many of Nirvana's songs are based on a sturdy melody which they then proceed to pummel into the ground. Kurt says there will be plenty more songs with a melodic bent on their next album; this is the direction they're been headed in for a while.

They won't "go metal." They hate it. ("I like heavy metal as a *concept*," corrects Kurt.)

After *Bleach* came the *Blew* EP on Tupelo/Sub Pop, the aforementioned "Sliver"/"Dive" single, a split single with the Fluid (a live cover of Vaseline's "Molly's Lips") and contributions to the recent Kiss and Velvet Underground tribute albums. Oh yeah, before all that was the first single, "Love Buzz," but you can't find it for under $40 anymore.

It's official that Nirvana has fled the Sub Pop stable and if all goes well on DGC, their records will receive the big money push from now on. In the meantime, they're as broke as ever. They're about to embark on a "mini tour" of the Northern U. S. and Canada and are wondering how they'll get their van fixed. When their new album comes out later this year, they'll tour with Jane's Addiction, presumably under more comfortable circumstances, and they hope to do a lot of headlining dates as well.

Turns out they were more than willing to speak to us and I'm glad my last interview, at least for this magazine, was with one of the Northwest's best bands. I'll skip over the part about puking up Twinkies (it wasn't that interesting) and get right to the meat of my conversation with vocalist/guitarist Kurt Cobain, bassets Chris Novoselic and their latest drummer, Dave Grohl.

Dawn: So how did you hook up with DGC?

Kurt: They called us up and took us out to dinner. I think they maybe got a clue from when we toured with Sonic Youth. We have the same manager as they do.

Chris: I guess MCA was the first to take an interest and then word got out all over Hollywood.

Dawn: So there was a lot of competition for you?

Chris: We averted it. We had so many labels to choose from and some of the choices were like, no way!

Kurt: But we still made them take us out to dinner.

Dawn: So what is it that made you go with DGC?

Chris: Well, they broke a lot of bands. DGC just seemed hip, you know, whereas if you go to a label like Capital they're pretty much dinosaurs. You've got these old Southern men working the radio promotion. . . . They have no idea where we're coming from at all. And DGC seemed like . . .

Kurt: They have an alternative, young staff. They have some credentials in the underground. Of course, it's like Russian Roulette anyhow; you never know if you've made the right choice. We have no idea if they're gonna promote us or not. We know they're not gonna make us dress up in monkey suits. . . .

Dawn: So what's the next step? Where and with who will you be recording?

Kurt: In March. We're going back to Madison to do it with Butch [Vig] and somebody else, maybe the guy who does Crazy Horse. But Butch will be the main producer. There will be a few songs that we'll pick out to be more commercial and we'll use other producers for those. I don't think it will really matter what producer we use. Most contemporary production sounds generic anyway.

Dawn: Someone told me you were gonna use the guy who did the last couple of REM records.

Kurt: Yeah, Scott Litt. We were talking with him. We're talking with a few different people.

Dawn: I also heard you were going to do some stuff at the Music Source.

Kurt: We already did. It didn't turn out very well. That place is good for making Nordstrom commercials. . . .

Chris: And Kenny G. We were gonna put out an EP, but that's not gonna happen. And Craig, our soundman, wanted a shot at doing the record and we thought we'd give him a chance, but it worked out kinda screwy. But it was free; we didn't pay for it.

Dawn: How did Sub Pop react to you leaving them?

Chris: They cashed in!

Kurt: I think we just passed them up. We were talking to Susan Silver and said, "You know, we got this 30-page giant contract from Sub Pop, what should we do?" And she said, "I think you should get a lawyer. I'm going down to LA tomorrow; maybe you should go down, too." So she flew down and we drove down and she introduced us to people and we got a lawyer. That was our big education. We were really ignorant of a lot of things before we got that lawyer and then we got a manager and the whole shebang, and we just sort of passed them up. So we flew the coop. It's too bad, really.

Dawn: So basically you just wanted to be on a bigger label?

Kurt: We wanted to be promoted! We weren't being promoted very well. I challenge anybody to find a *Bleach* ad.

Chris: Six or seven months after the record came out, we said, "Let's start promoting it, O.K.?" And they said, "No, you've gotta get something new out." Plus, Sub Pop was maybe gonna sign with a major . . .

Kurt: And we had no say about what major they went with.

Chris: So this way, we picked the label we wanted to be on.

Kurt: Another thing is, we've never known how many records we've sold on Sub Pop; we don't know how many copies of *Bleach* we sold.

Dawn: Everyone's going to be asking you the sellout question and you're gonna get really sick of hearing it, but it has to be asked. Will DGC expect you to change your sound to be more commercial?

Kurt: In our contract, we were dealing from a position of strength because there were other labels competing for us, so we get complete, 100 percent creative control. So we can do whatever we want. There's no pressure.

Chris: It's also a case of if something works, why fix it?

Dawn: And no one's telling you you should start trying to look prettier?

Kurt: Oh, no way!

Dave: The worst thing in the world is trying to make an ugly guy look pretty.

Photographer [James Bush]: We just got a photo like that; it was five ugly guys wearing lipstick and it was bad news!

Dave: Like the singer for Great White—have you ever seen that guy? He looks like the Church Lady. And they've got this video that starts out with him playing piano and he's got these short fat fingers with rings on every one, and then it pans up to his face and he's got this big nose and feathered hair . . . fuckin' loser.

Dawn: (to Dave) So where did they find you?

Dave: Well, I was in Scream. . . .

Kurt: He was in a band called Dain Bramage before Scream.

Dave: Then I was in Scream for four years. On the last tour Scream did last summer we were in Hollywood and the tour sucked; we weren't making very much money and the bass player started getting back together with his girlfriend over the phone and we woke up one morning and he was gone, she had wired him money and he flew home, so we were stuck in Hollywood and couldn't find another bass player. And then I talked to Buzz from the Melvins and he said, "I think Nirvana might call you because they need a drummer." They didn't call, so I called them. And I've been playing with them ever since.

Kurt: We've been wanting someone who could sing harmonies for a long time.

Chris: And he plays some damn fine drums.

Kurt: Chad was more of a jazz drummer and he'd switch to a heavier thing with us, but still, he couldn't do it natural.

Dawn: What happened to Danny? Did he leave voluntarily? [Mudhoney's Danny Peters briefly played drums for Nirvana.]

Kurt: No. . . .

Dave: We had a fist fight over who was gonna be the drummer for Nirvana; he knocked me out and I hit him with a pole. . . .

Dawn: So that's why he walks funny!

Chris: Dave's style just suited us. Dan plays a small drum set, you know. . . .

Kurt: But Dan played on "Sliver" and helped us write it and I'm really glad he did, because I love that song. He was about to leave on tour with Mudhoney and Tad had just finished in the studio at Reciprocal, so the half-hour after they finished we went in there and used their equipment and recorded the song.

Chris: It was so spontaneous. The song kind of jelled together in three or four days, then we jumped right in there and recorded it.

Dawn: What happened to Jason? [Jason Everman was the band's second guitarist for awhile.]

Kurt: Could you write in the story that he never played on *Bleach*? His name and picture are on the record.

Chris: We met him and he was real nice and he lent us the $600 for the record—we still owe him the money. And we wanted to get another guitar player to thicken our sound and stuff.

Kurt: But it seemed like we just got more metal sounding.

Chris: Then we went on tour and we just couldn't communicate with him anymore. He was just gone all the time.

Kurt: He'd kind of get pissed off, because that was when we went through a phase where we were smashing stuff up all the time and he didn't like that.

Dawn: I was going to ask if that was true. Did you break guitars on stage?

Kurt: Oh, yeah, that was true.

Chris: We just had the guys from Coffin Break send us new ones. You know, Rob had a chance to stay at the Hilton, but he stayed in the dumpster behind CBGBs instead because of his punk rock ethics. And he walked around CBGBs with a sign that said "I slept in a dumpster because of my punk rock morals." No, actually, I like Rob.[1]

Dawn: Are you satisfied with everything you released?

Kurt: Umm . . .

Dave: I still listen to *Bleach*, even though I had nothing to do with it. I thought that was a great record.

Kurt: Well, I really didn't want that split single to be put out; I called up Jon at Sub Pop and asked him not to do it. It was just a throwaway. I

---

1. *Backlash* had run an interview with Coffin Break a few months before, in which bassist Rob Skinner was complaining about their touring conditions as compared to the bands on Sub Pop. He said, "Kurt Cobain from Nirvana breaks guitars, so they send him guitars on the road, and he breaks them. We don't have that back-up." Coffin Break had a reputation as punk purists.—D.A.

like the song, the performance just wasn't up to par. But part of the buy-out deal was that single. So we said, "O.K., we'll let you do the single," and they said, "Good, because we already have the test pressings." You know the word "later" [etched in the inner grooves] on the single? They wrote "later." We had nothing to do with it.

Dawn: Will people still be able to see you in Seattle clubs?

Chris: Sure, we'll still play the Off-Ramp and the North Shore Surf Club down here [in Olympia] and we still play parties all the time.

Dawn: Are you ever going to make another $600 album?

Kurt: Probably not.

During almost a decade as a rock writer, I've seen my tape recorder do some very strange things. But while transcribing this interview, which is quite possibly my last, it started acting *really* deranged, speeding up and slowing down, fading in and out, so the guys all sounded like they'd dropped acid and inhaled helium.

Weirdly, this began occurring just as I asked them to comment on the Gulf War. I thought I'd give them the chance since Chris was on a tirade about it during the drive from Tacoma to Kurt's house in Olympia—this seemed to have been set off when my photog had to stop and buy film at the Tacoma Mall, which was crawling with idiots. "*These people* are breeding?" he kept saying.

Chris: You can start out by talking about the war, but you just get sidetracked and start talking about China and Panama, I mean it's all related and it just shows that everything is all screwed up and ending the war would just be a Bandaid—just the whole world is screwed up, it's just a big capitalistic money trip, people are just concerned about paying off their cars and going to the malls and people are all suspicious of each other and they're all breeding like rabbits.

My recorder, by this time, was going berserk. I asked them one more question, something about whether the Seattle grunge scene was dying. "Things change, things evolve" was all I caught.

FROM *ROUTE 666: THE ROAD TO NIRVANA*

Route 666: The Road to Nirvana, 1993

The day after the Lollapalooza show in Arizona, I drove from San Diego to Los Angeles to interview Nirvana. Their manager, John Silva, had just Fed Exed me a package containing four songs from their upcoming release, at that time not yet titled *Nevermind,* but my rental car didn't have a tape deck, so I had to play it by dangling my tape recorder, on full blast, in front of my ear while I drove up Highway 405.

So I drove, and I listened, again and again, all the way through, then I hit rewind and listened again. I remember thinking, when I heard the first number—the words went *"Love myself better than you / know it's wrong, but what can I do?"*—that if the world was a different sort of place, it'd be a huge hit single. Then the next number began. *"One baby to another said, 'I'm lucky / I met you / I don't care what you think unless it is about me,'"*—and I got kind of excited. The next number, "Lithium," was one long lurch in the pit of my stomach, a disturbance in my physical self, a sensation somewhat akin to fright.

Then "Teen Spirit" began. You know those opening chords? You know the gas pedal? You know the first line, *"Load up on drugs and bring your friends / it's fun to lose and to pretend?"* When I first heard "Smells Like Teen Spirit" I didn't think, "Why, this will be a monster hit that will transform the record industry and subsequently my life." I just felt afraid. Oh, rock 'n' roll beguiles but it betrays as well. When I heard "Teen Spirit," I felt sick with love for that song, sick with the thought that other people might dare to criticize it. Here, I knew, was one more thing to go to bat for, one more band by which I'd measure truth, one more life-changing, attitude-shaping, bigger-than-its-parts song of surrender. I felt sick because it was a battle call, and battles are always bloody. Somebody always loses.

I listened to those four songs for two and a half hours. At the end of them, I reached my destination—the Beverly Garland Hotel—and saw, in the parking lot, the three people who'd sung them, standing around idly, waiting for me to show up. Chris was lurching around in the parking lot, all goofily, while he gestured me into a parking space. And I couldn't help thinking back to when I'd first met Nirvana. It was in another kind of parking lot: the DMZish asphalt area of a McDonald's in San Ysidro (rebuilt on a new site since the famous sniper massacre of several years ago). It was a parking lot full of sullen teens in beat-up Mavericks, a ton of screaming children and the inevitable Baptist church choir on its way to a sing-off or something equally improbable out in the sticks. Saturday afternoons at McDonald's are the same the world over, and that Saturday at the Dairy Mart Road McDonald's in San Ysidro was no exception.

Nirvana was on its way across the U.S. border for weekend gigs at a nightclub called Iguana's in Tijuana. Trailed by a square yellow truck that was serving as the equipment van for the headliner, Dinosaur Jr., the band pulled into the lot one afternoon in June. They were an hour late, owing to traffic in Orange County, and still looked half asleep. When their manager pushed me unceremoniously into one of the dirtiest, smelliest vans I've ever been in, no one even looked up to ask who I was. I looked around disconsolately. Pizza crusts, candy wrappers, a cooler full of warm water and crushed cans; graffiti all over the inside of the van and a pair of grotty hightop sneakers tied so that they hung out the crack of a window (presumably because they smelled so bad). The seats of the van had been ripped out and replaced by the kind of torn plaid sofas that you sometimes see out on street corners in San Francisco that even halfway houses have already rejected.

I sat down gingerly on one, surrounded by baleful stares. The atmosphere was positively foreboding. The only person who wasn't nearly comatose was David Grohl, Nirvana's drummer, who (typically, I soon discovered) managed to utter a semifriendly "Hi!" Then, as we pulled out of the parking lot, I reached up nervously and turned my black baseball cap, with its K Records logo on it, back to front, Sub Pop style. There was the slightest stir from the back seat, as Kurt Cobain sat straight up. "Where'd you get that cap?" he asked.

"Made it myself with liquid paper," I replied. Kurt didn't answer. Then suddenly, shyly, he thrust his arm out under my nose. On the back of it was a tattoo of the exact same symbol. "Dave did it with a pin," Kurt said proudly, glancing over at him.

"You didn't just get it 'cause your name begins with K, did you?" I asked suspiciously.

"No!" Kurt exclaimed at once. "That's not it at all. I like the K label a lot and what Calvin's doing, and I wanted a tattoo and I couldn't think of anything else. Besides, [K] exposed me to so much good music, like the Vaselines, who are my favorite band ever. They didn't influence me, it was just a reminder of how much I really value innocence and children and my youth. Beat Happening had a lot to do with reminding me of how precious that whole childlike world is. I have great memories of what it was like to be a little kid. It was a really good time, and I see a lot of beauty in it. I was happiest then. I didn't have to worry about anything."

That was my first meeting with Nirvana. Back when I'd first heard *Bleach,* I had thought, "This band is kind of like the Pixies crossed with Soul Asylum." When I saw them play that gig in TJ, I realized that what Nirvana actually equaled was the Pixies *times* Soul Asylum. ("Thanks," said Kurt. "That's very close, I'd say. I never liked Soul Asylum, but I went to see them once, and I think we're closely related in our live shows. The Pixies, I've felt a real musical bond with them. I was blown away by them. That's very close to what we were doing and are doing more so now.") Live that night, Nirvana threw off sheer power in enormous bursts, leaning over their guitars with the weight of their fury, smashing them down on the ground, sometimes hurling them at each other; its members leaping, guitars and all, onto a surface of human flesh, Kurt held upright, clutched by each leg, howling "Teen Spirit" to an enthralled cabal, bodies plunging literally over the chicken wire-encased third-tier balcony and then bouncing off the skin below. Sometimes it was as if the guitars themselves had become possessed by the music and, poltergeist style, were seizing their owners like the brooms in *Fantasia* or something, hurling them around so many stages I stopped counting. Once I saw Kurt leap on Chris's shoulders, forcing him to the floor with his unexpected burden, both still playing notes all ripped apart from impact.

All this brilliance couldn't come from a more unlikely set of guys. Nirvana's founders—bassist Chris Novoselic and guitarist Kurt Cobain (Grohl, from Washington, D.C., joined the group in 1990; he's their fifth drummer in as many years)—are the embodiment of small-town stoners, the American equivalent of the kids in England who angrily declared that they had No Future back in 1977. They are the type of self-described "negative creeps"—shy, weasel-faced, introverted—that it's practically impossible to imagine copping any of the classic rock poses of stardom. When they turn on like light bulbs onstage, there's an unfeigned freedom, an intuitiveness so inarticulate there's almost no point in interviewing them. They are a little hard to get to know. Kurt did once tell me his favorite books are by philosophers—"Bukowski, Beckett, anyone beginning with a B"—and that he once tackled Nietzsche, but didn't understand a word of it. But you can't tell me that the guy who wrote the words *"Love myself better than you / know it's wrong but what can I do?"* didn't absorb the tenets of Man and Superman, even if Novoselic does jeer at the idea.

"Oh yeah, we're pocket philosophers," Chris says, laughing.

"Well, blue-collar ones, maybe," Kurt adds defensively.

One thing I do know about Nirvana's talent and music: it comes of obsessiveness and determination—the kind of determination that saw the band, in its early days, traveling up to Seattle time and again in a Volkswagen with all its seats torn out, packed up with tiny amps, an old Sears trap drum set, cymbal stands that were originally music stands from high school, basically equipment that was the Melvins' scraps—not to mention the three band members themselves, one of whom is six foot seven. And it comes of a genuine love of the misfit status that growing up on the outside in Aberdeen, Washington, will give a kid with a brain, a craziness that can't be faked by anyone. If there is one single thread that holds all of their banal observations together, it is that of eccentricity. Nirvana has learned to love the feeling of not belonging, to the point where the very idea of actually belonging scares them. "I just can't believe," says Kurt, "that anyone would start a band just to make the scene and be cool and have chicks. I just can't believe it."

Unlike many grungy white-boy college rock bands today, Kurt Cobain and Chris Novoselic take great pride in the fact that they even graduated from high school. They met in Aberdeen, the way people in high school do: they just kind of knew each other. They say they were always attracted to people on the outside—misfits, outcasts, strangers with candy.

"The first concert I ever went to," recalls Chris, "was the Scorpions. I went with these gay guys 'cause I was the only one with a car. One guy was my age and the other was older. And we were driving up to Seattle, and I looked in the back seat and they were making out and I'm, like, 'Jeepers creepers.' I was seventeen. They didn't bug me or anything. I kind of laughed. I thought it was funny 'cause I never saw gay people before. So we went to the show, it was the Scorpions, and it was totally boring. I stood up front and threw my shirt on the stage. And afterwards I couldn't find the other guys, so I just left without 'em."

Kurt interrupts. "Hey, I was friends with that guy! Randall [not his real name], he was my best friend in tenth grade and everyone else assumed I was gay too. I didn't even know he was gay but everyone else did, so there was all these gay-bashing rumors going on, like they were going to beat me up, there were really bad vibes going on in my P.E. class and then my mom forbid me to hang out with him anymore because he was gay. Randall! He's a great guy. I was always attracted to him 'cause he was really different. He had a really different perspective."

But wasn't it odd that a gay guy would like the Scorpions?

"No. Everybody liked the Scorpions in Aberdeen. It's a small hick town, those are the only records you can buy there," Kurt says. "Scorpions or Ozzy Osbourne."

"Not me," says Chris. "I didn't like 'em. I liked 'em when I was way younger, but then they started coming out with—well, all their records were crappy, but *Blackout* was the crappiest. Then I liked prog rock, and then I discovered punk rock. In 1983, I heard a compilation tape made by a friend. And then I listened to *Generic Flipper* and it was a revelation. It was art. It made me realize it was art. It was valid, it was beautiful 'cause I gave things validity by going, like, 'Is it as good as *Physical Graffiti?*' And Flipper was suddenly, like, 'Sure it is! If not better. Well, they both have their moments.' It was a revelation!

"My friend Buzz gave the tape to me. He's in the Melvins. He was the punk rock guru of Aberdeen. He's the guy who discovered punk rock and spread the good news around town. But he only told it to the most deserving, 'cause a lot of people would discount it. And then I tried to turn people on to it, and they'd be, like . . . one guy I know, I remember he goes, 'Ah, that punk rock stuff . . . all it is is, "want to fuck my mom! want to fuck my mom!"' "

Kurt: "He probably wanted to fuck *his* mom. He probably wanted to fuck Randall!" (He and Chris collapse in giggles.)

Luckily for Chris, one of the deserving people to whom Buzz gave a tape was Kurt, who kind of knew Chris from around town. "I'd met Buzz probably around the same time you met Buzz," recalls Kurt. "And one night I went over to hear the Melvins practice before they were the Melvins and they were playing, like, Jimi Hendrix and Cream and stuff like that. And I was really drunk and I thought they were the greatest band I'd ever seen, it was really awesome, and right around that time Buzz started getting into punk rock. Then they started playing punk rock music and they had a free concert right behind Thriftways supermarket where Buzz worked, and they plugged into the city power supply and played punk rock music for about fifty redneck kids. And when I saw them play, it just blew me away, I was instantly a punk rocker. I abandoned all my friends, 'cause they didn't like any of the music. And then I asked Buzz to make me a compilation tape of punk rock songs and I got a spiky haircut."

Chris reflects on this information for a moment. "You know what happened is, punk rock kind of galvanized people in Aberdeen. It brought us together and we got our own little scene after a while, and we all hung out. Everybody realized—all the misfits realized—that rednecks weren't just dicks, they were *total* dicks. And punk rock had all this cool political, personal message, you know what I mean? It was a lot more cerebral than just stupid cock rock, you know? Dead Kennedys. MDC, remember?

Dead Cops! Corporate Death Burger! We were never exposed to any radical ideas, all the ideas came from, like, San Francisco, or Berkeley."

"My first rock experience was Sammy Hagar in seventh grade," Kurt says. "My friend and I were taken by his sister to the show in Seattle. And on the way there we drank a case of beer and we were stuck in traffic and I had to go so bad I peed my pants! And when we got into the concert people were passing pipes around, marijuana, and I'd never smoked pot before, and I got really high, and I had a Bic lighter in my sweatshirt, inside the pocket, and I was tripping out and I lit myself on fire. So I stunk of pee and I caught on fire . . . and I didn't really like the concert at all. It just wasn't the right type of music for me. I didn't understand it. I liked rock 'n' roll but not that concert, it didn't thrill me. He [Sammy] seemed really fake.

"When I was a little kid I had a guitar and I'd run around the house with it and sing Beatles songs and I'd have concerts for my family when they came over, on Christmas, and I'd play my guitar and play Beatles songs. I always wanted to be a rock star when I was a little kid. Then when I was a teenager, it was just different. . . . I still liked music a lot, but it wasn't what everyone else liked. I hated Kiss, I hated Boston, it was so fake . . . and at the time I couldn't understand why people liked it. I never thought about rock when I was a teenager.

"But when I saw the Melvins play that show and I started getting into punk rock, it really changed me. I wanted to start a band really bad, and I got an electric guitar and I was really into it, but I couldn't find anyone in Aberdeen to be in a band with. I was lucky to find Chris at the time. A few years after we'd been hanging out, I made a tape of some punk rock songs I'd written with Dale, the Melvins' drummer, and I played it for Chris at my aunt's house and he really liked it, and he suggested we start a band. It sounded *exactly* like Black Flag. Totally abrasive, fast, punk music. There were some Nirvana elements, some slower songs, even then. And some heavy, Black Sabbath–influenced stuff. I can't deny Black Sabbath. Or Black Flag."

For a while, the band was called Skid Row. "Our drummer," Kurt recalls, "was this stoner guy, but he had a drum set and we kind of coaxed him into joining the band, coming to practice. But we got really serious and he wasn't that serious. He'd get drunk, miss a lot of practices. So we had a lot of trouble starting out. It didn't seem like a real legitimate band, or as legitimate as we wanted it to be. We didn't even have enough money to buy records, and there were no stores in Aberdeen.

"The closest place to see shows was Olympia or Tacoma. Tacoma is seventy miles. Seattle was one hundred miles. We didn't get up there very often, just for the major punk rock shows, Black Flag and stuff. When I first started playing guitar, I just started writing songs right away. I knew one Cars song and 'Back in Black' and after that I just started writing. I didn't think it was important to learn other songs because I just knew I wanted to start a band.

"At the time the Community World Theater was a really good place for new bands to start out 'cause they'd let you play. But you know what?" he adds, "it was pretty easy to get booked. That was the thing about it. There weren't a lot of really popular bands coming into town. So it was mostly local bands that played. Olympia and Tacoma were kind of more punk rock that way—it was easier to play there than in Seattle."

But did anyone come see you?

"Oh no. Maybe twenty people. There was one show in Seattle where nobody came. We didn't even play. We loaded up our stuff and left."

Dave, who's been lying completely silent, soaking up the rays for the last hour, suddenly looks up. "Really, nobody came at all?"

Kurt grins, "Not one single person, except for Jon and Bruce. It was at the Central Tavern."

Jon, of course, is Jonathan Poneman. Bruce is Bruce Pavitt, who by that time had started Sub Pop Records. During that year, 1987 [*sic*], Nirvana got some money together, kicked their drummer out of the band, hired Dale Crover of the Melvins, and recorded a demo at Jack Endino's studio in Seattle in a single day. Poneman heard it and liked it, eventually offering to put it out.

"Jon put out our single about six months after talking to him," Chris recalls. "We didn't know anything about Sub Pop at the time. We just loved playing. It's just so totally *fun*. It was the most important thing in my life at the time. It was awesome!"

Still, for a tiny podunk band like Nirvana to put a record out must have been a pretty big deal.

Kurt shrugs. "We were excited, yeah, but after a while the excitement kind of left because it took over a year for our album to come out, 'cause we were waiting for Sub Pop to get enough money to put it out, and we ended up paying for the recording ourselves. It cost six hundred and six dollars. That's cheap. And still," he adds, "when we went on tour, kids would come up to us in flocks, going, 'Where can we get the record? We can't find it.' That's the only reason we decided to go with a major, is just the assurance of getting our records into small towns like Aberdeen."

Kurt still feels sort of bad about being on a major label. "But what were we going to do, stay on Sub Pop? You couldn't even find our last record! And we were under contract to them, and somebody had to have the money to get us out of the deal."

Nirvana's not ungrateful to Sub Pop. "The Sub Pop hype thing helped a lot, the Seattle Sound thing. We just kind of got caught up in it," says Chris.

Kurt adds, "In England we were always very popular. I mean, it's kind of an unusual thing for a band that's as young as us to have gone over there so soon, and Sub Pop did that for us. But going to Europe that soon [in 1988], it was exciting but it was hell at the same time. We didn't eat very much, it was a very low-budget thing. We were touring with Tad in the same van and three extra people. Eleven people. It was really grueling, 'cause we had three days off in seven and a half weeks. We were playing a lot and not eating too much."

What was the highlight?

Kurt (without even stopping to think): "Oh! That place in Austria! Up in the mountains, with all the trolls? The troll village!"

Chris: "Oh yeah! A bunch of inbred villagers going, 'Play some rock and roll, bay-bee!' There was a guy who looked like Mick Fleetwood with a big huge knife scar down the side of his face. And there was a guy with a machete in his hand, and it was some huge holiday and everyone was all wasted, people were passed out on the floor! There was this really fat troll, saying, 'Come on, bay-bee, play something hea-veee.' And there was this guy playing the blues machine. He rented himself out to, like, the Austrian version of bar mitzvahs. Oh God, I would love to rent him for our record release party. The guys in Mudhoney would go crazy."

Kurt adds, "We also played one of our best shows in this town called Redmond. It was just a party. And all these rednecks were there . . ."

Chris: "But they moved into the kitchen, they didn't like us at all. They were scared of us."

"We were really drunk," Kurt laughs, "so we started making spectacles of ourselves. Playing off of the bad vibes we were giving to the rednecks, you know—jumping off tables and pretending we were rock stars. And Chris jumped through a window. Then we started playing 'Sex Bomb' for about an hour, and our girlfriends were hanging on us and grabbing our legs and doing a mock lesbian scene, and that really started freaking out the rednecks!"

But why was this the best show ever?

Kurt thinks for a sec. "Oh, just because it was such a great vibe, I mean, we were totally wigging the rednecks out! And that was the idea of punk rock to us in the first place, was to abuse your audience. And what better audience to have than a redneck audience?"

By that time, Kurt had lived in Olympia for about a year, and Chris lived in nearby Tacoma, about twenty miles away. As Chris explains, at that time Sub Pop was talking about signing a big distribution deal with Sony (which eventually fell through). Nirvana got their own lawyer, who shopped them to various labels in Los Angeles. Eventually Geffen Records paid Sub Pop Records seventy thousand plus points for the privilege of licensing Nirvana.

Nirvana had initially recorded the songs for *Nevermind* as demos for Sub Pop. When they signed to Geffen, they re-recorded much of it—as well as adding tracks—at Butch Vig's studio in the spring of 1991. The band had two weeks of studio time booked, but it only took them a week and a half to lay it down. Kurt was still writing lyrics in the studio. "Endless, Nameless," the buried track on the CD version (it begins ten minutes after "Something in the Way" ends) was a bunch of experimental shit they laid down in the studio at that time. The cello part on "Something" was added at the last minute, when Kirk Canning, a member of the band Spoon, happened to stop by the apartment the band was staying at in Madison.

Thus, *Nevermind* was initially conceived and marketed by the major label as just another relatively low-budget alternative band project. Kurt shrugs. "The level of success we're on doesn't really matter to us. It's a fine thing, a flattering thing to have major labels want you, but it doesn't matter. We could be dropped in two years and go back to putting out records ourselves and it wouldn't matter, 'cause it's not what we were looking for. We didn't want to be staying at the Beverly Garland Hotel, we just wanted people to get the records. And we did do it on an independent level. That's the beauty of it."

Chris: "We should make a made-for-TV movie. 'The Nirvana Story.' Who will play you?"

Kurt: "Ernest Borgnine. Who'll be you?"

"Someone tall—Kareem Abdul Jabbar? We'll have these intense scenes. 'I'm in this band, and what I say *goes*!' We'll be throwing our wine goblets through the window. Then there'll be the love part: 'Baby, I'm sorry, I've got to go out with the band.' And she'll be, like, 'Don't you love me?' And I'm, like, 'Hasta la vista!' The love! The camaraderie! (That'll be in the van with Tad in Europe.) The triumph! Us onstage. The let-downs: '*Booo!*' We're getting shit thrown at us. And it'll be directed just like an ABC After School Special. 'You know I love you, baby, but I've got to put the band before anything.' 'Yes, I understand.' 'But you'll live in my heart forever.' 'Go, love of mine.'"

Kurt grins. "And then the end. Our manager will come by and go, 'You guys have been dropped. You're broke.' And the last line is, Chris picks up the phone and goes, 'Hello, operator? Give me Sub Pop!'"

EVERETT TRUE
STATION TO DEVASTATION: NIRVANA

Melody Maker, November 2, 1991

It ends with a knock on my door at eight in the morning.

Two obscenely aggressive security men storm into my hotel room, wanting to know if I'm hiding a phone anywhere. Seems one went missing the previous night after Kurt from Nirvana took exception to a painting hanging in Chris's room and threw it out the window. Shelves, tables, sheets, glasses, mirrors followed—and then, a quick trip to Kurt's room for more of the same. The televisions stayed, however (have you ever tried lifting one of those fuckers?). All of this culminated in a rather prompt departure from Washington DC the next morning, before the journalist even manages to rise.

My clothes are covered in vomit, someone's using the back of my head as a pinball machine, there's a barbecue happening at the end of my bed and the rats in the back alley are so fat and complacent you can use them as footballs. Just another day on the road with Nirvana.

Two days earlier, Monty, Nirvana's long-suffering tour manager, was picked up for questioning by police in Pittsburgh at two in the morning (just after David Letterman). The show earlier that night had ended with some harsh words spoken between band and club and later someone attempted to set the place alight—piling up cushions, seat covers and carpets in the dressing room downstairs and dowsing them in petrol—and the Man figured Nirvana might know something about it.

"That was a classic case of coked-out Pittsburgh mafioso promotion," Kurt assures me later. "That club was the type of place that would have John Cafferty And The Beaver Brown Band, Huey Lewis And The News and all those other professional bar bands. What's rock 'n' roll to them?"

Nirvana had nothing to do with it: not this time. Kurt had merely smashed some bottles in the toilet and thrown a couple of things around. But, fair do's, Nirvana have certainly been responsible for their fair share of trouble in the past.

"When we were in Europe," says Kurt Cobain, Nirvana's charismatic and perpetually tired singer, backstage at DC's infamous 9:30 Club, "we nearly set the tour van alight." Around us, various members of the Nirvana entourage, including drummer Dave Grohl and his cool mom, chow down on the 9:30's infamous "pizza rider."

"You see, no one knows it, but those Sonic Youth kids, they're wild," he continues, gleefully. "They were instigating violence and terrorism throughout the entire European festival tour. Their [and Nirvana's] manager, also. He antagonizes people and leaves us to take the rap, beating us up, tearing our pants, conking Chris [Novoselic, bassist] over the head with a bottle, turning beetroot red when he's drunk. He's wild."

Kurt is one of those people for whom the words "butter," "melt" and "mouth" were invented. He looks angelic. Yet last time I saw him, backstage at Reading, he had one arm in a sling after leaping backwards into Dave's drum kit, and the previous time, his manager was sent a bill for God knows how much, after the band completely destroyed an LA apartment.

Yes, Nirvana like to wreck stuff: Chris usually finishes a set by throwing his bass 20 feet into the air (and occasionally catching it). In Pittsburgh, Kurt rammed his guitar straight into the snare drum out of sheer frustration; in DC, he ran off the stage 10 minutes before the end to take a breather, it was so damn hot, before rushing back to destroy the drums. New York's Marquee was blessed with an encore that was just bass, drums and Kurt screaming melodically from somewhere in the audience, he'd fucked his guitars up so bad—and it still sounded as if there were six guitars playing.

Nirvana have a $750 equipment allowance per week. And Kurt hates cheap guitars! They live the classic rock 'n' roll lifestyle (rampant vandalism) because it's the only lifestyle they know. And because it's fun. And, along the way, they're responsible for some of the most invigorating rock music of the Nineties.

One listen to their new album, *Nevermind,* confirms this: I'm up to about 230 and still of the opinion that there's no better record this year. That's what honesty does for you. Songs like the terribly open "In Bloom," "Drain You" and the mind-numbingly fine single, "Smells Like Teen Spirit" (something to do with a girl sitting alone in a room, or is that the torching lament of "Come As You Are"? Fuck knows, fuck cares) are *my life*. No exaggeration.

All I have to do is hear the opening strummed acoustic chords to "Polly" (a disquieting tale of rape) or the all-out melodic, self-centered attack of "On A Plain" and my mind flips. One note from Kurt's torturously twisted, magically melodious scream on "Stay Away" and my heart beats at my chest and makes a try for the heavens. Works every time.

Meanwhile, back in the real world . . .

"Yeah, I lit the curtains in our tour van on fire while we were doing an interview," Kurt says. "This was a few hours after some other destruction. This representative for MCA gave us a gift, a wastepaper basket full of candy and magazines, with a little note welcoming us to Germany.

"The gift had been in the dressing room for two hours, while we'd been doing our set and eating our dinner. During this time, Kim Gordon [Sonic Youth] had written 'Fuck you' underneath the woman's signature on the note. So we saw this and thought, 'Gee, that's kinda peculiar, but we can make good use of the sweets.'"

Kurt is a complete candy freak. (Does *anyone* else buy those little wax bottles you drink about 1 cc of pop out of?)

"So we met the rep, thanked her and Chris proceeded to get drunker and drunker," he continues. "He shot off a fire extinguisher, ripped up the magazines and threw the candy all over the place and destroyed the whole room. Sonic Youth's dressing room, too. Classic rock 'n' roll angst."

So the band went outside, the MCA woman came back, saw the note, assumed Nirvana had written it and threw a fit, threatening to drop them from the label.

"By this time," Kurt goes on, "we'd been doing interviews in the van for about an hour and I lit the curtains on fire, and we opened the door and this bellow of smoke came into her face. She thought we'd set the van on fire. The rumours were a bit exaggerated when they finally got back to MCA to the extent that we'd assaulted the woman and destroyed the club and completely burned out our van."

Rock 'n' roll, eh kids? There ain't nothing like the real thing.

The left handed singer/guitarist then tells me about another time in Belgium where they swapped round all the name tags in the chic cafeteria tent, so the party of 12 Ramones and friends ended up sitting at a table for four and Shane MacGowen was left on his own.

"He was being spoon-fed Gerbers baby food because he couldn't chew," comments Chris maliciously. "So we gave him a plate of apples."

Everyone giggles.

"There were about 30 of us sitting in a party with Sonic Youth," the singer adds. "Someone throws a carrot stick and someone throws a grape. Then someone throws back some dressing and it turns into a huge big food fight. We completely wrecked the food tent, but it was a lot of fun and if there had been televisions there, we would have wrecked them too.

"We snuck into Ride's trailer and stole their champagne," he continues. "This guy who was with us, video-ing the tour, pee-ed in their champagne bucket. We stole all their flowers and candy too."

Isn't this all rather rock 'n' roll? Isn't this all opposed to what Nirvana are about? I thought you were meant to "hate the average American macho male" (not my quotes). I thought you'd abhor such boorish behavior as the province of prats like Axl Rose and his ilk.

"Well, no one actually does this stuff anymore," Kurt says. "They're too scared. But that isn't our point. We only do it 'cos we're bored and we want to have fun. And we do—real sincere fun!"

"I think the alcohol has a lot to do with it, too," Dave adds.

But doesn't this sort of behavior just lead meek Limey journalists like myself to assume you're just a bunch of redneck no-good delinquents?

"We're not boasting about it," Kurt retorts. "You asked us."

"I asked *you? Me?*"

"Yes, you did," he replies.

"You started the whole fucking thing!"

"But at the same time, who fucking cares?" Dave asks. Dave woke up this morning on his mom's couch to the strains of "Teen Spirit." It was being used as background music for an advertisement for antique cars. He thought that was kinda cool. "It's all entertainment," he adds. "The people who'd call us stupid rednecks, whatever, are the people who give us that champagne to pee in, are the people who put on those shows."

"Cham-pagne," Chris says disgustedly. "Like if there was a fifth of whiskey there, I'm going to drink cham-pagne!"

"Ride should have had that fucking champagne," Dave sneers. "Make them stop staring at their fucking feet the whole time, goddamn it!"

So how much do Nirvana love rock 'n' roll? Let's find out.

"Rock 'n' roll?" asks Dave perplexed.

Yeah!

"When they asked Jesus how much he loved the world, they nailed his hands to the cross—This much!" Chris comments.

C'mon guys. Let's talk about rock 'n' roll, for fuck's sake—Sammy Hagar, Van Halen, Warrant or whatever their damn names are!

"They're not even worth slagging," Kurt replies, aware that I'm trying to wind him up. "Let's just say I don't want to be associated with 99 per cent of rock 'n' roll bands."

"The Youth, the Honey, the Breeders, the Cross, the Knife, the Nails, Fugazi—they're the bands we like," explains Chris (the Knife are Shonen Knife, the three-headed pure punk pop goddesses from Japan).

Do you provide an alternative to heavy metal?

"Oh, we've been called an alternative band before," Kurt sneers. "But we eat meat so I think we're disqualified: chili dogs, corn dogs, Jimmy Dean Sausage Breakfast."

"When I first joined the band," Dave comments, "I was living on Kurt's couch and there was an AM/PM convenience store right down the street where you could get three corn dogs for 99 cents. I lived on them for a year."

"It kept him regular too," Kurt adds. "I knew when to avoid the bathroom, nine in the morning and 12 at night. He had to walk through my bedroom to get to the bathroom."

"That's right," Chris agrees. "I actually took a shit in your backyard once, because I didn't want to stink up your whole house. It was really pleasant: warm and wet. Sweet!"

So I ask Kurt if he thinks he's developing a rock star complex. It seems like an appropriate question.

"We talked about that," he replies evasively. "I can't remember what I said."

Yeah. You were saying sometimes you can't work out what the matter is.

"What did I say? Can you remember?" he asks pitifully, sounding like Courtney Love momentarily.

It's something to do with wanting to weed out certain elements of your audience. (If I wrote how many metal bands Nirvana have turned down as supporting slots, we'd be in litigation for a decade.)

"That's true," Kurt confirms. "The people who scream 'Naked of Creed' throughout the entire show, even after we've played it, and who talk really loud during songs like 'Polly.' Like, last night, that exact type of people were the ones yelling, 'Sell out' after we played because we didn't do an encore, because we didn't sign autographs. But what could be more rock 'n' roll than that?"

We also had a conversation a few days earlier, in that weird street in Philadelphia where every other building was a witchcraft store, where you said how little making music means to you anymore.

"That's partly true," Kurt replies. "That's because if we ever had any conscious goals, we've already gone past them. We now have guaranteed distribution, we've gone up to a pretty high level on the underground circuit and that's all we ever wanted."

"We're not going to be proud of the fact that there are a bunch of Guns N' Roses kids who are into our music. We don't feel comfortable progressing, playing larger venues."

You mentioned how people in Olympia ostracize you, for not being "pure" enough, now that you've signed to a major label. We spoke about the bullshit this industry gives up and you even had an inspired rant against "rockers" like Hagar and Halen in the van between NYC and Pittsburgh when there was nothing else to do but scarf junk food and flip through copies of *Sassy*.

Hell, you even told me something of your past in Olympia or wherever it was you grew up, how you would get bored out of your skull and go round and break into people's homes, trash them, not steal anything, just trash them, graffiti the walls, break up the furniture, smash the adornments—anything for a thrill, the buzz. Sounded pure Jimmy Dean to me. You mentioned the buzz you get from the after-effects of your trouble-making, the exhilaration of being confronted by a truck-load of angry officials.

As I watch him fall asleep at a moment's notice, I wonder, how can this cherub-faced misfit, this sulky boy be responsible for such brutal, poignantly touching music?

"I'm disgusted with having to deal with the commercial side of our band at the moment and as a reaction, I'm becoming more uptight and complain more. And it feels like I'm adopting a rock star attitude," Kurt says. "But I still fell guilty about it, because I'm bumming people's days."

So we're talking your classic white middle-class liberal guilt complex here, right?

"What?" Dave asks affronted. "The only guilt that I have is that I'm bumming other people's fun," Kurt explains. "I'm not pleasant to be around in those situations and I'm concerned that my band-mates might be having a bad time."

Why are you doing this right now?

"Because I'm under contract," the singer responds. "Because I'm in fear of having to go to court if I were to leave the band."

What would you be doing if you weren't doing this?

"I'd be a street musician, definitely. That's my goal in life."

PATRICK MACDONALD
IN SEARCH OF NIRVANA

The Seattle Times, March 8, 1992

Aberdeen, Grays Harbor County—the first thing you see coming into this town is dead trees. Thousands and thousands of dead trees, stacked in pyramid piles along the mouth of the Chehalis River, where it empties into Grays Harbor. This is timber country.

"This Business Supported By Timber Dollars" say green, stenciled placards in the windows of most of the surviving stores and shops in the downtown area. "For Sale" signs are in the windows of the many empty storefronts.

Residential parts of town are dominated by small houses where many windows display the same sign: "This Family Supported By Timber Dollars."

"This is the ultimate redneck town," says Dana James Bong as he waits on the porch for his friend Greg Hokanson, who is upstairs getting some videotapes. The two long-haired guys in their late 20s are among many in the close-knit Aberdeen music community who are longtime friends, fellow musicians and fans of Kurt Cobain and Chris Novoselic of Nirvana, the hottest rock band in the world.

The emergence of the punkish, anarchistic, brooding, powerful trio (which also includes East Coast drummer Dave Grohl)—whose *Nevermind* album has been at the top of the charts since the beginning of the year—has given new validity to the scene here.

"Nirvana's not the first band to come out of here," advises Bong as the wind picks up and a light rain starts to fall outside the porch. Just a few minutes ago, it was sunny.

"The Melvins [a top alternative band] came from here and so did Metal Church [a heavy metal band]," he explains as Hokanson arrives with tape in hand. "Kurdt Vanderhoof [of Metal Church] lives just down the street, and the Melvins used to practice a few blocks from here."

As we head to the car, a tall, skinny woman in a polka-dot dress walks down the sidewalk carrying an umbrella in one hand and an armful of manila envelopes in the other. "There's one of the town's crazies," Bong says. "One of our log ladies."

Across the street, a house in the corner has a garden filled with brightly painted wood cutouts of flowers. Painted wood birds are attached to the trees. Painted wood squirrels and ducks stand motionless in the well-tended yard.

"Yeah, there's a lot of *Twin Peaks* in this town," Bong allows.

We are on our way to the Polish Hall Tavern, because it has a wide-screen TV. Bong lugs a suitcase of videos and a cardboard box containing a VCR. Along the way, he and Hokanson point out Nirvana tourist sites—the vacant lot where one of the houses Cobain used to live in once stood; the second-story window Cobain once jumped from during a party (he didn't get hurt too badly because he was drunk, Bong says); an abandoned house Cobain used to crash in.

"Kurt used to live there," Hokanson says, pointing to a blue boarding house across the street. "He lived all over town. I don't think he ever slept at home passed the age of 15."

Cobain stayed in Hokanson's house for six months, sleeping on the couch or on the floor in Greg's room. That was about the time Nirvana started in 1986, Hokanson says, as we go into the tavern's back room. On the big TV, Bong plays a video of Nirvana's first performance, at the Hoquiam Eagles Hall in 1986.

That concert has reached near-mythic status in Aberdeen. Every rock fan you meet here claims to have been there, although most admit they went for the Melvins, who headlined, more than Nirvana. The Melvins, now based in San Francisco, introduced live punk rock to the rock fans of Aberdeen, mostly metalheads, and turned on a lot of people—including Kurt Cobain—to the rage, energy and tortured eloquence of punk.

But people who were there will never forget Nirvana. In the video, it's apparent that back then the group already had a certain spark, a unique way of blending punk, metal and pop, and a strong sense of outrageousness. Novoselic, the 6-foot-7-inch bassist, played the entire set in his underpants. Cobain arrived on stage with his neck painted bright red.

On the tape, the band crunches out a song called "School." In place of the refrain "No recess," Cobain screams, "No Dana! No Dana!" while glaring into Bong's video camera. Bong turns up the volume and starts dancing around the pool table, flinging his arms in the air and jumping on one foot.

"This is the Chris Novoselic dance," he yells over the music.

The library of Weatherwax High School is a stately, high-ceilinged room dating to 1906. A few students sit at tables, working quietly. The morning sun streams through the tall windows. I whisper to a librarian that I'm looking for yearbooks with Cobain and Novoselic in them.

"Chris was not in school very often," a librarian offers.

How about Kurt?

"Oh, yes. He was in here a lot."

She holds up a copy of *Spin* magazine with Nirvana on the cover. "We've started a file," she said, pulling it out of a shelf behind her. It includes some clippings from *The Aberdeen World* and a feature from a recent *Rolling Stone.*

Novoselic and Cobain managed to get through high school without ever having their pictures in the *Quinault,* the school's yearbook. Head librarian John Eko brings out copies of *Ocean Breeze,* the school paper, from 1983 to 1985, when the two were enrolled. Again, nothing.

"Nirvana's success is the best thing to happen to Aberdeen in years," Eko says. "They're something I can point to and tell kids that there's all kinds of possibilities out there." I tell him Cobain once told me he secretly started writing poetry in junior high, but hid it from friends for fear of being teased.

Eko's eyes brighten. "That's great. I never knew that. Now maybe I can get some kids to read poetry."

One of the *Daily World* stories quotes Weatherwax art teacher Bob Hunter as saying Cobain was one of the most talented students he ever had.

A librarian tells me she once saw Cobain when he was very down. She asked him what was the matter and she said his father had smashed his guitar because he was playing too loud.

"Sounds like his father was his first critic," says Eko. Maybe that's why he still smashes guitars on stage.

Maria's Hair Design, on M Street, is a blue, two-story house on the edge of downtown with a small black Nirvana sticker in a corner of the front window.

Maria is Chris Novoselic's mother. A tall, perky redhead, she's bubbling with enthusiasm over her son's good fortune.

"I still can't believe it," she says, with a trace of an accent. "I still can't believe it's happening."

Maria Novoselic put the sticker in her window two years ago, when Nirvana released its first album on the Sub Pop label, *Bleach*. No one paid much attention to the sticker until late last year, when *Nevermind*—the band's second album and its first for a major label, Geffen—was released. Now Nirvana fans come into the shop, wanting to take her picture.

"Chris was here for Christmas," she says. "He couldn't even go to the store, because people just make such a big fuss over him. And Chris is a very down-to-earth kid, he doesn't want all this fuss."

Chris Novoselic was born 26 years ago in Compton, Calif., after his parents emigrated from Yugoslavia. The family came to Aberdeen in 1979.

"There are lots of Croatian people here, and that's why we are here," Maria says. "We are not Yugoslavian anymore, we are Croatian."

Chris Novoselic speaks fluent Croatian. When he was 14, he went to school in Croatia for a year, living with relatives. When he and his mother talk—which they do frequently on the phone—they speak Croatian.

When Novoselic started hanging out with Cobain, his mother didn't like it. "I remember Kurt as just this little skinny kid, and I thought, 'Oh, my God, who's this?'"

She said Kurt was shy and never spoke to her, but Chris assured her, saying Kurt was talented and was going to be somebody. Knowing her son's love of music, she approved—until she came home one evening and found the house full of kids listening to Chris and Kurt jam with some friends.

"I just yell and scream, 'Get these kids out of here!' I didn't understand. I was protecting my property."

For a while, Novoselic worked as a house painter, but was always more interested in music. About four years ago, he and Cobain moved to Olympia to concentrate on making Nirvana happen.

Two years ago, Novoselic married his longtime girlfriend. They recently bought a house in Seattle and furnished it with antiques, most of them collected in Aberdeen thrift shops. Novoselic, who loves working on cars, bought a junker for $100, and fixed it up himself.

"Chris is just a sweetheart," says his mother. "He respected me so much. I'm not bragging. He is just a super son. He helped a lot of people. He's not bratty, he doesn't smoke. He's a strict vegetarian for years. If anybody deserves this, it's Chris."

The Pourhouse Tavern is Aberdeen's hottest rock spot. On weekends, the old tavern—with a long bar, an old wooden phone booth, a small stage and a pool room in the back—is just about the only place in town to hear live rock music. All the best local bands play here, mixing original tunes with popular cover songs.

"Kurt played here once," Greg Hokanson says, straining to be heard over the music. He doesn't remember the name of the band, because Cobain was in so many before Nirvana was formed: Ted Ed Fred, Bliss, Pen Cap Chew, Skid Row.

Before hooking up with Cobain, Novoselic was lead singer and guitarist in a band called the Stiff Woodies that also played the Pourhouse. Hokanson remembers hearing them do a great song called "Vaseline and Gasoline."

Hokanson introduces me to his mother, a young-looking woman who easily fits in with the mostly 20s crowd. What was it like having Kurt Cobain living in her house?

"Like living with the devil," she shoots back.

Cobain had one of his destructo raids in her son's bedroom, destroying furniture and scrawling things on the wall (he still does the same thing, but now it's hotel rooms). But she was impressed by his intelligence and talent, she said. He read a lot and could talk about anything. Greg Hokanson adds, "Kurt read more books than anybody I ever knew."

One day he rented the video of *A Clockwork Orange* and watched it with Cobain. "The next day he went to the library and got the book and read the whole thing, and then read it a couple more times, then read everything by Anthony Burgess," Hokanson said.

Earlier, Bong said, "Kurt Cobain was the only young kid I knew who did not smoke, did not drink beer and did not smoke pot." But, he added, he did all of those things later. In excess.

Performing Artists Services is an old building on the edge of town that a group of Aberdeen musicians are converting into band practice rooms and a recording studio. One of those involved in the project is Aaron Burkhart, Nirvana's first drummer. Like so many other musicians here, he once lived with Kurt Cobain.

"He had a bathtub full of turtles," Burkhart recalls, as Nirvana's "Smells Like Teen Spirit" blares from huge speakers. Cobain collected the turtles at nearby lakes and streams. "One of the little ones escaped once, and he accidentally stepped on it and squished it."

Burkhart takes me into one of the practice rooms. "I live here some of the time," he says. The back seat of an old car rests on the floor, with blankets and a pillow. Burkhart talks about jamming with Cobain at the Melvins' house and says that some of Nirvana's old equipment is still there.

Burkhart's big moment with Nirvana was a show in Seattle at the Vogue in 1987. Shortly thereafter he was kicked out of the band after he borrowed Kurt's car and was arrested for driving while intoxicated.

Burkhart, who now heads a band called Attica, says he has no regrets. "I was the first one," he says. "They had four drummers after me."

"I'm just proud I was a part of it."

In New York, the mad have been set free. Let out into the city, they are difficult to tell apart from the rest of the punks, junkies, addicts, winoes, or down-and-outs who inhabit it. It is difficult to see why a city as crazy as this one would keep its mad in the shadows, why it would withdraw from circulation specimens of a madness which has in fact, in its various forms, taken hold of the whole city.

—Jean Baudrillard, *America* (translated by Chris Turner)

Crashing mashing intensified dense rhythms juxtaposed with filmic mood pieces. Evoking an atmosphere that could only be described as expressive fucked-up modernism. And so forth.

—Thurston Moore, describing the music of Sonic Youth in their first press release

Sonic Youth released the double album called *Daydream Nation* in 1988. It was their last release by an independent label. The cover featured paintings of candles by the German artist Gerhard Richter—paintings so acutely detailed that they seem almost like photographs. They exemplify what Richter calls "photo/paintings" and, as commentaries on art and vision, they display a blatant pop/postmodern sensibility. As with Andy Warhol's earlier sampling of the worlds of advertising and fashion, Richter's work comments on the social world as it challenges the very nature of painting. When photography was first invented it changed painting—to compete with the "perfect" image of the photograph artists moved inward and towards abstraction. Richter turns the entire history of painting on its head by going back to the camera image and creating paintings that duplicate the ideal world of the photograph. In response to the stuff of his art, Richter calls his work "Capitalist Realism."

The placement of Richter's paintings on the cover of *Daydream Nation* is indicative of Sonic Youth's understanding of their place within postmodern rock and art. It is also a comment on the Reagan years, which ended officially in 1988 but lingered into the next decade. Just as Richter turns visual art on its head by bringing its evolution and contradictions to the surface, Sonic Youth embraces and disrupts the course of rock 'n' roll. This is the importance and the strength of Sonic Youth: they are astute readers of their own place within rock in particular and American pop culture in general. And they use this knowledge in their music. As the bedrock of the underground throughout the 1980s—their first album came out in 1982—Sonic Youth is like those mumbling, possessed ones at the end of *Fahrenheit 451*: they kept something alive through persistence and resilience. If anyone ever writes a science fiction novel about Sonic Youth they should steal the first sentence from Bradbury's book-burning future to describe their approach to rock: "It was a pleasure to burn." Or, to steal more and steal better, maybe the description should be taken from Walter Pater:

> Not the fruit of experience, but experience itself, is the end. A counted number of pulses only is given to us in a variegated, dramatic life. How may we see in them all that is to be seen in them by the finest sense? How shall we pass most swiftly from point to point, and be present always at the focus where the greatest number of vital forces unite in their purest energy? To burn always with this hard, gem-like flame, to maintain this ecstasy, is success in life.[1]

The candle of Sonic Youth set a thousand bands with a thousand songs on fire.

The inclusion of the following interview with Sonic Youth in a book about Nirvana is necessary because it points to one of the origins of Nirvana. The music of Nirvana is not taken directly from Sonic Youth—listen to Flipper, the Melvins, the Pixies, Black Flag, Black Sabbath, and the Vaselines for immediate influences—but Nirvana's sound would have been impossible without Sonic Youth. This is true for an entire generation of bands. In the particular case of Nirvana, Sonic Youth promoted them and took them on tour. Sonic Youth's signing with Geffen in 1990 led to the label's interest in Nirvana. And in 1992, Kim Gordon coproduced Hole's first album, *Pretty on the Inside*. When asked what kind of success they wished for, the members of Nirvana always pointed to Sonic Youth—a success that fostered creativity and disregarded the pressures of the market.

Sonic Youth is important because in many ways they are the bridge between the New York punk of the late 1970s and the music of Nirvana, Soundgarden, the Pixies, Pavement, late Beastie Boys, Hole, Sebadoh, Babes in Toyland, Gumball, Pussy Galore, My Bloody Valentine, the Breeders, and Dinosaur Jr. Emerging from No-Wave post-punk, Sonic Youth combined together the sounds that were all around them—the far-off experiments in noise offered by the Velvet Underground, then, a little closer, the music of Television and the guitar eruptions of Glenn Branca.

---

1. Walter Pater, *The Renaissance* (Oxford and New York: Oxford University Press, 1986).

By experimenting with guitar tunings, Sonic Youth created an entirely new musical world for others to explore. But, as the following interview shows, this new way of using guitars was only one of the physical manifestations of Sonic Youth's art. Their importance lies deeper, further, beyond, and all over the music that used to live underground.

JOE GORE

KILL YR TUNINGS

Guitar Player, July 1994

Scattered around the lobby of Manhattan's Sear Sound, the members of Sonic Youth idly thumb through a stack of music magazines, nibble Mexican takeout, and pass around a copy of Michael Azerrad's *Come As You Are: The Story of Nirvana.* Kurt Cobain is still alive, and the musicians have been scrutinizing their depiction as early boosters, touring buddies, and label mates of the Seattle trio.

The night before guitarist Thurston Moore cornered Azerrad after a Royal Trux gig at CBGB's, telling him that his book erroneously reported that Sonic Youth mixed in layers of white noise to help their last album, *Dirty,* live up to its name. Might Moore, who thrives on tweaking earnest journalists, have uttered such a fib in much the same spirit that he told *Guitar Player* readers that he attended Berkeley and studied with Bill Frisell? "Maybe," he allows.

Producer Butch Vig, veteran of Nirvana's *Nevermind,* Smashing Pumpkins' *Siamese Dream,* and *Dirty,* calls in the musicians one at a time for level checks. It's well past midnight when he asks the quartet to run down one tune so they can listen with fresh ears tomorrow. They plow through "Doctor's Orders" and then return to the console for a playback. The sound, with absolutely no processing, is stunning, the oddly tuned guitars alternately barking and glistening. "Wow," murmurs bassist Kim Gordon. "It sounds like it's mixed already."

Six months later *Experimental Jet Set, Trash, And No Star* is about to be released. A giddy blend of fastidiously arranged pieces and off-the-cuff rave-ups, Sonic Youth's ninth album (excluding EPs and gray-market bootlegs) recalls *EVOL, Sister,* and *Daydream Nation,* the late-80's LPs that helped elevate the quartet from fringe avant-gardists to post-punk's most influential guitar band. Many of *Experimental*'s songs are downright beautiful, full of eerie harmonies, precise ensemble work, and ravishing guitar textures. There's even a solo acoustic cut. "Geffen says they don't hear a single, but we love this record," enthuses co-guitarist Lee Ranaldo. Tomorrow morning Cobain's body will be discovered; today the band is in high spirits.

Gore: Did everything go as smoothly as that first night?

Thurston: It started easy, then we decided to make it harder, then we went back to Easyville.

Lee: Which is to say, as much as we enjoyed our quick rough mixes, we felt we couldn't trust them, so we spent two weeks and 25 grand doing proper mixes . . .

Kim: But we ended up using the half-hour rough mixes.

Gore: There's an amazing mix of sublime, pretty stuff and bonehead punk rock.

Lee: "Bonehead?"

Thurston: Well, we're trying to eradicate the bonehead parts as we go along.

Gore: "Skink" and "Bone" use the guitars and bass in one big, resonant choir.

Kim: Both of those are based on guitar riffs of mine—there's no bass on those cuts. It's the same tuning I use with [side band] Free Kitten: B, E, D, D, and two low Bs on top.

Gore: It's cool how "Bull in the Heather" makes pop hooks out of abstract gestures like cluster harmonics and behind-the-nut strums.

Thurston: That's a behind-the-bridge strum. Behind-the-nut is for arty, pretentious people. Behind-the-bridge is rock; behind-the-nut is art school. Stay away from the nut.

Gore: Has anyone compared that song to Creedence's "Fortunate Son"?

Lee: Yeah, that's what the main guitar riff is.

Thurston: What?

Kim: I don't hear that, but "Sweet Shine" was originally called "Lindsey" because it sounds like Fleetwood Mac.

Gore: *What are the noises on "Starfield Road," the ones that sound like toy ray guns?*

Thurston: Toy ray guns.

Gore: *Come on, man—I've seen you lie to journalists before.*

Lee: And then five years later some guy in France is going to say, "Deed you evair do more with ze toy ray gun sound?" That effect is my newest toy, a Maestro ring modulator. My other favorite is the Ibanez AD80 analog delay stomp box I use all over the album. We've been really into old effects pedals.

Thurston: I use Sovtek Big Muffs pedals for all the "bonehead" chords. I've also got a '70s Mu-Tron Fuzz/Wah and a Mu-Tron phase shifter that just makes a scratchy whistling sound. I used some Turbo Rat for your classic distortion, but I'm thinking of abandoning that in favor of just clean and cranked Big Muff.

Gore: *You're using mostly high-quality guitars now instead of the pawn-shop trash you used to play.*

Lee: Yes indeed. My biggest recent discovery has been the Les Paul; almost all my parts on the record were written on it. I love it so much; everything it does is perfect. I also used my usual Travis Bean aluminum-necks and early-'70s Tele Deluxes. My main amp is a new Fender Tone Master; I really like the way it has the simplest controls possible. Now I'm going to investigate early Fender Deluxes. I'm definitely leaning towards cool smaller amps, though I need something like the Tone Master to blast live.

Kim: My main bass was a Fender Precision through a Mesa/Boogie amp and some tube direct box.

Thurston: I just used the same old same old, mostly a couple of Jazzmasters and a 160-wat Peavey Roadmaster. We have to go on tour so I can have one of our roadies change the tubes.

Lee: See, we haven't had to do that stuff ourselves in so long, we don't know how.

Thurston: I changed a string myself the other night. It took five hours, man. I run the Peavey through a '60s Marshall 4x12 bottom. I need more so I can build a wall out of them—or at least some coffee tables.

Gore: *What's the acoustic guitar on "Winner's Blues?"*

Lee: That's Thurston playing my Carson J. Robison acoustic, which was made by Gibson in the '30s. It's an amazing guitar.

Gore: *What's the tuning?*

Thurston: E, E, B, E, G♯, B, low to high. But they're not tunings; they're secret codes.

Lee: Tunings talk is passé. Every article you read, whether it's Pearl Jam or whoever the fuck, they all use tunings at this point. It's not important. I mean, it's great for guitarists to know that those things exist, but at this point it's very secondary to what we do.

Kim: Now tunings are just part of the vocabulary that everyone uses. A tuning is just an extension of the guitar. Wouldn't it be great if the guitars people bought on 48th Street all came in weird tunings, and you were committed to that tuning for the life of the guitar? What would happen?

Gore: *Now that you've dismissed tunings, tell us which ones you used.*

Lee: We used so many fewer guitars and tunings than ever before— maybe two or three each. For about 60% of the record, I use the Les Paul in a new tuning, G, G, C, G, C, D. Two other recent faves are G, G, B, D, G, A, and C♭, F♯, C♯, F♯, A♯, B. All my tunings are restrung— I never used any gauges smaller than .017. I used E, E, B, B, E, F♯ for "Sweet Shine." I call it "Wooden Ships" tuning because it sounds so Jefferson Airplane/Crosby, Stills & Nash.

Thurston: I used a lot of the "Brother James" tuning [G, G, D, D, E♭, E♭]. "Skink," "Screaming Skull," "Tokyo Eye," and "Sweet Shine" are all in the "Dirty Boots" tuning [E, G, D, G, E, D, with the second string tuned lower than the third] that Kim came up with. I'm using

Pavement's tuning for every song I'm writing now, but they'll get bummed if I disclose it.

Lee: Tell!

Thurston: Okay, it's C, G, D, G, B, B.

Lee: This time around we wanted to expedite the writing process and skip the weeks of searching for tonal centers and so forth. At this point we have a collection of guitars and tunings that work well together; why not just utilize them?

Thurston: Didn't you see the quote on the back of our CD? It's from Jack Brewer, the singer from Saccharine Trust. He said, "Once the music leaves your head, it's already compromised." I don't know, man . . . I remember reading an interview with Greg Ginn years before I knew him. They asked him what his favorite guitars were, and he said he didn't have any favorites because he didn't consider himself a guitar player. He just happened to pick up guitar because it was around.
J Mascis is like that too.

Gore: *You mean musicians referring to themselves as "guitarists" is like novelists calling themselves "typewriters"?*

Thurston: Yeah. That's what Charles Bukowski always used to say: "I'm a typewriter." So I agree with Greg Ginn. I'm not a guitarist.

Gore: *So how come* Guitar World *pronounced Sonic Youth the "eighth most important" fixture on the guitar scene, in between Jimmy Page and Ace Frehley?*

Lee: They did? Cool! But how do they rationalize that? We're not what they're all about.

Thurston: Yeah, but some things you can't deny! [Laughs.] Hey, I like playing guitar. It's a cool instrument, in a way.

PART TWO

Vandalism—As Beautiful as a Rock in a Cop's Face

This whole world . . . wild at heart and weird on top. I wish you'd sing me "Love Me Tender." I wish I was somewhere over the rainbow. Shit, shit, shit.

—Lulu in David Lynch's *Wild At Heart*

Hey, Hullabalooza isn't about freaks. It's about music and advertising and youth-oriented product positioning.

—Kim Gordon in *The Simpsons* (Episode #3F21)

Nevermind took the number one slot on the *Billboard* charts on January 11, 1992. It was the beginning of a strange and wild year for Nirvana. The video for "Smells Like Teen Spirit" became a fixture on MTV. In April, the band appeared on the cover of *Rolling Stone*. They were still the same band but everything had changed.

The writing in this section describes the changes that occurred and the wild world Nirvana was thrown into. Everett True's "In My Head I'm Not Ugly" caught Nirvana just as things started to get out of control. Nirvana still enjoyed performing at this point, reflected in the beautiful fury L. A. Kanter encounters when he attends a Nirvana show. Kanter also explores one of the underrated aspects of Cobain's music—his ferocious, passionate, and riveting guitar work.

But fame came and its pressures quickly closed in. Everett True was one of the first writers to report on the tensions the band was facing—in "Come As You Aren't" he witnesses it on stage, and in "Crucified By Success" the band tells him about it.

Darcey Steinke talked to Cobain and Novoselic when things were at their worst: the *Vanity Fair* debacle was still haunting Cobain (more on this in the last section of this book, where True interviews Cobain and Love), and rumors of Cobain's heroin use were everywhere—from *MTV News* to *Entertainment Tonight*. Steinke's article is important because it goes into what is really important—the music that inspired Cobain. Cobain picks through his record collection and comments on the music he loves (Leadbelly, the Shaggs, Black Sabbath) and even points to Nirvana's future performance of the Meat Puppets' "Lake of Fire" during the *MTV Unplugged* recording.

From the pages of *Billboard* comes Craig Rosen's report on the controversy that surrounded the post-production of *In Utero*—a controversy instigated by *Newsweek*. It was a media-generated controversy indicative of the constant scrutiny that Nirvana had to endure.

This section ends with my thoughts on Cobain's connection to William S. Burroughs and a selection from Burroughs's "cut-up" novel, *The Ticket That Exploded*. Burroughs exploded literature, and his artistic example fascinated Cobain—any consideration of how Nirvana exploded popular music would be incomplete without a discussion of Burroughs's work.

Dear Mr. Bukowski:
Why don't you ever write about politics or world affairs?

—M.K.

Dear M.K.:
What for? Like, what's new?—everybody knows the bacon is burning.

—Charles Bukowski, "Politics Is Like Trying to Screw a Cat in the Ass"

CLOV: What is there to keep me here?
HAMM: The dialogue.

—Samuel Beckett, *Endgame*

DUTCH: The chimney sweeps take to the sword.
1ST DETECTIVE: Control yourself.
2ND DETECTIVE: The doctor wants you to lie quiet.
DUTCH: But I am dying. . . .
DUTCH: French Canadian bean soup.

—William S. Burroughs, *The Last Words of Dutch Schultz*

IN MY HEAD I'M SO UGLY

Melody Maker, July 18, 1992

For logistical reasons, this interview took place in Kurt Cobain's LA apartment during the second week of June, a couple of weeks before his band's short tour of Europe.

The day's cloudy, the room dim and slightly messy. Scraps of diaries containing lyrics and ideas from both Kurt and his wife, Courtney Love, plus a couple of guitars and amplifiers, litter the main room. A few weird-looking stick dolls, made by Kurt for use in a future video, nestle next to multi-coloured bird feathers and jars full of flowers.

In the front room, where Kurt lounges in an armchair, looking studious in his "geek" glasses and short, bleached hair; a Patti Smith record plays quietly in the background. A small kitten darts about, tigerish. Courtney, several months pregnant, is asleep in the bedroom with her TV tuned quietly to daytime MTV.

Earlier, Kurt had shown me the video to Nirvana's new single, "Lithium," on the same TV set. Compiled from live footage of the band from last year's Reading Festival, a gig in Seattle, and a show in Rotterdam where he first romanced Courtney, it's breathtakingly ferocious. Live videos usually suck, this one doesn't. Work it out for yourself.

As you join us, Kurt's been telling me how, the older he gets, the more affinity he feels for feminine people.

"I was more of a feminine person when I was young, I just didn't know it," he says, taking a sip of strawberry tea. "Then, when my hormones started swinging around and I started getting facial hair, I had to let off my male steam somewhere, so I started smoking pot and listening to Black Sabbath and Black Flag. It took the Pixies to put me back on the right track and off the whole macho punk rock trip."

The trouble with punk was that it thought it was cool to put down women. I could never relate to that. Here was this movement which was supposed to be right on, but it excluded over half the people I knew.

"Definitely," he agrees. "That was something I realized later, 'cos I didn't experience punk in the Seventies. There was this live record, *Night of the Living Dead Boys,* where Stiv Bators was spewing off about how some girl was sucking his cock while he was on stage. That was the common accepted thing."

Watching *Headbangers Ball* on MTV, nothing seems to have changed. Music, especially metal, still reinforces all the scummiest aspects of being a male.

"It might be getting a little better because of bands like Soundgarden, who are obviously metal," says Kurt. "They have a good, healthy attitude, and maybe others will follow them. Even Pearl Jam, who were obviously cock rock poseurs down on the Strip last year, are preferable."

The singer pauses, struck by a thought.

"You know, there's an LA band called Love Buzz [title of the first Nirvana single], and their first album is called *Grunge*. I want to get that album real bad," he laughs.

Does feminism have any bearing on your life? Courtney has already gone on record as stating that she views herself as a feminist. What does a statement like that mean to you?

"It means women controlling their own lives, and me not standing in their way by being a male," Kurt responds. "It's not so much of an ideal as a sense. It doesn't seem like there's such a thing as a recognizable feminist movement like there was in the Seventies, more a collective awareness. It's in the way you live your life."

What would you say are the main differences between having a masculine and feminine outlook are? Kurt carefully considers his words before replying.

"Being aware of not offending women and not supporting sexist acts," he offers. "But not so you become so paranoid that you can't feel comfortable in a woman's presence. Sexist jokes are harmless as long as you're aware of them, but I also know a lot of people who put on this pretend macho redneck act 24 hours a day—they use the redneck lingo and spew out sexist quotes—and then they claim that they're simply trying to remind you that's how rednecks are. I've noticed that if someone does that too long they turn into a redneck."

That was one of my main bones of contention with Sub Pop a couple of years back, that they didn't realize they were turning into the people they aped.

"Absolutely," Kurt agrees. "That's the main reason I never got along with very many people in the Sub Pop world."

It was funny for a while, but then you started wondering whether they meant it or whether that even mattered. Dwarves (West Coast scum punk band who give interviews about shoving various items of furniture up pregnant women's orifices) are a good example of that.

"I kind of respect people who go out of their way to act like an ass-hole when they're really intelligent, though," Kurt counters. "It's a nihilistic statement, like saying there's no point in trying to be a human any more because things have gotten so out of hand. It's a very punk rock attitude, but I also think it'd be boring to be Johnny Rotten after all these years. I'm not talking about sexism, but that kind of negative attitude when you're no longer able to appreciate passion or beauty."

You've retained certain aspects of the punk attitude, though.

"Of course," replies Kurt. "Because, even though Black Flag were too macho, I still love the music."

You've talked in recent interviews about how you want to help to build up the underground network of alternative bands so that they become better known by name-dropping other bands like Bikini Kill and Sebadoh.

"Yeah," Kurt sighs, heavily. "That's one of the few good things we can do, except for pleasing people with our music. The corporate side of our image is so exploitative, it's one of the only ways we can retain our dignity. One of the main things I regret about the success of this band is . . . this crap." He brandishes a copy of a Nirvana comic book and a Nirvana poster booklet. "We're being totally raped by these people, we have no control over this stuff. They sell hundreds of thousands of those magazines and we don't get a dime out of it, we don't have any say-so in what pictures are used and what quotes are re-written."

"The comic book's quite funny," he adds, "but then, you have to laugh, don't you?"

Do you feel any responsibility towards the people who buy your records?

"Not until people started telling me that I did," Kurt states honestly. "That, and the realization that we have letters from nine-year-old kids coming in all the time. I can't talk about smoking marijuana in interviews, I can't talk about drugs. I can't talk about things that'll influence these kids, but I don't want to be so aware of it that it stops me from saying anything."

"So when I am outspoken and I say nasty things about Pearl Jam," he continues, "I get a lot of flak, and people condemn me and call me an ass-hole. There are so many people who hate my guts because I put down Pearl Jam. But what value do these people have in my life? I have to speak the truth, I have to tell them what I feel. I'm being honest and people aren't used to that, especially in the metal world."

But isn't the problem that then someone like Inger Lorre can come along and claim that she too is telling the truth, totally abusing people's credulity, so that they end up not knowing who to believe? It's difficult for people to differentiate.

"I can see that."

The phone rings. It's someone from a radio station, wanting to know what type of music Kurt listens to. He tells them, "Adult-Orientated Grunge." It rings again. It's Corey from Touch & Go, seeking Kurt's advice over a problem which has arisen with Kurt's management over a projected joint Nirvana/Jesus Lizard single on his label. Kurt listens carefully and promises he'll resolve the situation with his manager.

Despite reports to the contrary, Kurt looks a lot healthier than the previous times I've met him. I wouldn't say that he glows, but he definitely radiates something—happiness in his new-found marriage, perhaps?

I suggest to him, when he eventually comes off the phone, that he seems much more relaxed.

"Oh yeah," he replies. "But that's because when we last met (in October of '91), I'd been on tour for five months, and I haven't played for a while now. Plus, I was getting pissed off doing commercial radio station interviews with all these DJs with their finely sculptured moustaches, talking in professional American radio DJ voices and not having any idea who the fuck we were. How much exposure does one band need?"

Granted. At one point, around the start of this year, it seemed that you couldn't pick up a British music magazine without Nirvana being on the cover, usually with a rehashed or 10-minute interview inside.

"Right," Kurt agrees. "I practically adopted the J. Mascis Fifth Amendment, because I couldn't deal with so many interviews."

He laughs.

"I don't have narcolepsy."

Who started that?

"I did. It's the only defense mechanism I have."

The phone rings again. It's for Courtney, but we aren't mean enough to wake her. Talk turns to Kurt's recent marriage.

How much did meeting Courtney change you?

"Totally," Kurt says, emphatically. "I'm not as much of a neurotic, unstable person as I was. I used to feel I was always alone, even though I had lots of friends and a band that I really enjoyed being with. Now I've found someone I'm close to, who's interested in the things I do, and I really don't have many other aspirations."

Did you know who she was before you met her?

"Not really, no" he replies. "I'd heard about her, though—some nasty rumors, that she was this perfect replica of Nancy Spungen."

Kurt laughs again.

"That got my attention," he remarks, maliciously. "Like everyone else, I loved Sid 'cos he was such a likable, dopey guy. I've often felt that many people think of me as a stupid, impressionable person, so I thought that maybe going out with someone who was meant to be like Nancy would stick a thorn in everyone's side, 'cos it's the exact opposite of what they would want me to do."

"Courtney certainly helped me to put Nirvana in perspective," he adds, "to realize that my reality doesn't entirely revolve around the band, that I can deal without it if I have to. Which doesn't mean I'm planning on breaking up the band or anything, but that the minimal amount of success I strived for isn't of much importance any more."

Has the success put any pressure on the band?

"I don't know," Kurt says slowly, considering his words. "Because of my reputation for being this pissy, moody person, I feel that everyone is expecting me to freak out and develop some kind of ego or quit the band. But there's no way I'm going to do that. I still like playing with Chris and Dave, and I know our new songs are really good and I can't wait to record the next album. And the album after that."

To infinity?

"At least," he laughs. "but I'd also like to have a side project. When you've been working with the same people for a while there's not much more you can do, even though I feel we have succeeded in coming up with some new styles. It'd be fun to play with someone else. But every time I do that, I end up regretting it. Because, if it sounds good, I wish that Nirvana had done it."

Kurt starts flicking through the Nirvana comic, and pauses, struck by a sudden thought.

"People think I'm a moody person, and I think it's lame that there are only two kinds of male lead singer," he complains. "You can either be a moody visionary like Michael Stipe, or a mindless heavy metal party guy like Sammy Hagar."

I tried to portray you as a mindless party animal type [see "Station to Devastation" on page 31 of this book—the interview that went on about Nirvana's smash-fests during the summer] and you got annoyed.

"Oh, okay," Kurt laughs. "I guess it is better to be called a moody visionary than a mindless party animal. I tried to become an alcoholic once, but it didn't work."

We wander through to the bedroom, to see if Courtney's awake yet. Just. The box in the corner is still dribbling out MTV. Talk drifts to how MTV totally controls the American rock world.

"I want to get rid of my cable," Kurt declares. "I've done that so many times in my life, where I decide I'm not going to have television, become celibate. It usually lasts about four months."

I was going to ask you about your fondness for smashing up guitars. Don't you ever get bored with it?

"No," replies Kurt. "I don't do it nearly as much as everyone thinks I do. I just wait for a good time to do it—like when I'm pissed off, or if I want to show off in front of Courtney. Or if I'm appearing on TV, just to piss the TV people off. I have my guitar-smashing room in the back, where I practice four hours a day."

PAUSE. Kurt's building up for another rant.

"You know what I hate about rock?" he asks me. "Cartoons and horns. I hate Phil Collins, all of that white male soul. I hate tie-dyed tee-shirts, too. You know there are bootleg tie-dyed tee-shirts of Nirvana? I hate that. I wouldn't wear a tie-dyed tee-shirt unless it was dyed with the urine of Phil Collins and the blood of Jerry Garcia."

Courtney overhears this last comment from her bedroom.

"Oh God, Kurt, how long have you been thinking about that one?" she castigates him, annoyed.

"Well, fuck," he whines. "No one ever prints it."

"It's fifth grade!" Courtney yells. "It's so boy!"

"Well, ex-ker-use me!" Kurt shouts back, sarcastically.

Courtney's up and about now. This means it must be time to close the interview soon, because there's no way my tape recorder can compete with the demands of a Courtney Love in full flight. Sure enough, Courtney suddenly appears with a book written by her father—a road manager for the Grateful Dead in the Sixties—which includes postcards sent to him by Charles Manson. Weird. Then she produces the original lyrics to "Teen Spirit," scrawled on a scrap of lined paper.

"Thought you might enjoy seeing these, Everett," she announces blithely, oblivious to hubbie's annoyance.

"Can Everett have this, Kurt?" she demands. He growls.

Time for one last question, then.

What's the new album like?

"Like the tape you heard," Kurt tells me.

Oh, yeah, the tape I heard. It sounded like the melodies of *Nevermind* melded to the grunge of *Bleach* on a fast listen. It sounded pretty fucking awesome.

"We haven't decided on a studio yet," he continues. "I'd like to do at least 50 per cent of it on an eight track. Then, hopefully, it will be exactly like *Bleach* and *Nevermind* split down the middle (see, told you). It will definitely sound a lot rawer than *Nevermind*."

Any regrets, Kurt? Have you ever felt like turning the clock back and reclaiming the past?

"If I wanted to, I could," the singer replies. "If, after this dies down, we started putting out records which were unpalatable to the general public, we'd eventually start playing smaller places and . . ."

You'd be the new Beastie Boys.

"Yeah."

Chris Novoselic

For practical reasons, this interview took place the morning of the big Nirvana show in Stockholm, in the band's hotel. The show two days ago in Oslo was slightly lackluster, contrary and full of unanswered questions as to Nirvana's role as a stadium rock band. Chris bounced, barely.

In conversation, Chris is friendly, sincere and thoughtful. He's more committed than ever to his humanitarian causes: actively fighting the new Washington anti-erotic music bill (the one which deems it illegal for shops to sell any record which might contain "erotic material" to minors), speaking up against whaling Norway and taking part in "Rocking the Environment." He gave up drink for three months at the start of the year because his raging moods coupled with Nirvana's success made for a volatile combination (he, the man who once declared he got a cold if he missed a morning's drinking). He's still a firm vegetarian.

The noises you can't hear are those of the hotel staff clearing away the remains of breakfast. As you join us, Chris is talking about the pressures of success.

"People thought we'd self-destruct, but we haven't," he tells me. "I kind of thought that, too, because we took off in such a fury. Our record came out, it was flying up the charts and we were flying in the stratosphere—I know I was, messed-up drunk. Then we had a three month period where we chilled out, and everything was okay. I don't know . . . it seems we're a lot tamer right now, almost going through the motions. What we need to do is put out a new record, play some new songs."

You were saying that the band are unable to play new songs live right now.

"That's right, they'd be bootlegged in an instant," Chris sighs. "But I don't have a problem playing to large audiences, I'm not going to pull my hair out about being unable to play clubs anymore. We should have stayed with Sub Pop if that's what we wanted, and kept playing the Astoria. I try to look at our role in the mainstream positively, like we're helping integrate it."

Do you think a lot of your audience is false?

"What, like we're a fad?" he asks, worried. "I don't know. I'm optimistic about people, to the point of being naive. If they liked *Nevermind*, that's cool, but the next record isn't going to be like that. I see that record as being a litmus test towards our audience. It's going to be a good record but, in terms of mainstream appeal, it won't have the glossiness of *Nevermind*. If we lose those people, that's too bad, but they won't give a shit because they'll be satisfied watching Extreme, or whoever."

You must have had a lot of people who used to know you, who now completely ignore you.

"Yeah," Chris answers, softly. "That's too bad. We're not into playing the role, like driving around in limousines, going to Grammy parties or playing MTV softball like Motley Crue, you know? We still operate on the same level—the only difference is that we sell a lot more records and play to a lot more people. But most of our old fans have stuck with us and understand what's going on."

How do you judge success?

"Peace of mind."

The previous night, Nirvana had managed to escape the pressures of being a world-famous band on tour for a few brief hours. A bunch of us clambered up a hill, stood around on the top rolling a joint, feeling for all the world like we were playing hooky from school, and then found a deserted adventure playground to let off steam in. Both Dave and Chris picked up on this as one of the happiest incidents in the last year-and-a-half of touring. Small things DO matter.

"I have this weird sense of liberation now," Chris continues. "Did it take money to liberate me, or was it just that I got older? I'm not going to bust my ass for the Man ever again, that's for sure. Even if I'm broke, I'm not going to return to that mainstream culture—I'll join a commune, go and get a thatched hut in the woods."

Do you feel like you're a spokesman for a generation?

"I don't know what our generation is about," he replies. "I've never seen any identity to it. Everybody's got rock 'n' roll, everybody's got their own genre. The parents have got Mark Knopfler and Bruce Springsteen and Genesis, and the kids have Nirvana—it's all rock 'n' roll. Maybe I shouldn't give those old fuddy-duddies the credence of calling it rock 'n' roll, maybe it's just entertainment. We try and give it some energy, some enthusiasm. I don't know, man . . . I don't know about leaders."

Maybe you are leaders by default? That's the only way anybody ever seems to get elected nowadays.

"Exactly. A society, by default."

Dave Grohl

For logical reasons, the interview with Dave took place in the same room as the interview with Chris. Dave's great. Having been thrust almost immediately into the Nirvana whirlwind upon leaving his old Washington, D.C. band, Scream (Dave joined shortly before the recording of *Nevermind*), he seems the one least affected by it all. Maybe it's because he's the youngest. Who knows?

We sit down opposite each other and our eyebrows read, "so?" Dave leans forward and starts to speak.

Did success fuck with your mind?

"Not as much as it fucked with everyone's around us," the drummer replies. "Everybody was so astounded at what had happened, they were going crazy. It fucks with me sometimes, when we're driving out of a festival and people are banging on the windows and girls are screaming. That stuff scares me, just because I don't understand it. If anything, our success gave me a dose of humility, the realization that we're just as normal and fucked up as everyone else."

You're the only non-married member, though . . .

"And I plan on keeping it that way," Dave quickly interrupts. "I can't imagine marrying anybody, especially now. Why the fuck would anyone want to get married in the middle of such an insane situation. It's crazy." My lips remain sealed. "You never have time to do anything. You wake up, do a soundcheck, play, travel, barely eat. You don't have time to have real lives."

"I'm still planning on having a life in a year or two," he continues. "When I go back to school and shit. When I dropped out of high school, I was so stoned that I had no idea what I was studying. I was interested in graphic arts and commercial design, but that doesn't yank my crank anymore. A lot of people don't think school's important, but to me it is."

He pauses, takes a sip of tea, and sighs.

"All of this doesn't make sense," he adds. "When I was kid, I always thought of movie stars and rock stars as famous. Famous was a picture in a magazine, or being on the nightly news or on the radio. But once it started happening to the band, it just destroyed that image—these three scrawny little losers come out and sell a bunch of records."

It gives hope to all the losers, doesn't it?

"Sure," he replies. "And everybody's a loser, one way or another. If fucking Michael Jackson's a loser, all of us are. I don't want to flatter myself by saying that our music inspired anyone, but it just goes to show that anyone can be in a band. Maybe that made a lost of kids feel good about themselves."

Dave pauses again.

"I think Kurt has something no one has," he opines. "His way of writing is simple, childlike, minimalist tunes that stick. But that just shows that you don't have to be so accomplished to impress. Anybody can do Kurt Cobain, anybody can do Chris Novoselic . . . I dunno. None of us were cut out for this."

Maybe that's why people picked up on you. The last people who should have power are those who want it.

"Any musician would be lying if they said that they didn't want people to appreciate their music," Dave responds carefully. "But something on this scale is just too perverse and too bizarre to accept sometimes, especially for us."

"We definitely aren't the ones who wanted this. I just don't want this whole fiasco to ruin my life."

KURT COBAIN'S WELL-TEMPERED TANTRUMS

Guitar Player, **February 1992**

It's a Saturday night at San Francisco's Warfield Theater, and an impatient crowd is waiting for Nirvana. An anticipatory buzz charges the air. Even before the trio takes the stage, an enormous mosh pit forms, whirling to its own internal anti-logic.

Finally, the curtain rises and Nirvana kicks into a scorching, punked-out cover of the Vaselines' "Die For You." The crowd's pent-up tension erupts in one desperate exhalation of energy. The pit's tidal motions become positively oceanic, as the crowd surges forward and all three tiers of the hall begin to bounce.

Guitarist Kurt Cobain checks it out from behind his scraggly all-very-blue bangs. He appears unimpressed, even bored. He turns his back on the audience and tears into a blistering, out-of-key solo, ending with a passage of noisy sustained feedback that pushes the crowd even higher. All night long Cobain remains aloof, ambivalent. Finally, at the conclusion of the band's final encore, the ultra-frantic "Territorial Pissings," he rips his guitar off his chest, flings it into the drum kit and marches off the stage, his amp feeding back behind him.

The next morning I turn on MTV to see Nirvana's super-cynical "Smells Like Teen Spirit" sandwiched between—no kidding—videos by Mariah Carey and Paula Abdul. Kurt Cobain hasn't seen the video yet, at least not on MTV, and he isn't looking forward to it. In fact, the very idea that his band is appearing alongside such mainstream successes elicits a low, slightly pained groan from the guitarist.

"We've been lucky enough not to see MTV," he says, a dry sarcastic tone creeping into his voice. "We're not really aware of exactly how much hype is going on. We've been told about it by a lot of people—mainly by our friends making fun of us."

Cobain is in the enviable position of having his attitude and profiting from it too. After all, Nirvana's major-label debut, *Nevermind* (Geffen), went gold in only six weeks after its initial release—an unlikely feat for a group still fresh from the underground. The band's tight hybrid of punk rock energy, grinding metallic riff, and catchy pop songcraft—"the Knack and the Bay City Rollers being molested by Black Flag and Black Sabbath," as Cobain likes to put it—has hit big with college radio fans, modern rockers, and metalheads alike, propelling the album into the Top 10.

To be sure, Nirvana's sound is neither new nor revolutionary. Bands like Hüsker Dü and Dinosaur Jr. have worked similar turf for years without half the acclaim. Similarly, Nirvana's dynamic range recalls that of the Pixies; both groups move eloquently between spare bass-and-drum grooves and shrill bursts of screaming guitars and vocals. But what makes Nirvana's ambivalent anti-anthems so intriguing is the multitude of contradictions that they embody and embrace. The songs are fueled by an uneasy coexistence of apathy and rage, boredom and titillation, innocence and ennui, irreverence and profundity. They move with surprising logic between dirge and groove, singing and screaming, melody and noise.

Kurt's guitar work is rooted in the same contradictions. He alternates between extremes of restraint and overkill with astonishing ease. Dry strumming exists alongside fat, aggressive power chords; haunting minor-key lines explode into major-key choruses; smoothly melodic lead lines turn into furious power drill attacks. Snaking inside the deep, muscular grooves of bassist Chris Novoselic and drummer Dave Grohl, Cobain is just as likely to use his guitar for quick bursts of punctuation as for dense walls of sound.

Nonetheless, there are few extended solos on *Nevermind,* far fewer than on the band's debut, *Bleach* (Sub Pop). "I didn't feel there was a reason to have many solos on this album," says Cobain. "It all depends on what I feel is needed for each song. There are some songs that just shouldn't have a solo, just some fills that remind you of the melody. What solos there are are a bit out of it, a bit weird and strange."

On *Nevermind*'s first single, "Smells Like Teen Spirit," for example, Kurt's brief solo is a near-masterpiece of restraint. You keep expecting him to take off into typical upper-register runs; instead, he remains note-faithful to the melody throughout the eight bar phrase, driving an already catchy melody even deeper into your brain.

Contrast that with his solo on the punk/metal rave "Breed," where he bends a simple F♯-*to*-A groove out of shape with twisted tremolando chromaticisms that give the song a strange, increasingly atonal edge. It may not make much musical sense, but considering that the song is supposedly about "marrying at age 18, getting pregnant, stuck with a baby—and not wanting it," the solo makes an even greater kind of sense.

"That solo is really out of key," says the guitarist. "In fact, I can't play it live until I learn it. But I'm too lazy to learn it." Call this laziness or negative capability, but the furious, tossed-off quality of Cobain's work befits the energy and immediacy of Nirvana's songs—something carefully planned just wouldn't work. "I never practice a solo," claims Kurt. "For every guitar solo I've ever recorded, I've always just played what I wanted to at the time and then just picked out the best takes."

On *Nevermind,* Cobain had quite a bit of freedom to pick and choose. While *Bleach* was recorded in less than a week for $600, Nirvana stretched out on *Nevermind,* taking one month and spending about $20,000 before finishing. The production by Butch Vig (Smashing Pumpkins, Slayer) makes Nirvana sound not so much produced as edited; the sprawling mania of *Bleach* is still there, but all the unnecessary baggage has been carved away, leaving a series of carefully honed, tightly focused musical statements. "We think along the same lines, on the same level," says Cobain of Vig. "So every suggestion he had, there was no conflict at all. A few songs weren't finished so he helped us with arrangements, cutting them down to the average three-minute pop song."

Cobain, not surprisingly, has a typically punk attitude about his equipment. "I guess I've never considered musical equipment very sacred," he says when asked about his set ending outburst at Warfield. He says he's probably broken 300 guitars—a casual attitude indeed for someone who claims his left-handedness makes it difficult to find instruments he enjoys playing.

"I've resorted to Japanese-made Fender Stratocasters, because they're the most available left-handed guitar," explains Kurt. "I like guitars in the Fender style, because they have skinny necks." Cobain runs his guitar through a Roland DS-2 distortion pedal and a Carver power amp driven by a MESA/Boogie preamp. He plays "Polly," *Nevermind*'s stark acoustic tune, on a $20 pawnshop guitar.

In fact, Cobain harbors a rather twisted fascination for crappy equipment. "My favorite guitar in the world is the Fender Mustang," he maintains. "They're really small and almost impossible to keep in tune. They're designed terribly. If you want to raise the action, you have to detune all the stings, pull the bridge out, turn three little screws under the bridge, and hope that you've raised them the right amount. Then you put the bridge back and tune all the strings. If you screwed up, you have to do the whole process over again."

"But I like it," he continues. "That way things sound fucked-up, and I stumble onto stuff accidentally. I guess I don't like to be that familiar with my guitar."

A NOTE ON KURT'S JAG-STANG

> "Mother, my joy," he would say, "there must be servants and masters, but if so I will be the servant of my servants, the same as they are to me."
>
> —Fyodor Dostoyevsky, *The Brothers Karamazov*

Kurt Cobain was more than just influenced lyrically by the Burroughs/Gysin cut-up technique. In February of 1993, Cobain "cut and pasted" a guitar—Fender's Jag-Stang was designed by Cobain (though he requested that his name be kept off the instrument). Cobain met with Fender to talk about his vision for an instrument that would combine his two favorite types of guitars—Cobain's hands desired to fondle a Jaguar's bottom and stroke a Mustang's neck. This demanded an operation, a fusion of the Jaguar and the Mustang. To provide the designers with an idea of his vision, Cobain used a Polaroid to take two separate pictures of each guitar. He then cut them in half and pasted them together. Less concerned with the new guitar's tone and shape, Cobain expressed the most interest in the fit of the Mustang's neck.

Cobain played this guitar almost exclusively for the last three months of his life. Scentless and senseless, purging power chords through paroxysms of energy, trailing his callused fingertips up and down the guitar's neck, Cobain created a guitar as he played it. His energy is forever entombed within the Jag-Stang.

EVERETT TRUE
COME AS YOU AREN'T

Melody Maker, July 25, 1992

Nirvana
Isle of Calf Festival, Oslo
Sjohistoriska Museum, Stockholm 1992

They don't deserve this.

Forget any reports you have heard that rock is alive and kicking. The world's only credible arena rock band is close to cracking. Kurt Cobain is barely able to cope with the restraints of his position, the kids who are out there watching his band because Guns N' Roses aren't in town till next week and Bryan Adams was on yesterday. His band is afraid to play any new songs knowing that, if they do, bootlegs will hit the streets running. So, numbed by the intensity of their unlooked-for role as some kinda spokesmen, Nirvana attempt to inject meaning into the old as best they can.

Which means: no emotion shown, if that's the only way they can retain self respect.

First night in Stockholm, I'm watching MTV with Kurt and Courtney in their hotel suite, waiting for the new Nirvana video to come on. Eddie Murphy flashes by, typically unfunny. "He used to be funny once, didn't he?" Kurt remarks. "Back before he became famous and complacent, back when he was struggling to be heard, back when he had to try." There's no need for Kurt to elaborate. We know who he's talking about.

But Kurt still tries. Otherwise, why is he in so much pain? Not for the first time this year, I begin to realise why Bono and Axl and Bruce and all those other would-be rock messiahs are so much crap. The market forces, the record buyers, ARE that powerful—you either succumb or you go insane. Is there a third choice? Nirvana are struggling against it—they're struggling real hard and they're struggling real strong—but it's impossible to make sense of much of this confusion.

In Oslo, Kurt simply stands immobile as 20,000 kids go berserk, uncaring as to what reaction his band may or may not be exacting. And the audience, with their ritualised clapping and banners and shoes tossed in the air couldn't give a damn about how good or otherwise the band on stage are. Why should they? This is corporate entertainment, however much the band decry it. To most of these serenely beautiful, sun-kissed Scandinavians, it doesn't matter that it's Nirvana up there. It could be anyone. It's a festival, see. They couldn't give a damn about Flipper or Shonen Knife of punk or Courtney Love or any of the things so close to Nirvana's heart. Why should they? What matters is size.

Festival crowds know what to expect, or so they think. They had the parameters of how they choose to spend their leisure time mapped out long ago. On this scale, art counts for virtually nothing. Rebellion? How can anyone be rebellious once they've conquered the American market? By throwing it all away again? Then you're just termed "a failure," or worse, "a one-hit wonder."

In Oslo, for all it matters, Kurt could be rampaging drunk and breaking equipment, Chris could be throwing his bass 10 feet into the air and

Dave moshing hard, like they used to. But they aren't (okay, Dave is). Sometimes Kurt flicks his floor switch from reverb to normal, sometimes Kurt looks across to see if Chris is playing the correct bass part, sometimes Kurt'll try and make a self-deprecating remark and fail. There's precious little emotion, humour, angst here—a bunch of incredible songs turned to shimmering dust, some brutally beautifully evocative lyrics which now mean less than shit, now that the whole world has learnt its part and reduced them to the everyday, the mundane. Shit happens.

Yet Nirvana still sound glorious.

Yet "Polly" and "Stay Away" and "On a Plain" still evoke, chastise, berate, uplift. Fuck knows why. Maybe familiarity doesn't always blunt. Maybe we're talking love.

In Stockholm, Kurt at least tries, buoyed by the news shouted across the stage by his wife that the concert has been undersold by 6,000. "Hey! We're on our way out," he gleefully shouts at the British press, stumbling across stage to change guitars. But then, Stockholm isn't part of a two-day festival like Oslo—it's a Nirvana show, for fans only. So Kurt changes the set list seconds before taking the stage, starting with a classic American punk number, "Money Roll Right In" (irony!), playing an impromptu "D7" upon request AND "Molly's Lips," even making a few jokes. Dave and Chris look happier as well: for the encore (a searing, purposeful "Teen Spirit" and a rampant "Territorial Pissings"), they drag 50 kids waiting by the back gate on stage—and, hell, spontaneous bonhomie can work on this level. Even if it does recall something off of *The Arsenio Hall Show.*

But the main set is still as bad as I've seen Nirvana play, in terms of spirit, excitement, inspiration (everything Nirvana used to have in spades). Even if I am damn near crying during "Lithium" (it seems so appropriate, somehow). And Oslo was way, way worse.

Contrast the difference in attitude between Nirvana and Teenage Fanclub at the Stockholm soundcheck. First, Nirvana: a roadie stands in for Kurt as the band runs through a lackluster "In Bloom" and a flat "Teen Spirit," sounding weirdly like Weird Al himself. Then, Teenage Fanclub—all the band present and visibly enjoying life, running carefree through a Todd Rundgren number, a Sixties bubblegum pop classic, Alex Chilton, anything and everything they've loved. Once, Nirvana delighted in their togetherness, forged through years of constant touring through the cesspits of America. Now, it seems Kurt would rather be anywhere than hangin' with Chris and Dave.

Pressures, dude. But Nirvana still sound life affirming.

How could they sound otherwise? Especially when *Nevermind,* as awesome as it was/is, never did justice to the excitement and genuine power of their live sound.

So, Oslo is a mess of contradictions and contrary emotions. The day's so glorious, the babes so beautiful, the sound so exemplary, Teenage Fanclub's support slot so buoyant and inspirational, it'd take some kinda churlish fool or pining Aberdeen type not to enjoy themselves. Yet, even with the inspired choice of Tori Amos's version of "Teen Spirit" as an intro tape, it's apparent that Kurt is torn—torn between his loyalty to the kids who genuinely appreciate and love his music, and those who are into them as a fad, as a cuter, punkier Ugly Kid Joe alternative.

His voice is still inexhaustibly expressive, emotive, his guitar still bleeds angst, but his demeanour . . . remember, this is the band who built a whole career out of being rampant on stage, whose new video mythologises the whole guitar-smashing ethos with a grandiose finality. Kurt won't even admit he has any frustrations left. Not in public. But he has. Oh, man.

Second night in Stockholm, the assembled Nirvana and Fanclub crews are watching an MTV clip of Eddie Vedder going off the rails in Denmark. There's no appreciable glee at a well-publicised rival losing it, just a sad empathy, a feeling of genuine pity that perhaps here is another singer who is unable to cope with the lies and pressures and traumas of fame, who loathes and despises the distance forced between him and his audience, who can't see any way out of the trap, the role forced upon him simply because he's written lyrics that reach people (it's not his fault his band sucks). Pearl Jam canceled the remainder of their European tour the same day. Bet Kurt was jealous.

The way people talk it right now suggests that, even if Nirvana aren't going to split up, Reading will be their last show for a very long time. (On the phone the next week the singer flatly denies this. "We'll be touring in November," he tells me, "but no festivals this time. Definitely no festivals. And, if Chris wasn't in Greece, we'd be in the recording studio laying down tracks for the new album right now.")

Let's hope to fuck that Nirvana learn how to adapt and survive. We desperately need people like them up there to give people like us down here hope, hope that you don't need to be an Extreme or an INXS or a Bryan Adams to succeed.

NIRVANA: CRUCIFIED BY SUCCESS?
Melody Maker, July 25, 1992

The interview with Nirvana takes place in a dressing room on the edge of a river in Stockholm. The day is cloudy, with occasional flashes of sunshine. People are drinking coke, and, in Chris's case, red wine. Chris and Dave are sitting on one couch, Kurt on another. A bowl of chili-roasted peanuts and some fruit nestles on the table. Someone's smoking.

The band seem awkward in each other's presence, slightly wary of one another. When Chris speaks, his eyes are looking anywhere but in Kurt's direction. When Kurt speaks, he does so almost defensively, as if he feels a need to justify himself in front of Chris. When Dave speaks, you know he can feel the uneasiness, but he's trying to ignore it.

Apart for a brief spot on Swedish TV earlier today, this is the first interview Nirvana have given as a band for a long while. This might account for the subdued atmosphere—although many people have pointed to Nirvana's success as creating cracks, friction within the band. Certainly, Kurt seems warier than when I last met him—photographer Steve Gullick has to go through a ridiculous rigmarole of hoods and bleached hair and agreements before he's allowed to take any shots.

The noise you can't hear is the support band, Teenage Fanclub, soundchecking for tonight's show. Nirvana's concert is lacking in any real excitement or emotion, although the encore is inspired [see "Come As You Aren't" on page 68 of this book]. It seems they still have some way to go before playing arenas becomes second nature to them. It's obvious the band aren't happy with this state of affairs, but equally obvious that they aren't prepared to compromise their principles just to make people feel easier.

As you join us, Kurt is talking about Nirvana's forthcoming album.

"We're going into the studio as soon as we get back to Seattle," says Kurt. "What I'd like to do is to go into Reciprocal with Jack Endino [the engineer on *Bleach*] and rent exactly the same equipment as was there when we recorded *Bleach*. We record the songs with Jack on an eight track, record them somewhere else on a 24 track with Steve Albini, and then pick the best."

So you're aiming for a rawer sound on the next album?

"Definitely less produced," says Chris.

"As long as it doesn't sound like *Nevermind*," adds Kurt.

Why? Are you fed up with it?

"No, I really like that album," Kurt replies. "And it doesn't matter what kind of production it had because the songs are good. But it would have been better rawer. It doesn't sound very original."

"We don't want to find ourselves in Slayer's situation," Dave explains, "where the same people produced their last three records and they all sound identical. That's stupid."

When you talk about how different you want your next record to sound, isn't there an element of wanting to challenge your audience about that statement? (The implication is that, because Nirvana have become fed up with their audience, they want to alienate them.) Kurt denies this.

"It's not like that," he says. "It's more like challenging ourselves, making a record exactly as we want to. Whether our audience likes it or not doesn't really matter. We don't want to be writing 'In Bloom' for the next five years."

"Maybe the next record will be the one where we can judge how much impact we've actually made," Chris wonders aloud.

"Yeah, but we know that at least 50 per cent of people who like us now aren't going to like our next record if it has a lot of abrasive, inaccessible songs on it," replies Kurt, scornfully. "If they do . . . man, that proves our theory that you can shove anything down the mainstream's throat and they'll eat it up."

"But that's what I always thought of our second record as being," interrupts Dave. "Something way less produced, where we can push the sound even further and see if we can get a noisy LP on the charts."

"But do you think that would happen?" Kurt asks him. "Let's pretend we haven't released 'Endless, Nameless' yet, and it's our first single off the next album—if people bought it, wouldn't if just prove that they like us 'cos it's cool to?"

"No," Chris replies. "That argument just doesn't hold any water. They wouldn't be that mindless."

("Endless, Nameless" is the 10 minute long noise-fest grunge track which appeared on limited quantities of *Nevermind,* and on the B-side of "Come As You Are.")

Do you think you'll have another single as big as "Teen Spirit?"

"No," states Kurt, firmly. "We haven't written any songs as good—or as poor—as that. We might write one right before we finish recording the album, because 'Teen Spirit' was written just weeks before *Nevermind,* but we're not going to try."

Kurt disappears momentarily to find a cigarette. Someone (the promoter? a roadie?) pokes his head round the door, looking for Alex, Nirvana's exuberant tour manager. The strains of Teenage Fanclub's "The Concept" drift in through a window, glorious in the early evening air. Dave cracks open another can.

Earlier, a bunch of us had gone for a stroll down by the river while Kurt and Courtney traversed the town, looking for Nirvana bootlegs to liberate and then give to kids wearing official Nirvana tee-shirts. One seller became freaked out and started yelling at Courtney—but there was no repeat of the ugliness in Ireland, where Kurt was repeatedly punched by a bouncer after going to stop an altercation between security and a fan.

It's apparent that there are two distinct camps in Nirvana: the newly-wed couple—and everyone else. Still, that's no reason to start believing all the malicious stories that have plagued Nirvana, and, more particularly, Kurt Cobain, since the band's rapid rise to the top. Drugs? What the fuck does it have to do with you, punk?

Chris stretches his legs and sighs. This is gonna be a long interview. Kurt comes back, and we continue.

When I saw your static performance in Oslo two days ago, I kept thinking back to what Kurt told me last year: *"We're not going to be proud of the fact there are a bunch of Guns N' Roses kids who are into our music. We don't feel comfortable progressing, playing larger venues."*

"We can't," Chris agrees. "We're always treated people with that mentality with a little bit of contempt and cynicism, and to have them screaming for us . . . Why are they screaming? What do they see in us? They're exactly the same kind of people who wanted to kick our arse in high school."

"It's just boring to play outdoors," explains his singer. "I've only just gotten used to playing large venues because the sound is at least tolerable. But, outside, the wind blows the music around so much that it doesn't feel like you're playing music, it feels like you're lip synching to a boom box recording. Plus, these festivals are very mainstream—we're playing with Extreme and Pearl Jam, you know? Ninety per cent of the kids out there are probably just as much into Extreme as they are into us."

"I try it every night," he continues, "but I just can't fool myself. I'm not going to smile and pose like Eddie Van Halen, even though he's a miserable drunk. That doesn't mean it'll be that way next month [Reading, England], but that's how it is, right now."

Do you feel any responsibility?

"For what?" Kurt asks.

The masses. The people who bought your record. Because you've been given this power to use.

"To me," Dave begins, tentatively, "our main responsibility is not to be something we're not. I don't think pretending to be a professional rock unit really works. If we're gonna have a shitty show, then let's have a shitty show. I can see there's a lot of responsibility playing massive shows, but other kinds? I don't know."

"It's rock 'n' roll to be irresponsible," Chris adds.

I know.

"Once you start considering this to be a responsibility, it becomes a burden," muses the drummer.

Silence.

We've reached a brief impasse. Kurt starts leafing through a crap metal rag and spots a picture of the Melvins (his early mentors), to his delight. Courtney sticks her head round the door to ask if we've seen *Siren* because Inger Lorre slags her in it. Someone throws her a copy.

Dave starts telling me about the interview that they've just done for Swedish TV.

"They thanked us for saving rock 'n' roll," he laughs. "For throwing a bomb into the rock 'n' roll establishment."

Do you feel you've done that?

"Maybe we blew up a paper bag and popped it," sneers Chris.

From where I'm standing, you don't seem to have changed very much. Murmurs of agreement come from the assembled.

What do you hate most about being famous?

"Kids with Bryan Adams and Bruce Springsteen tee-shirts coming up to me and asking for autographs," Kurt says. "When people in the audience hold up a sign that says 'Even Flow' (a Pearl Jam song) on one side and 'Negative Creep' (a Nirvana song) on the other."

Silence from the other two.

Okay. What's the best thing about being famous?

"You know, that's a really good question," answers Kurt, ironically.

"We might get some perks here and there," his bassist ventures. "A free drink or two, maybe."

Do you get many groupies?

"When I was about 12," replies Kurt. "I wanted to be a rock 'n' roll star, and I thought that would be my payback for all the jocks who got girlfriends all the time. But I realized way before I became a rock star that that was stupid."

"Maybe it's flattering to all these heavy metal bands, but we find it kind of disgusting," adds Dave, Nirvana's only unmarried member.

How about drink?

"I came into this tour with a fresh perspective," Chris muses. "I used to get stressed out, drink a whole lot and react to everything. Now I just go with the flow."

"I've always loved the spontaneity of being frustrated and pissed off . . ." Kurt challenges him.

" . . . and drunk," finishes Chris. "Oh yeah! I've had some of my best inspirations intoxicated—it's a different reality. It's like living in a movie or a cartoon, where your subconscious takes off. That's where all the good stories come from. But it's such a hell on your body."

Has the sudden fame appreciably changed your lifestyles?

"Definitely," responds Kurt, vehemently.

"It hasn't changed mine," his bassist disagrees. "I can still go down to the Safeway, buy fruit and vegetables, walk around town. I don't care if people stare at me or whatever."

"You don't," Kurt asks him, "at all?"

"No," Replies Chris. "And the more they see me, especially in Seattle, the more . . ."

"Oh yeah, eventually they'll get tired of sniggering at you and talking behind your back." Kurt finishes his sentence for him. "Well, I've been confronted by people wanting to beat me up, by people heckling me and being so drunk and obnoxious because they think I'm this pissy rock star bastard who can't come to grips with his fame."

"I was in a rock club the other night," he continues, "and one guy comes up, pats me on the back and says, 'You've got a really good thing going, you know? Your band members are cool, you write great songs, you affected a lot of people, but, man, you've got to get your personal shit together!' Then another person comes up and says, 'I hope you overcome your drug problems.' All this happens within an hour while I'm trying to watch the Melvins, minding my own business."

"There were about five or six kids sitting around, very drunk, screaming 'Rock star! Rock star! Oh, look, he's going to freak out any minute! He's going to have a tantrum! He's going to start crying!' Then this other guy comes up, puts his arm around me and says, 'You know, my girlfriend broke up with me and took my Nirvana album, so you should give me $14 to buy a new CD, 'cos you can afford that now you're a big rock star.' And I said, 'Gee. That's a clever thing to say. Why don't you fuck off?'"

"But you have to ignore them," Chris warns him, "or it becomes an obsession. I have dreams about being nude in public, and I interpret them as worrying about sticking out. Forget it! It can become a preoccupation. I was like that, too, when I used to see someone famous. . . ."

"Yeah, but did you pitch them shit?" Kurt interrupts him.

"No," Chris replies. "I didn't, but that incident you mentioned seems to be pretty isolated."

"It's not isolated," snarls Kurt. "It happens to me all the time—every time I go out, every fucking time. It's stupid. And, if it bothers me that much, I'm going to do something about it. Fuck it, rock doesn't mean that much to me. I still love to be in a band and play music with Chris and Dave, but if it means that we have to resort to playing in a practice room and never touring again, then so be it."

Chris and Dave fall silent. The mood in the room has turned dark.

"I have to hear rumours about me all the time," the singer growls. "I'm totally sick of it. If I'm going to take drugs that's my own fucking prerogative, and if I don't take drugs it's my own fucking prerogative. It's nobody's business, and I don't care if people take drugs and I don't care if people don't take drugs."

"It all started with just one article in one of the shittiest, cock rock–orientated LA magazines," he continues, "where this guy assumed I was on heroin because he noticed that I was tired. Since then, the rumours have spread like wildfire. I can't deny that I have taken drugs and I still do, every once in a while. But I'm not a fucking heroin addict, and I'm not going to . . ."

He trails off, momentarily wordless.

"It's impossible to be on tour and to be on heroin," he begins again. "I don't know any band that could do it, unless you're Keith Richards and you're being given blood transfusions every three days, and you have runners going out and scoring drugs for you."

Kurt glowers in anger.

"I never realised that mainstream audiences react towards mainstream rock stars in this manner, because I've never paid attention before," he rails. "I don't mean to complain as much as I do, but it's a load of shit. It's really stupid. I've had days where I've considered this to be a job, and I never thought that would happen. It makes me question the point of it all. I'm gonna bitch about it for another year and, if I can't handle it after that, we're gonna have to make some drastic changes."

SMASHING THEIR HEADS ON THAT PUNK ROCK

Spin, October 1993

Fame has a vaporizing effect. It lifts and floats the celebrity into our most private venue: dreams. But for Kurt Cobain, our collective obsession seems like a car's stark headlights, freezing its unassuming victim in the glare. "In my dreams, there's always this apocalyptic war going on between the right and the left wing," he says, sitting on the plush burgundy couch in his Seattle living room. "The last dream I had like this was two nights ago. Courtney and I were in the Hollywood Hills, and Arnold Schwarzenegger was my neighbor. I was completely disgusted by the whole idea of living next to these people." Cobain speaks in a lilting Pacific-Northwestern drawl, like a grungy Quentin Crisp. "So I went down to where the oppressed people were starving on the streets, killing each other for a quarter. In one part of the dream I was being honored for something and the ceremony was at an S/M club, but it was a really nice one. It didn't have chains on the walls, just beautiful flowers. Lost of stars were there." Cobain glances up at the small plastic doll in a nun's outfit propped up on the mantel, one of the hundreds of dolls that he and his wife, Courtney Love, leader of the band Hole, have collected. "I had to make an entrance from the top of the stairs, and because of the way people think of Courtney, she happened to be this two-foot-tall black midget with huge feet. She waddled like this. . . ." Cobain sways back and forth like Charlie Chaplin. "As soon as she made her appearance someone kicked her down the stairs. I just started screaming."

As it would with anyone, the past 18 months have taken a fierce toll on Nirvana and the Cobains. They've struggled coming to terms with their gargantuan stardom, straining to get their footing on the unfamiliar and sometimes brutal landscape of fame. The terrain has been dotted with obstacles: some mere potholes, some treacherous landmines. With the follow-up to *Nevermind, In Utero,* due on September 14, the Seattle-based trio hopes to trade in its celebrity status for the more comfortable role of rock band. But erasing the lunacy of the months gone by may require more than a bracing blast of punk rock.

Last September, *Vanity Fair* ran a much-publicized piece on Love. The article quoted her as saying, among other things, that she used heroin while pregnant with their now one-year-old (and healthy) daughter, Frances Bean, which she later denied. Cobain refers to Condé Nast, which publishes the magazine, as "a bunch of right-wing, high-fashion,

Christian Satanists. They have the power to eliminate anything that threatens them."

Cobain tends to go to extremes when discussing the abuse he's taken from the mainstream media. His outrage borders on a persecution complex, but the press has left him feeling terminally unprotected, his day-to-day life and love compromised in ways he never imagined. He's horrified about rumors that have been circulating concerning a recent trip to New York City, where he and Love were supposedly so high they were puking in the back of a cab, and when they got out they left little Frances Bean behind in the backseat. The story continues with the cabby driving around for hours not knowing there was a baby in the car.

"It's like the Rod Stewart semen story," I tell him. "You're a part of modern folklore."

"Geez," Cobain says. "I could live with *that*, Kurt Loder saying, 'There was a half gallon of semen found in Kurt Cobain's stomach.' That at least is funny."

Notoriety doesn't really bother bassist Chris Novoselic. He says he makes himself available so often he's gotten over any phobia, but he admits to awkwardness when meeting people. "If you introduce yourself they say, 'I know who you are.' And if you don't they think you're arrogant."

Dave Grohl, Nirvana's drummer, figures the reason he's seldom recognized is because people can't really see him behind his drums and his long hair. Though he's never been stopped on the street, something he recently heard did freak him out. "There's a guy in New York City that goes into this record store every single Sunday and claims he's my father. It's creepy."

Both agree that while stardom is sometimes hard for them, it's hell for Cobain. "It's a load of shit on Kurt's mind that he doesn't deserve," Grohl says. "You can tell when he's upset and it ends up bothering all of us."

"You know how Tabitha Soren's delivery is usually kind of flat and calm? I've noticed whenever she reports anything on us, she *really* gets into it—her eyebrows raise, and she gets this venom in her voice." Cobain says this as we settle into a booth with Novoselic at the Dog House Restaurant, a diner in Seattle that's been open since 1934. A sign above the counter says ALL ROADS LEAD TO THE DOG HOUSE. Cobain's intensity is startling, practically electric, like the hum from overhead power lines. A bad case of scoliosis as a child has left him permanently hunched, and in his plaid hunter's cap, flaps down over his ears, and visor pulled low for privacy, his ice-blue eyes are transfixing. His black tennis shoes have "Fugazi" written on the toes in black magic marker, each foot with a different spelling. He lights yet another cigarette, his fingernails a splatter of chipped red nail polish.

Cobain is referring to a July 12 MTV news segment based on a piece in the *Seattle Times*. The article reported a domestic disturbance at the Cobain home, claiming the couple were physically fighting over their possession of several handguns and an AR-1-5 rifle.

Cobain shakes his head. "I was just so surprised to find the police report so detailed, yet so completely wrong." He sinks deeper into the booth. "What really happened was that Courtney and I were running around the house screaming and wrestling—it was a bit Sid and Nancy–esque, I have to admit—but we were having a good time. And then we get this knock on the door, and there are five cop cars outside, and the cops all have their guns drawn." His voice mirrors the absurdity of the situation. "We were in our pajamas. I was wearing this long black velvet pipe-smoker's jacket. Not the most desirable thing to be arrested in. . . ." The police explained a new Washington State law that requires that someone be arrested in cases of domestic violence. "That's when we did start arguing, about who was going to jail. I said, 'I'm going,' and Courtney said, 'No I'm going.' And I said 'Noooo, *I'm* the man of the house. They always arrest the man.'" Cobain smiles. "I kind of regret that now, because the idea of Courtney as a husband-beater is kind of amusing," he says wryly. "She did throw juice at me and I did push her, but it was about who was going to jail."

Novoselic, tall and Abe Lincoln–like, listens sympathetically. "Just as we were going out the door," Cobain continues, "the police said, 'By the way, do you have any firearms in the house?' And I said no, because I didn't want this to turn into an even bigger deal. But Courtney said yes." Cobain's cheeks flush, his narrow shoulders tense. "I'm in full support of that law though. I've witnessed that kind of domestic violence. On one occasion my mom's boyfriend was beating up on her. He'd done it before, but I only witnessed it once. He was this huge Yugoslavian macho man who drank a lot of booze. She had two black eyes and had to go to the hospital." Cobain's own eyes grow as big as saucers, as it becomes painfully clear why this accusation has affected him so deeply. "I am sympathetic to this new law," he says quietly.

Novoselic has a calming effect on Cobain, bolstering him verbally, talking him down when he grows too paranoid. He tells how the *Seattle*

Times called his mother for her comments regarding the Cobain-Love allegations. Mrs. Novoselic refused to say anything; Novoselic has trained her not to talk to the press, promising to "give her a new roof on her house" if she kept quiet.

Grohl, on the other hand, deals with the treadmill of catastrophes by staying out of the loop. "I love to play music with Chris and Kurt, but I don't like all the hubbub that surrounds it," he says. "Some people have to have psychodrama, but I have to *not* have it."

This current rock 'n' roll juggernaut is a long way from the band's humble beginnings. Cobain's early years were spent in a trailer park in Aberdeen, 100 miles south of Seattle. Novoselic grew up in Los Angeles before moving to Aberdeen at age 14, where his mother still runs Maria's Hair Design.

In high school Cobain won a scholarship to art school, but he chose not to attend. He was more interested in music, specifically in local sludge-rock heroes the Melvins. Cobain incessantly watched the band rehearse, and eventually wrote and recorded songs with the Melvins' drummer, Dale Crover. Novoselic, also a Melvins insider, was impressed by the tape, and in early 1987, he asked Cobain if he would like to start a band together. After forming this early incarnation, both left Aberdeen: Novoselic moved to Tacoma, finding work as a house painter, while Cobain settled nearby in Olympia, a place he'd always thought of as a "cultural Mecca," eventually working as a janitor in a dentist's office.

They gigged in the area, and soon after booked recording time at Reciprocal Recording with producer Jack Endino. There they recorded a demo tape, which Endino passed along to Sub Pop's Bruce Pavitt, who was duly impressed. "Love Buzz/Big Cheese," the band's first single, was released in October 1988, followed by 1989's *Bleach*, their debut LP, which they recorded in only three days for a mere $600. It wasn't until 1990, after going through a handful of drummers, that Cobain and Novoselic drafted Grohl, whom they spotted at a gig behind the kit for the D.C. hardcore band Scream.

As a result of their fans having a difficult time finding their records, and their label, Sub Pop, prowling for a distribution deal, Nirvana began entertaining the idea of jumping to a major label. The band shopped the songs that would end up on *Nevermind*, recorded by a Madison, Wisconsin studio owner named Butch Vig. A subsequent bidding war broke out, culminating in Geffen buying out its Sub Pop contract, and offering the band a reported $287,000 spread over two records.

Vig eventually produced *Nevermind,* with Andy Wallace handling the final mixes. *Nevermind,* which record executives expected would sell around 300,000 copies, flew out of stores at a breakneck pace. MTV endlessly aired the video for "Smells Like Teen Spirit" (later even saturating America with its parodic partner, "Weird Al" Yankovic's "Smells Like Nirvana"). The single went straight to the top of the charts, and *Nevermind* went on to sell five million copies in four months (it has now exceeded nine million worldwide). The record's unparalleled success has altered the course of music, fashion, the recording industry, and deodorants. Nirvana went from being just another punk band schlepping around from gig to gig in its van to *the punk band.* Nirvana's sound helped create and define a category of music. *Nevermind* also made the band members Rock Stars.

"I really miss being able to blend in with people," Cobain says wearily. "It's just been lately that I could even handle being recognized."

Cobain tells me about an incident that took place when he went to see a Melvins show in Orange County, California. "One by one, those drunk, sarcastic twentysomething kids would come up to me and say, 'Aren't you in the B-52's?' Just trying to start a fight. One guy came up, smacked me on the back, and said, 'Hey, man, you got a good thing going, just get rid of your pissy attitude. Get off the drugs and just fucking go for it, man.'"

There are times when Cobain yearns to take his fans aside, explain the endless complications, pressures, and compromises of stardom, prove to them that in his heart he's still the same lonely Aberdeen kid whose life was irrevocably bettered by punk rock. Once in a while he doesn't have to. "There were these, like, ten-year-old kids at a Butthole Surfers concert. They had green hair, they were skater punks who had made their own T-shirts with their favorite bands written on them. I could tell we had some kind of impact on them, and so had punk rock, because they didn't want autographs. They just wanted to shake our hands and say thanks. I got a thrill meeting kids who are into alternative music. To be that advanced at that age makes me so envious."

Cobain is clearly pleased that he's helped nurture a subculture, one that was much less accessible when he was their age. Still, with Nirvana's new record, *In Utero,* about to be released, it's impossible not to wax nostalgic about life pre-*Nevermind,* pregrunge.

"It was just so much simpler then," Cobain says. "I was just getting out of this heavy period of depression. . . . I lived in bed for weeks, reading Beckett, writing in my journal. Dave and I were living in a tiny apartment eating corn dogs and potatoes. The place was a mess, cigarette butts everywhere, half-eaten food. Chris and I pawned all our equipment. Once I even had to go to the hospital, get hooked up to an IV because of dehydration . . . but as soon as we got to L.A. to record *Nevermind,* all that lifted. It was totally warm and kind of tropical. We stayed in the Oakwood Apartments, most of which were filled with *Star Search* mothers and kids. Kind of gross, but it was such a relief. They had a weight room and I cooked fish dinners." He pauses and sighs. "This time, with *In Utero,* it seems like it's taking forever. I feel like I'm stuck in a void."

At around 4:30 in the morning, Geffen publicist Luke Wood volunteers to drive me from Cobain's house back to my hotel. Cobain, whose 1990 Volvo has come up lame, says he wants a ride to a friend's house. Wood asks if he wants to call his friend, make sure he's awake. Cobain shakes his head no. We drive down Interstate 5. The few lights left in the hills surrounding Seattle make the water glitter—the place has a dreamy feel, like Oz. We pull off the highway, then, following Cobain's instructions, zigzag from one side street to another. It's an older neighborhood, three-story wood houses nestled side by side. "This is it," Cobain says. "I'll get off here." He opens the door. It's drizzling. All the houses are dark, quiet. I say good-bye, leaving him standing on the wet pavement, lit by a lone street light, preoccupied and exhausted.

The ghostly spectre of Cobain, adrift in suburbia, with dawn still an hour away, is mirrored by his uncertainty over *In Utero.* "I haven't heard enough positive feedback. The initial tapes from the studio didn't give me the same chill. With *Nevermind,* we were so musically validated it was almost embarrassing, but with this record, because of the production [infamously recorded by Steve Albini], the songs, and the way we approached the record, you really have to listen a few times to be able to understand it."

Cobain, though hesitant, is genuinely proud of *In Utero.* "The lyrics on the new record are more focused, they're almost built on themes," he says. "With *Bleach,* I didn't give a flying fuck what the lyrics were about. Eighty percent were written the night before recording. It was like 'I'm pissed off. Don't know what about. Let's just scream negative lyrics, and as long as they're not sexist and don't get too embarrassing it'll be okay.' I don't hold any of those lyrics dear to me. *Neverinind* was an accumulation of two years of poetry. I picked out good lines, cut up things. I'm always skipping back and forth to different themes. A lot of bands are expected to write as a whole. One song is supposed to be as cut-and-dried as a *Dragnet* episode."

The songs on *In Utero* are indeed more concentrated lyrically. "Scentless Apprentice," co-written by all three members of Nirvana (a process Cobain refers to as "a breakthrough in our songwriting") is based on Cobain's favorite novel, Patrick Süskind's *Perfume. Perfume*'s main character is Jean-Baptiste Grenouille, a strange, odorless monster of a man with an acute sense of smell who works as an apprentice to a perfumer, and in his spare time kills virgins in order to steal their scent. The song's lyrics paraphrase from the book ("Most babies smell like butter," goes one line), as Cobain brutally connects his own discomfort with the world to Grenouille's horrific deeds. ("Go away, get away, get away," Cobain begs). Besides, both Cobain and Love are way into scents, from the rank gymnasium stench of "Smells Like Teen Spirit" to the Love-penned ode to odors in a recent *Mademoiselle*. "I'm really interested in smells," says Cobain. "I think I'd like to own a perfumerie someday."

"Rape Me," which carries a quiet biblical angst, is the song the band wanted to play on last year's *MTV Music Awards* instead of "Lithium." Cobain conceived it as a life-affirmative rape song. "It's like she's saying, 'Rape me, go ahead, rape me, beat me. You'll never kill me. I'll survive this and I'm gonna fucking rape you one of these days and you won't even know it.'"

Nirvana has been an active, outspoken promoter of social causes, openly condemning homophobia in print ("I'm definitely gay in spirit, and I probably could be bisexual," Cobain told the *Advocate,* a gay and lesbian magazine) and headlining a recent benefit for Bosnian rape survivors, which was Novoselic's idea. Cobain hopes *In Utero* will change the misogyny so endemic to rock 'n' roll. "Maybe it will inspire women to pick up guitars and start bands. Because it's the only future in rock 'n' roll. I've had this negative attitude for years. Rock 'n' roll has been exhausted. But that was always male rock 'n' roll. There's a lot of girl groups, just now, within the last few years. The Breeders and the Riot Grrrls all have a hand in it. People are finally accepting women in those kinds of roles."

The band's new album is certain to be scrutinized like a virus under a microscope. Even months before the scheduled release there was a raging controversy. In late spring, word leaked in the *Chicago Tribune* that Geffen wasn't happy with the record. One industry insider called it stridently anticommercial in *Newsweek*. Some say the leak sprang from the band; others say it was producer Steve Albini who complained to a journalist. Albini says that "the rumors of the trouble came from the record company. They were trying to undermine the band's confidence." He feels Geffen tried to pressure Nirvana to add some commercial gloss to his defiantly monochromatic production. The band, on the other hand, alleges the remixes had nothing to do with corporate intervention, but that *they* were the ones who decided the vocals on two songs were too abrasive. (Scott Litt, who works with R.E.M., remixed "All Apologies" and the album's first single, "Heart-Shaped Box".) Following the *Newsweek* article on the conflict that exacerbated it further, Nirvana rebutted the media's claim with a full-page ad in *Billboard* magazine.

"I was happy with the recording process, for the most part," Cobain says. "Albini was great but he's an opinionated guy. Basically the whole media thing was an ego boost for him, a way for him to get out of the fact that he had anything to do with us. He's so into being Mr. Punk Rock. It didn't surprise me. He's an extremely paranoid person. But he may have reason for that . . . many major labels do fuck with their artists."

Guttersniping and bickering aside, *In Utero* was finally given the September 14 release date, and Nirvana is ready for a long stint on the road. "I'm totally excited to tour," Cobain says. "But we don't know yet what kind of venues we'll be playing. We don't know how well the record will sell. Because of the backlash, and the general negative attitude toward our band the past year, we can't expect to book arenas."

They've had offers to play with U2, and this past summer rejected a possible $6 million paycheck from Lollapalooza. Instead, they want to tour with a myriad of their favorite bands. The Breeders will open some shows, as will longtime mates Mudhoney, and, they hope, TAD and Sonic Youth. "It can get monotonous seeing the same people for several weeks," Cobain says. "We don't want to take any chances of getting into fights with our friends."

In the wee small hours of the morning, Cobain is rifling through his record collection. Novoselic left hours ago; the next day he's going to try to track down a female cello player for a scheduled band practice, and his cleaning lady is coming by early.

Hundreds of records are stacked against the wrought-iron rail that looks over the living room. The record player is perched on an old black trunk. The painting from the cover of *Incesticide* leans against one wall, a giant telescope in front of it. On the floor, near a big cardboard box overflowing with papers, is a bound black journal with a polariod of Frances glued to the front, sandy-haired and adorable. "The Bean," as Cobain sometimes calls her, has flown off with the nanny today to see her mother in England, where she's playing with Hole at the Phoenix Festival. There are reminders of both of them everywhere: Love's guitar, painted red with Victorian flowers, her '70s fake-fur coat in the closet, Frances's playpen, her stroller, her little dirty baby socks all over the place.

Showing off his records, Cobain appears more at ease. He proudly hands me the cover of one of his Daniel Johnston records, titled *Hi, How Are You,* and puts it on the turntable. "He's an insane person, been in and out of mental hospitals. . . . I have a videotape of him playing. He sits down at this organ—you know, the kind Christians had in their homes in the late '60s, the ones with the colored plastic tempo buttons. He starts crying about midway through the first song. It's just so touching, you feel so sorry for him, but at the same time you're so intrigued."

Next is the new Royal Trux record. "It's basically New York scum rock." And then "The 'Priest' They Called Him," a record he collaborated on with one of his heroes, William S. Burroughs. "It probably pleases me more than it pleases anyone else." Burroughs's familiar warble comes on and Cobain's feedback wails underneath.

He passes me a Wipers record. "I got this in Europe." And then a Meat Puppets album. "Leave that out" he says to me, "we're gonna do a cover of 'Lake of Fire.'" There's the Kyoto monks, and a Half Japanese record. "Jad Fair is gonna open for us a few times in the fall." A very worn copy of *Revolver* balances against the brown box in the center of the room, and there's a smashed Knack record near where Cobain squats, flipping through vinyl.

He loves the new P.J. Harvey record. I put on the new Hole EP, *Beautiful Son.* On the cover is a school picture of a young Cobain, framed by pink and blue bows. "No one's supposed to know it's me," Cobain confides. Love sings, "What a waste of sperm and egg." "Man, if I could get that girl to publish her poetry, the world would change," Cobain beams.

He holds up *The Flowers of Romance* by PIL. "This is a great record, it's just totally uncompromising. It's a bunch of drum beats, Johnny Rotten yelling over it all, but it works somehow." *Never Mind the Bollocks, Here's the Sex Pistols* follows. "This is still the best-produced record in the world. I want to work with the guys who produced this on our next record." He sits back on his ankles. "But if they've been progressing with technology, their production might suck now."

He grabs a Smashcords record. "I found this in Aberdeen." Then Black Sabbath's *Born Again.* "They got Bill Ward out of the asylum to play drums." I tell him I like the cover, a purple-and-red devil baby. He tells me his mom didn't want him to have the record in the house, that he had to hide it.

He picks up Mark Lanegan's solo record. "He has the greatest voice." A Jandek record is next. On the cover there's a very blurry photo of a man sitting in a lawnchair. "He's not pretentious," Cobain says, "but only pretentious people like his music."

Cobain says he listened to the Shaggs' *Philosophy of the World (Third World)* every day for months. The three girls on the front have '60s hairdos and wear plaid pleated skirts. "The first records are good but then they started taking it seriously and really trying to learn how to play their instruments and it wasn't as good."

He moves to the far wall. "Time to get the Leadbelly records out." Cobain hands me one, a deep blue duotone adorning the time-worn jacket. "I think he's still most popular among intellectual Jewish communists from the East Coast," he says jokingly. One of the rarest of his Leadbelly records is cracked, and he explains Courtney isn't always so good at taking care of records. Recently, Cobain says, a lawyer representing the Leadbelly estate phoned up, offering him the only guitar Leadbelly ever had. "But it was $500,000. I can't afford that." He shrugs his shoulders, moves over to another stack of albums, and smiles sarcastically. "I just wish there was some really rich rock star I could borrow the cash from."

CRAIG ROSEN

NIRVANA SET HAS SMELL OF SUCCESS

Billboard, September 25, 1993

Los Angeles—"Teen-aged angst has paid off well / Now I'm bored and old," sings Kurt Cobain on "Serve the Servants," the opening track of Nirvana's new album, *In Utero.*

With 1991's *Nevermind* having sold more than 4.6 million copies in the U.S., according to SoundScan, DGC is cautiously optimistic that *In Utero,* due Tuesday [9/93], also will pay off. Yet the label is taking a low-key approach to marketing the album in an effort to avoid hype.

Robert Smith, head of marketing for Geffen/DGC, says, "We want this record to be discovered in the same way that *Nevermind* was—through the music and how powerful the band is."

In order to do that, Smith says the label "will set things up, duck, and get out of the way," as it did for *Nevermind.*

Geffen/DGC set up *In Utero* with a street campaign that included pre-release snipes with the album's title posted in major cities such as New York, Boston, Detroit, and Los Angeles. In addition, the label distributed stickers of the cover art—a rendering of the transparent "Visible Woman" model, with angel's wings—at the New Music Seminar in July, and at various alternative retail outlets across the country.

In keeping with the alternative market, Geffen/DGC will also issue the album on vinyl.

The label has been advertising *In Utero* with an eye toward the alternative audience. "We're going with *Alternative Press* as opposed to *Entertainment Weekly,*" Smith says.

On the television front, the band is set to perform on the Saturday season premiere of *Saturday Night Live,* and is also planning an appearance on MTV's *Unplugged* later this fall.

While Nirvana undoubtedly will be supported whole-heartedly by alternative accounts, even the chains are gearing up for the release.

"We're buying it like any other superstar product," says Mark Michel, director of purchasing for the 21-store, Miramar, Fla.–based Peaches Entertainment chain.

The track "Heart-Shaped Box" was serviced to college, alternative, and album rock radio in early September, although there currently are no plans for a commercial single release. The track entered at the Modern Rock Tracks chart at No. 7 and the U.K. singles chart at No. 5 last week, and already is generating a significant buzz.

"We're playing it all the time," says Steve Masters, MD at modern rock KITS (Live 105) San Francisco. "It's performing really well. It's our most requested song." Masters characterizes the whole album as "brilliant."

At this point, Geffen isn't actively courting top 40, which jumped on the "Smells Like Teen Spirit" band-wagon following MTV's support of the video. "Inevitably, top 40 will be involved," Smith says. "[But] Nirvana didn't sell nearly 5 million because of a hit single. They sold that many albums because of who they are."

Nirvana is, of course, one of the more controversial acts to top the Billboard 200 in recent years, and, in keeping with the band's past, controversy erupted over *In Utero* months before its release. *Newsweek* reported that Geffen/DGC was unhappy with the album, which Nirvana recorded with former Big Black member and noted underground producer Steve Albini. Scott Litt, known for his work with R.E.M., eventually was called in to remix "Heart-Shaped Box" and "All Apologies."

Geffen/DGC took out a full-page ad in *Billboard* on the band's behalf, slamming the *Newsweek* piece (*Billboard*, May 22).

With hindsight, Nirvana bassist Krist Novoselic (who recently changed the spelling of his first name from Chris to reflect his Croatian heritage) and Albini both say the whole controversy was blown out of proportion.

According to Novoselic, he, Cobain, and drummer Dave Grohl jammed frequently over the last two years before settling on the material for *In Utero*. Since the majority of the songs where in an aggressive vein, Cobain suggested Albini.

"After I heard the way the songs turned out, it was like, 'Yeah, Albini would be cool. He would be the man for the job,'" Novoselic says. "And he was easy to deal with. He didn't have to negotiate points and an advance, because he totally operates autonomously from the music industry. That was a relief. . . . We didn't trust anyone else."

In Utero was recorded and mixed in about 12 days, in a studio in the woods 10 miles from Minneapolis. Albini has yet to hear the final master of the album, so he declines to comment on the finished album.

"The band and I were both trying to make a record that was very straightforward, very accurate, powerful, hi-fi recording of the band, without doing the contemporary studio tricks," Albini says. "The band recorded essentially live in the studio."

Although Albini says he wasn't a fan of *Nevermind*, he says that he now has "way more respect for the band, after having met them and dealt with them, than I did after hearing that record."

After finishing the sessions, Nirvana wasn't completely happy with the album. "I was really happy with the record, but 'Heart-Shaped Box' irked me," Novoselic says. "It just wasn't right. There was a horrible effect on the guitar. Then Kurt wanted to add more background vocals."

Novoselic says that both Albini and Andy Wallace contacted them to help make the changes. "We wanted to do it right away, so I called up Scott Litt," he says. "I really like the way that [R.E.M.'s] *Automatic For The People* and *Document* sound."

The remix was done in Seattle at Bad Animals studio. When "Heart-Shaped Box" was completed, the band also elected to remix the album-closer "All Apologies," Novoselic says.

While some of *In Utero* is closer in spirit to the band's 1988 debut on Sub Pop, *Bleach,* the album isn't a drastic departure from *Nevermind*. A few songs feature cello. "It's not too left-wing," Novoselic says. "It's pretty much straightforward. It's not like some experimental grunge record. It's not prog-grunge."

Lyrically, *In Utero* sees Nirvana grappling with the pains that accompanied its sudden success, including Cobain's stomach problems. Those struggles occasionally are couched in childbirth imagery. (Cobain and his wife Courtney Love, lead singer of Hole, had a baby girl last year.)

Novoselic says success has its ups and downs. "Right now it's on an up-swing. The downs are when your private life is invaded."

The band has also split with some of its closest business associates. Although Danny Goldberg left his Gold Mountain management firm to become senior VP of Atlantic Records, Novoselic says, jokingly, that Goldberg is still the band's "spiritual guru." He adds that the recent move by Gary Gersh, who was the band's A&R man at Geffen, to become president/CEO of Capital Records was "kind of screwy. It was terrible when it happened, but life goes on, people part ways."

Nirvana was in Los Angeles recently to shoot the "Heart-Shaped Box" video with Anton Corbijn, and to collect a trophy for the best alternative video at MTV's *Video Music Awards*. But Novoselic is tired of it all.

"The whole thing sucks," he says. "The *MTV Awards* and all the schmoozing, and all the people who are just in this to be popular and make money, they don't want to express themselves, they are just out for some kind of ulterior motive."

In mid-October, the band will embark on its first tour in two years. "We're chomping at the bit," Novoselic says.

Joining the band on tour will be guitarist Pat Smear, best known as a member of the legendary L.A. punk band the Germs. "He's got a lot of spirit and spunk, and that rubs off on the band," Novoselic says. A cellist also will join the band on a few numbers.

"We will probably do a quiet part of the show," he adds, "where we dim the lights, break out the candelabras and have special appearances by James Taylor, Art Garfunkel, and Burl Ives—who lives in Washington, by the way."

A NOTE ON THE CORN DOLLY

The Corn-mother plays an important part in harvest customs. She is believed to be present in the handful of corn which is left standing last on the field; and with the cutting of the last handful she is caught, or driven away, or killed.

—James G. Frazer, *The Golden Bough*

They give birth astride of a grave, the light gleams an instant, then it's night once more.

—Samuel Beckett, *Waiting for Godot*

The corn dolly had many names. Among them were: Corn-mother, Harvest-mother, Great Mother, Grandmother, Mother of the Grain,

Mother-sheaf, Old Woman, Old Wife, the Caillech, the Hag, the Queen, the Bride, the Maiden, the Ceres, and the Demeter.

—Barbara Walker, *The Woman's Dictionary of Symbols and Sacred Objects*

All over the cover of *In Utero* are feminine power symbols taken from *The Woman's Dictionary of Symbols and Sacred Objects*, by Barbara Walker. These symbols reflect the fertility imagery that appears throughout the artwork on Nirvana's albums—the baby underwater chasing the dollar bill from *Nevermind* (has there ever been a more prescient cover in rock history?); the painting of a mutant doll-baby clinging to its spectral parent, which Cobain did for the cover of *Incesticide*; and the anatomical woman with angel's wings on the front of *In Utero*.

The title of the latter album resonates with the birth imagery that runs through songs such as "Breed" and "Pennyroyal Tea." The back cover of *In Utero* features a collage of fetuses, organs, and flowers designed by Cobain, which became "controversial" when Wal-Mart and K Mart refused to carry the album because of it and the song entitled "Rape Me." (That song is, of course, an *anti*-rape statement—an important fact that apparently eluded the comprehension of the moronic corporate giants.) Cobain was clear about this imagery when he spoke to Michael Azerrad in the biography of Nirvana, *Come As You Are*: "So it's sex and woman and *In Utero* and vaginas and birth and death." (Beckett in *Waiting for Godot*: "Astride of a grave and a difficult birth. Down in the hole, lingeringly, the gravedigger puts on the forceps.")

The most prominent symbol on the cover of *In Utero* is that of the Corn Dolly—it appears on the back with the other symbols and inside the cover in a larger drawing. The Corn Dolly was made by ancient peoples out of wheat, barley, or oats—all collectively called "corn"—and used as a fertility power symbol. She was either burned, doused with water, or hung in the farm house to insure a good harvest. The anatomical figure with angel's wings on the front cover of *In Utero* is a modern, plastic version of the Corn Dolly.

The prominence of the Corn Dolly could also be a Nirvana inside joke. Cobain and Grohl lived off of corn dogs when they were poor and living together. Corn dogs kept them alive and may have even provided the fertilizer for their art.

CLOSING THE CIRCLE: THAT PUNK WITH BURROUGHS

1997

> I am not a punk and I don't know why anybody would consider me the
> Godfather of Punk. How do you define punk? . . . I think the so-called
> punk movement is indeed a media creation. I did however send a letter
> of support to the Sex Pistols when they released "God Save the Queen"
> in England because I've always said that the country doesn't stand a
> chance until you have 20,000 people saying BUGGER THE QUEEN!

> —William S. Burroughs, in conversation from *With William Burroughs:*
> *A Report from the Bunker,* by Victor Bockris.

> As always the lunch is naked.

> —William S. Burroughs, *Naked Lunch*

In the liner notes to *Incesticide* Kurt Cobain ("the blonde one") thanked
Thor Lindsay of Tim Kerr Records for giving him "a signed first edition
of *Naked Lunch*." This was an indication of Cobain's literary interests
and it signaled the closing of a rock circle. Whenever Cobain mentioned
the writers he liked the three Bs constantly came up: Burroughs, Beckett,
and Bukowski. William S. Burroughs was one of the original and most
provocative of the Beats; Bukowski was Bukowski ("I met Kerouac's boy
Neal C. shortly before he went down to lay along those Mexican railroad
tracks to die" [438]). And Beckett came before them all. This essay traces
the circle Cobain drew from Burroughs to himself. A look at the life and
writing of Burroughs sheds light on Cobain's words, his aesthetic interests,
and the overall world of punk. To connect the dots on the circle we must
go from the music of Nirvana to the music of the Beats. It is a tale full of
sound and fury, signifying what this literature meant to Cobain and how
it influenced his music. It is a circle we still watch turn around itself.

    Naked Lunch is Burroughs's masterpiece, and it embodies the most
experimental qualities of the Beat literary movement. The Beat movement
was named after Jack Kerouac, Allen Ginsberg, and Burroughs came into
contact with a Times Square hustler, petty criminal, and drug user named
Herbert Huncke. It was Huncke who first used the term "beat" to
describe his own life on the streets; the word was initially used by itiner-
ant jazz musicians to describe their "beaten" life on the road. Huncke is
the person in Ginsberg's "Howl" who "walked all night with shoes full of
blood" (128) (he appears as Herman in Burroughs's first book, *Junky,* and
as Elmo Hassel in *On the Road*). Huncke provided Burroughs with his

first look into the dark world of drugs and street life, a world that fascinated Burroughs and gave him an alternative to a society he had always felt was suffocating. Huncke's world was a way out, a way *through* a culture Burroughs found constricting in a moral and aesthetic way. Burroughs came from a privileged background: his grandfather invented an adding machine that still bears his name (the name was Lee, and Burroughs used it as a pseudonym when he first published *Junky*). This invention gave the family plenty of money and they went almost untouched by the Depression. Burroughs went to Harvard and then to Vienna to study medicine. He had a trust fund. He moved to New York City in 1943 and soon met Kerouac and Ginsberg.

Coming to New York provided Burroughs with his first encounter with the underworld of drugs and crime, but his coming also opened up a new universe for Kerouac and Ginsberg. As John Tytell describes it in his seminal study of the Beats, *Naked Angels,* Burroughs provided a vital stimulus for the emerging movement; Ginsberg and Kerouac had been studying literature at Columbia, but it was Burroughs who introduced them to

> Blake, Rimbaud, Hart Crane, and Auden. Burroughs gave Ginsberg his copies of Yeats's *A Vision* and Eliot's poems and presented Kerouac with Spengler's *Decline of the West*. He introduced his new friends to writers like Kafka and Céline, to Cocteau's writing about opium, to books like *The Cancer Biopathy* by Wilhelm Reich and *Science and Sanity* by Count Korzybski. Soon both Kerouac and Ginsberg were sucked into Burroughs's vortex, and he began to effect subtle changes in their outlook. (39)

It is this "vortex" of provocative literature and the underworld of drugs and crime that inspired the Beats. The work they produced had a profound influence on Cold War America and the emerging form of rock 'n' roll. This is not to say that the books they published were one and the same: the work they produced often contrasted sharply in technique and content. In conversation, Burroughs often made it a point to distance himself from the Beat movement: "I don't associate myself with it at all, and never have, either with their personal objectives or their literary style. . . . You couldn't find . . . writers more different, more distinctive" (*Job* 43). But they always had the same motive behind everything they wrote: an intense honesty in the depiction of their lives, loves, and losses.

Kerouac's novel of "the mad ones" ("mad to live, mad to talk, mad to be saved" [9]) called *On the Road* appeared in 1957. Ginsberg's "Howl"—the poem that defined their generation ("angelheaded hipsters burning for the ancient heavenly connection to the / starry dynamo in the machinery of night" [126])—was first read by him in public in 1955, and *Howl and Other Poems* was published a year later. *Naked Lunch* was first published in 1959 but it soon ran into legal trouble and was declared "obscene" by the Superior Court of Boston. This ruling was overturned in 1966 at a trial in which Ginsberg and Norman Mailer appeared to show support for the book. (This trial was historically significant because *Naked Lunch* became the last work of literature to be censored by the post office and a state government; it effectively made censorship of literature in the U.S. a thing of the past.) Mailer made it clear that the novel was important for the modern reader:

> Just as Hieronymus Bosch set down the most diabolical and blood-curdling details with a delicacy of line and a Puckish humor which left one with a sense of the mansions of horror attendant upon Hell, so, too, does Burroughs leave you with an intimate detailed vision of what Hell might be like, a Hell which may be waiting as the culmination, the final product, of the scientific revolution. ("On Trial" xviii)

But before Burroughs could give us Hell, he had to go through his own personal Inferno.

Before *Naked Lunch* could describe "The Algebra of Need" its author had to face himself. After his exposure to the drug underworld in New York, Burroughs took off for other parts of America to pursue his interests: guns, drugs, books, freedom. Traveling with him was Joan Vollner Adams, a woman he met in New York who would become his common-law wife. His relationship with Adams was intense and complicated by his homosexuality, his drug use, her young daughter (and later a son from Burroughs), and her addiction to Benzedrine. After America became too small for them—after authorities in New Orleans found a pile of illegal guns and drugs on his farm—Burroughs and Adams moved to Mexico with the two children. (William S. Burroughs Jr. later became a writer; this is how he described his father while visiting him in Tangier: "There was an orgone box in the upstairs hall in which my father would sit for hours at a time smoking kif and then rush out and attack his typewriter without warning" [446–47].) Initially, Mexico provided the freedom Burroughs was looking for, but things started to go wrong: "And for every real cop there were two or three professional brothers of cops with huge badges in their pockets and .45s stuck down into inside holsters as I have seen only in Mexico" ("The Name" 10). And then things went really wrong. On September 7, 1951, late at night at a party, Burroughs shot his wife in the head. After asking her if they could perform a "William Tell" trick, Adams had placed a glass on her head. Burroughs missed.

Her death shattered Burroughs. The Mexican authorities did not prosecute for murder and Burroughs jumped bail at the first opportunity. Thus began his years of exile in Tangier, South America, Paris, and London. His wife's death was an accident, but it haunted him. He tried to find relief by experimenting with yage, the mystical hallucinogen administered by shamans in the jungles of South America. (In "Letter from a Master Addict to Dangerous Drugs" he describes the drug as a way to get over a painful event: "Yage induces a state of conscious anesthesia, and is used in rites where the initiates must undergo a painful ordeal like whipping with knotted vines, or exposure to the sting of ants" [230].) He tried to find relief in heroin—he lived for an entire year in Tangier without changing his clothes or washing or doing anything but shooting up and staring at his shoes ("I could look at the end of my shoe for eight hours" ["Deposition" xxxix]). He tried to find relief in travel. But the only relief he found was within himself and it gave him a voice to write. He lost his wife, the children, and his family's financial support because of the accident. As Tytell puts it, this event "freed Burroughs from his own past. His use of drugs, his consort with criminals, and finally his shooting Joan—all were steps in outcasting himself, becoming unacceptable to a society which he had already rejected" (46). As Burroughs himself put it, the accident enabled him to write:

> I am forced to the appalling conclusion that I would never have become a writer but for Joan's death, and to a realization of the extent to which this event has motivated and formulated my writing. I live with the constant threat of possession, and a constant need to escape from possession, from Control. So the death of Joan brought me in contact with the invader, the Ugly Spirit, and maneuvered me into a lifelong struggle, in which I have had no choice except to write my way out. (Morgan 199)

And the first way out was *Naked Lunch*.

Burroughs began what would turn into *Naked Lunch* in 1955. He maintained that because of his use of junk, he had "no precise memory of writing the notes which have now been published under the title *Naked Lunch*" ("Deposition" xxxv). The beginning consisted of fragments, sketches he wrote describing street life, the drug hustle, hallucinations, insect-monsters sucking the life out of those around them, sexual nightmares, junk madness, bureaucratic idiocy, and addiction in all its forms (drugs, sex, power, hypocrisy, morality, government, religion). The writing was a descent into the hell of addiction and the hell of trying to beat addiction ("One more shot—tomorrow the cure" [91]). In 1957, Kerouac and Ginsberg journeyed to Tangier and journeyed into Burroughs's nightmare: Ginsberg discussed its beauty with Burroughs while Kerouac, the supertypist (he typed-wrote *The Subterraneans* in three days!), typed up sections of it.

In 1958, Burroughs left Tangier and moved to Paris with the massive, patched-together manuscript. What he felt he needed to do at this point was to read through all the sections and put them into an order for final publication. But this never occurred. An editor named Sinclair Beiles who worked for a publisher who was interested in the book suggested that the manuscript be submitted in the haphazard order Burroughs was carrying it around in. Burroughs accepted the idea immediately because he realized that this "order" would convey the experience and ideas he wanted the book to give. His descent into his nightmares was put into book form following the "order" of a descent into Hell. Looking back on the book, looking back on the addiction he had kicked, looking back on the death of his wife, Burroughs defined the title of the book and thus defined his career: "I did not understand what the title meant until my recent recovery. The title means exactly what the words say: NAKED Lunch—a frozen moment when everyone sees what is on the end of every fork" ("Deposition" xxxv).

It was this "frozen moment" and the overall rebellion of the Beats—rebellion against Cold War America, rebellion against accepted morality, rebellion against the "rules" of conventional art—which influenced and inspired the early practitioners of what came to be known as rock 'n' roll. This is the beginning of the circle (do circles have beginnings?): Bob Dylan fused the Beat approach to life and art with the folk tradition of Woody Guthrie. The Beats put the "Beat" in the Beatles (and Dylan put the Beats into their heads when he turned them on to pot). As the punk inheritor of Lennon—a legacy he almost single-handedly embodies—Cobain knew his roots. This is the reason for his approaching Burroughs through Thor Linsdsey; and what came out of it was *The "Priest" They Called Him*. It is a chilling and beautiful combination of Cobain's guitar and Burroughs's voice telling the story of an "immaculate fix," an epiphany on the dark side. It was an important collaboration for Cobain: he told Darcey Steinke that it "probably pleases me more than it pleases anybody else."[1] Cobain

---

1. See Darcey Steinke's "Smashing Their Heads on That Punk Rock" on page 78 of this book. *Ed.*

wanted Burroughs to appear in the video for "Heart-Shaped Box" as the crucified man. Burroughs refused but the two met in Lawrence, Kansas, the home of Burroughs since 1981. This is how Burroughs described their meeting:

> I waited and Kurt got out with another man. Cobain was very shy, very polite, and obviously enjoyed the fact that I wasn't awestruck at meeting him. There was something boyish about him, fragile and engagingly lost. He smoked cigarettes but didn't drink. There were no drugs. I never showed him my gun collection. (Sandford 299)

The two also exchanged gifts: Burroughs gave Cobain one of his paintings—Burroughs had turned to the canvas in his later years—and Cobain gave him a biography of Leadbelly. Cobain's gift is an interesting curve on the circle: instead of giving Burroughs one of his own paintings, Cobain gave him a book about the life of another American artist who influenced him. It was almost as if Cobain was introducing his artistic fathers to each other. But that is how America goes: curves all over the place and edges far away. We need to jump back on the circle to the '70s.

In 1974 Burroughs moved back to New York City and settled in a cavernous and windowless apartment he called "the Bunker." It was three blocks from CBGBs. It was a fitting location. New York punk grew on the small stage at CBGBs and Burroughs provided the scene with a presence, an artistic figurehead. However, it was from the stage at the St. Marks Poetry Project that Patti Smith announced that Burroughs was back in town as she "performed" her poetry with guitar accompaniment. It was a short step from Smith reading her poetry—words partly inspired by Burroughs—to singing in a rock band—an act partly inspired by Burroughs. After seeing her on stage, Burroughs was stuck by the fact that Smith's words came alive when "performed":

> You see, Patti started out as a poet, then turned to painting, and then she suddenly emerges as a real rock star. Which was strange, because I don't think she could have gone very far either in her poetry or her writing, just from scratch. But suddenly, she's a rock star. There was no question of that. (McCain 161)

Smith's words gained their power through their performance. It was the punk "performance" which established it as a movement in New York and helped it spread to Britain. It was a "performance" in opposition to standard musical practice, standard mainstream entertainment. It was more than entertainment. It was an *act* against conventional society and Burroughs was one of its inspiring forces. This was made clear when Burroughs became the only established writer to send a letter of support to the Sex Pistols after they released "God Save the Queen" and everyone in Britain was screaming for their blood. The Sex Pistols could not even perform in their homeland anymore, but Burroughs saw their song—their punk *act*—as a healthy aesthetic reaction to a dead culture. In an essay called "Bugger the Queen," Burroughs made this perfectly clear: "The Queen is the fountainhead and motherload of a snobbery that poisons the dank air of England with the smell of brussels sprouts cooking in a soggy green paste" (79–80). It was Burroughs's concern with directly confronting conventional morality and suffocating shibboleths that inspired the punk movement. Patti Smith began part of the circle and she ended a curve of it with "About a Boy," a song written for Kurt Cobain. But we must skip back on the circle to the late '70s and a performance artist called Genesis P-Orridge who provides another spin on the Burroughs wheel.

Genesis P-Orridge turned to music while he lived in a place called the "Death Factory" because it was next to a 17th-century mass grave filled with victims of the bubonic plague. With his then girlfriend and fellow performance artist Cosey Fanni Tutti, P-Orridge fashioned what is now called "industrial" music—a term that came into circulation along with the band they formed called Throbbing Gristle. Following on the death of British punk, the band was an extension of their work as performance artists. As P-Orridge put it, they were after a

> larger target: the mass media and, in particular, popular culture. Being a child of the radical Sixties, I was—and still am—an idealist about wanting to liberate young minds from the feeling that they are not able to achieve and express everything they feel inside. In other words, countermanding the orders of society. So that led to choosing either television or popular music. (di Perna 29)

In their music and live performances Throbbing Gristle attacked the conventional standards of just about everything. The topics taken up in their "songs" included war atrocities, mutilations, burn victims, pornography, the occasional confession of a murderer, child abuse, Charles Manson, Charles Manson, and Charles Manson. Their music was the beginning of industrial and trance-dance. It mixed in noise with snippets of dialogue from various sources including television. What is significant about their work is that they consistently referred to Burroughs—and Burroughs later gave P-Orridge some of his paintings and championed his later band, Psychic TV. In 1982, P-Orridge put together *Nothing Here But the Recordings*, a fascinating compilation of Burroughs's recorded words. The reason for Throbbing Gristle's debt to Burroughs is that they took their basic working method of attacking mainstream culture from him. This method was called the "cut-up."

It was the artist Brion Gyson who first introduced Burroughs to the method of the "cut-up": he sliced a newspaper up and put a text together from the pieces in a random order. (This was in the late '50s, a jump back on the circle.) Burroughs immediately seized upon this technique as a way to completely destroy traditional narrative. Based on this method, he constructed the great "cut-up" trilogy: *Nova Express, The Soft Machine,* and *The Ticket That Exploded.* Burroughs moved these experiments into the verbal and used tape recorders to construct sound "cut-ups," the precursor to the sampling common in industrial, house, and techno.[2] To those who called the use of the "cut-up" akin to plagiarism (Beckett replied to the method thus: "You're using other people's words!" [Bockris 214]) Burroughs made the case that all writing is in a sense "stealing" and that a modern writer must steal with impunity:

> Everything belongs to the inspired and dedicated thief. All the artists of history, from cave painters to Picasso, all the poets and writers, the musicians and architects, offer their wares, importuning him like street vendors. They supplicate him from the bored minds of school children, from the prisons of uncritical veneration, from dead museums and dusty archives. . . . Words, colors, light, sounds, stone, wood, bronze belong to the living artist. They belong to anyone who can use them. ("Les Voleurs" 21)

Naked Lunch had subconsciously set the stage for the "cut-up" because of its random "ordering" and Burroughs's "use" of scenes from writers he admired—Joseph Conrad, James Joyce, Samuel Beckett—throughout the nightmare of the book.

The "cut-up" was important for Burroughs because he felt that it broke through the "control" the mass media placed on people, a "con-

---

2. A fascinating section of *The Ticket That Exploded* called "the invisible generation" appears on page 103 of this book—it uses the "cut-up" method to explain how the method works.—*Ed.*

trol" often sweetened under the guise of information and entertainment. (In *Naked Lunch,* Burroughs distances his work from the world of mass culture: "Insofar as I succeed in *direct* recording of certain areas of psychic process I may have limited function. . . . I am not an entertainer" [200].) As Tytell describes it, the "cut-up" was the knife Burroughs used to cut through the white noise of mainstream culture:

> "Cutting the word-lines" means severing the hypnotizing authority of newspapers, magazines, radio, and television, whose sources of power are obscured. It becomes a way of resisting the constant bombardment of images to which modern city man is subject that blunts his receptivity, dazes his senses with a permanent image haze. As a means of exploring subliminal awareness, the cut-up can establish fresh connections between images. (116)

It was the concern with breaking through the "permanent image haze" which attracted Cobain to the work of Burroughs. This is what connects Cobain to Burroughs; it is not drug use or the possession of guns which closes the circle. The circle Cobain drew from himself to Burroughs was based on artistic vision and it can be seen all over the music of Nirvana. And this begins at the basic level of Cobain's songwriting. As he told Steinke, he approached writing lyrics as an exercise in collage: "*Nevermind* was an accumulation of two years of poetry. I picked out good lines, cut up things. I'm always skipping back and forth to different themes." This is the strength behind the songs: they are scintillating chunks of poetry combined together under the critical mass of roaring music. The music keeps the words together and the words always threaten to rip the music apart.

Cobain combined the literary experiments of Burroughs with the energy and honesty of punk. But Cobain's debt to Burroughs does not come from a complete submission to his techniques. One cannot patch together the "importance" of Nirvana from their lyrics, or somehow paste Cobain's life together from the songs. The genius behind Cobain's music lies in the fact that he went beyond Burroughs and punk by applying the intensity of Burroughs's literary *honesty* and "stealing" from the Melvins, Flipper, Beckett, the Beatles, Bukowski, Sonic Youth, the Vaselines, the Meat Puppets, Scratch Acid, the Butthole Surfers, the world of Aberdeen, Devo, Courtney Love, the United States of America, the Pixies, fish beer, history, his family, Buddhism, Black Flag, the Velvet Underground, Patrick Süskind's *Perfume,* the Pacific Northwest, Shocking Blue, drugs,

Mudhoney, Francis Farmer, the Germs, the Cold War, *The Andy Griffith Show*, Leadbelly, John Lennon, William S. Burroughs, and his own life. He stole from our world to give it back to us. He took the career of Burroughs as a model because the author of *Naked Lunch* took the dark side of America and the dark side of himself and turned it into art. It was an intensely personal process that produced a distinctly passionate form of expression. This is what Cobain brought to rock and, as Lester Bangs told us, it is the essence of that thing called punk:

> Rock & roll is not an "art-form"; rock & roll is a raw wail from the bottom of the guts. And like I said, whatever anybody ever called it, punk rock has been around from the beginning—it's just rock honed down to its rawest elements, simple playing with a lot of power and vocalists who may not have much range but have so much conviction and passion it makes up for it ten times over. Because PASSION IS WHAT IT'S ALL ABOUT—what all music is about. (104)

It was the passion of Nirvana that made them a great band. To define the passion requires listening very closely to their music: listening beyond the distortion, the thundering bass, the drums on fire. Listening beyond the instruments being smashed. Listening beyond Cobain's screams. Listening beyond him asking us about ourselves: "What is wrong with me?" The passion of Nirvana comes from the tiny sound of a circle being closed.

WORKS CITED

Bangs, Lester. "In Which Another Pompous Blowhard Purports to Possess the True Meaning of Punk Rock." In *The Penguin Book of Rock 'n' Roll Writing,* edited by Clinton Heylin. New York: Penguin Books, 1992.

Bockris, Victor. *With William Burroughs: A Report from the Bunker.* New York: St. Martin's/Griffin, 1981.

Burroughs, William S. "Bugger the Queen." In *The Adding Machine: Selected Essays.* New York: Arcade Publishing, 1986.

———. "Deposition: Testimony Concerning a Sickness." In *Naked Lunch.* New York: Grove Press, 1990.

——— with Daniel Odier. *The Job: Interviews with William S. Burroughs.* New York: Grove Press, 1970.

———. "Letter From a Master Addict to Dangerous Drugs." In *Naked Lunch.* New York: Grove Press, 1990.

———. *Naked Lunch.* New York: Grove Press, 1990.

———. "Naked Lunch on Trial." In *Naked Lunch.* New York: Grove Press, 1990.

———. "The Name is Burroughs." In *The Adding Machine: Selected Essays.* New York: Arcade Publishing, 1986.

———. "Les Voleurs." In *The Adding Machine: Selected Essays.* New York: Arcade Publishing, 1986.

Burroughs, William Jr. "Kentucky Ham." In *The Portable Beat Reader,* edited by Ann Charters. New York: Penguin Books, 1992.

Bukowski, Charles. "Notes of a Dirty Old Man." In *The Portable Beat Reader,* edited by Ann Charters. New York: Penguin Books, 1992.

di Perna, Alan. "Jackhammer of the Gods: Industrial Revolution." *Alternative Guitar* 3 (1996): 26–33, 89.

Ginsberg, Allen. "Howl." In *Collected Poems: 1947–1980.* New York: Harper and Row, 1984.

Kerouac, Jack. *On the Road.* New York: Signet, 1957.

McNeil, Legs and Gillian McCain. *Please Kill Me: The Uncensored Oral History of Punk.* New York: Penguin Books, 1996.

Morgan, Ted. *Literary Outlaw: The Life and Times of William S. Burroughs.* New York: Henry Holt and Co., 1988.

Sanford, Christopher. *Kurt Cobain.* New York: Carroll and Graf Publishers, 1995.

Steinke, Darcey. "Smashing Their Heads on That Punk Rock." In *The Nirvana Companion,* edited by John Rocco. New York: Schirmer Books, 1998.

Tytell, John. *Naked Angels: The Lives and Literature of the Beat Generation.* New York: Grove Press, 1976.

WILLIAM S. BURROUGHS
THE INVISIBLE GENERATION
The Ticket That Exploded, 1966

what we see is determined to a large extent by what we hear you can verify this proposition by a simple experiment turn off the sound track on your television set and substitute an arbitrary sound track prerecorded on your tape recorder street sounds music conversation recordings of other television programs you will find that the arbitrary sound track seems to be appropriate and is in fact determining your interpretation of the film track on screen people running for a bus in piccadilly with a sound track of machine-gun fire looks like 1917 petrograd you can extend the experiment by using recorded material more or less appropriate to the film track for example take a political speech on television shut off sound track and substitute another speech you have prerecorded hardly tell the difference isn't much record sound track of one danger man from uncle spy program run it in place of another and see if your friends can't tell the difference it's all done with tape recorders consider this machine and what it can do it can record and play back activating a past time set by precise association a recording can be played back any number of times you can study and analyze every pause and inflection of a recorded conversation why did so and so say just that or this just here play back so and so's recordings and you will find out what cues so and so in you can edit a recorded conversation retaining material which is incisive witty and pertinent you can edit a recorded conversation retaining remarks which are boring flat and silly a tape recorder can play back fast slow or backwards you can learn to do these things record a sentence and speed it up now try imitating your accelerated voice play a sentence backwards and learn to unsay what you just said . . . such exercises bring you a liberation from old association locks try inching tape this sound is produced by taking a recorded text for best results a text spoken in a loud clear voice and rubbing the tape back and forth across the head the same sound can be produced on a philips compact cassette recorder by playing a tape back and switching the mike control stop start on and off at short intervals which gives an effect of stuttering take any text speed it up slow it down run it backwards inch it and you will hear words that were not in the original recording new words made by the machine different people will scan out different words of course but some of the words are quite clearly there and anyone can hear them words which were not in the original tape but which are in many cases relevant to the original text as if the words themselves had been interrogated and forced to reveal their hidden meanings it is interesting to record these words words literally made by the machine itself you can carry this experiment further using as your original recording material that contains no words animal noises for instance record a trough of slopping hogs the barking of dogs go to the zoo and record the bellowings of Guy the gorilla the big cats growling over their meat goats and monkeys now run the animals backwards speed up slow down and inch the animals and see if any clear words emerge see what the animals have to say see how the animals react to playback of processed tape

the simplest variety of cut up on tape can be carried out with one machine like this record any text rewind to the beginning now run forward at arbitrary intervals stop the machine and record a short text wind forward stop record where you have recorded over the original text the words are wiped out and replaced with new words do this several times creating arbitrary juxtapositions you will notice that the arbitrary cuts in are appropriate in many cases and your cut up tape makes surprising sense cut up tapes can be hilariously funny twenty years ago i heard a tape called the drunken newscaster prepared by jerry newman of new york cutting up news broadcasts i can not remember the words at this distance but i do remember laughing until i fell out of a chair paul bowles calls the tape recorder god's little toy maybe his last toy fading into the cold spring air poses a colorless question

any number can play

yes any number can play anyone with a tape recorder controlling the sound track can influence and create events the tape recorder experiments described here will show you how this influence can be extended and correlated into the precise operation this is the invisible generation he looks like an advertising executive a college student an american tourist doesn't matter what your cover story is so long as it covers you and leaves you free to act you need a philips compact cassette recorder handy machine for street recording and playback you can carry it under your coat for recording looks like a transistor radio for playback playback in the street will show the influence of your sound track in operation of course the most undetectable playback is street recordings people don't notice yesterday voices phantom car holes in time accidents of past time played back in present time screech of brakes loud honk of an absent horn can occasion an accident here old fires still catch old buildings still fall or take a prerecorded sound track into the street anything you want to put out on the sublim eire play back two minutes record two minutes mixing your message with the street waft your message right into a worthy ear some carriers are much better than others you know the ones lips moving muttering away carry my message all over london in our yellow submarine working with street playback you will see your playback find the appropriate context for example i am playing back some of my dutch schultz last word tapes in the street five alarm fire and a fire truck passes right on cue you will learn to give the cues you will learn to plant events and concepts after analyzing recorded conversations you will learn to steer a conversation where you want it to go the physiological liberation achieved as word lines of controlled association are cut will make you more efficient in reaching your objectives whatever you do you will do it better record your boss and co-workers analyze their associational patterns learn to imitate their voices oh you'll be a popular man around the office but not easy to compete with the usual procedure record their body sounds from concealed mikes the rhythm of breathing the movements of after-lunch intestines the beating of hearts now impose your own body sounds and become the breathing word and the beating heart of that organization become that organization the invisible brothers are invading present time the more people we can get working with tape recorders the more useful experiments and extensions will turn up why not give tape recorder parties every guest arrives with his recorder and tapes of what he intends to say at the party recording what other recorders say to him it is the height of rudeness not to record when addressed directly by another tape recorder and you can't say anything directly have to record it first the coolest old tape worms never talk direct

what was the party like switch on playback

what happened at lunch switch on playback

eyes old unbluffed unreadable he hasn't said a direct word in ten years and as you hear what the party was like and what happened at lunch you will begin to see sharp and clear there was a grey veil between you and what you saw or more often did not see that grey veil was the prerecorded words of a control machine once that veil is removed you will see clearer and sharper than those who are behind the veil whatever you do you will do it better than those behind the veil this is the invisible generation it is the efficient generation hands work and go see some interesting results when several hundred tape recorders turn up at a political rally or a freedom march suppose you record the ugliest snarling southern law men several hundred tape recorders spitting it back and forth and chewing it around like a cow with the aftosa you now have a sound that could make any neighborhood unattractive several hundred tape recorders echoing the readers could touch a poetry reading with unpredictable magic and think what fifty thousand beatle fans armed with tape recorders could do to shea stadium several hundred people recording and playing back in the street is quite a happening right there conservative m.p. spoke about the growing menace posed by bands of irresponsible youths with tape recorders playing back traffic sounds that confuse motorists carrying the insults recorded in some low underground club into mayfair and piccadilly this growing menace to public order put a thousand young recorders with riot recordings into the street that mutter gets louder and louder remember this is a technical operation one step at a time here is an experiment that can be performed by anyone equipped with two machines connected by extension lead so he can record directly from one machine to the other since the experiment may give rise to a marked erotic reaction it is more interesting to select as your partner some one with whom you are on intimate terms we have two subjects b. and j. b. records on tape recorder 1 j. records on tape recorder 2 now we alternate the two voice tracks tape recorder 1 playback two seconds tape recorder 2 records tape recorder 2 playback two seconds tape recorder 1 records alternating the voice of b. with the voice of j. in order to attain any degree of precision the two tapes should be cut with scissors and alternate pieces spliced together this is a long process which can be appreciably expedited if you have access to a cutting room and use film tape which is much larger and easier to handle you can carry this experiment further by taking a talking film of b. and talking film of j. splicing sound and image track twenty four alternations per second as i have intimated it is advisable to exercise some care in choosing your partner for such experiments since the results can be quite drastic b. finds himself talking and thinking just like j. j. sees b.'s image in his own face who's face b. and j. are continually aware of each other when separated invisible and persistent presence they are in fact becoming each other you see b. retroactively was j. by the fact of being recorded on j.'s sound and image track experiments with spliced tape can give rise to explosive relationships properly handled of course to a high degree of efficient cooperation you will begin to see the advantage conveyed on j. if he carried out such experiments without the awareness of b. and so many applications of the spliced tape principle will suggest themselves to the alert reader suppose you are some creep in a grey flannel suit you want to present a new concept of advertising to the old man it is creative advertising so before you goes up against the old man you record the old man's voice and splices your own voice in expounding your new concept and put it out on the office air-conditioning system splice yourself in with your favorite pop singers splice yourself in with newscasters prime ministers presidents

why stop there

why stop anywhere

everybody splice himself in with everybody else yes boys that's me there by the cement mixer the next step and i warn you it will be expensive is programmed tape recorders a fully programmed machine would be set to record and play back at selected intervals to rewind and start over after a selected interval automatically remaining in continuous operation suppose you have three programmed machines tape recorder 1 programmed to play back five seconds while tape recorder 2 records tape recorder 2 play back three seconds while tape recorder 1 records now say you are arguing with your boy friend or girl friend remembering what was said last time and thinking of things to say next time round and round you just can't shut up put all your arguments and complaints on tape recorder 1 and call tape recorder 1 by your own name on tape recorder 2 put all the things he or she said to you or might say when occasion arises out of the tape recorders now make the machines talk tape recorder 1 play back five seconds tape recorder 2 record tape recorder 2 play back three seconds tape recorder 1 record run it through fifteen minutes half an hour now switch intervals running the interval switch you used on tape recorder 1 back on tape recorder 2 the interval switch may be as important as the context listen to the two machines mix it around now on tape recorder 3 you can introduce the factor of irrelevant response so put just anything on tape recorder 3 old joke old tune piece of the street television radio and program tape recorder 3 into the argument

tape recorder 1 i waited up for you until two o'clock last night

tape recorder 3 what we want to know is who put the sand in the spinach the use of irrelevant response will be found effective in breaking obsessional association tracks all association tracks are obsessional get it out of your head and into the machines stop arguing stop complaining stop talking let the machines argue complain and talk a tape recorder is an externalized section of the human nervous system you can find out more about the nervous system and gain more control over your reactions by using the tape recorder than you could find out sitting twenty years in the lotus posture or wasting your time on the analytic couch

listen to your present time tapes and you will begin to see who you are and what you are doing here mix yesterday in with today and hear tomorrow your future rising out of old recordings you are a programmed tape recorder set to record and play back

who programs you

who decides what tapes play back in present time

who plays back your old humiliations and defeats holding you in prerecorded preset time

you don't have to listen to that sound you can program your own playback you can decide what tapes you want played back in present time study your associational patterns and find out what cases in what prerecordings for playback program those old tapes out it's all done with tape recorders there are many things you can do with programmed tape recorders stage performances programmed at arbitrary intervals so each performance is unpredictable and unique allowing any degree of audience participation readings concerts programmed tape recorders can create a happening anywhere programmed tape recorders are of course essential to any party and no modern host would bore his guests with a straight present time party in a modern house every room is bugged recorders record and play back from hidden mikes and loudspeakers phantom voices mutter through corridors and rooms word visible as a haze tape recorders in the gardens answer each other like barking dogs sound track brings the studio on set you can change the look of a city by putting your own sound track into the streets here are some experiments filming a sound track operations on set find a neighborhood with slate roofs and red brick chimneys cool grey sound track fog horns distant train whistles frogs croaking music across the golf course cool blue recordings in a cobblestone market with blue shutters all the sad old showmen stand there in blue twilight a rustle of darkness and wires when several thousand people working with tape recorders and filming subsequent action select their best sound tracks and film footage and splice together you will see something interesting now consider the harm that can be done and has been done when recording and playback is expertly carried out in such a way that the people affected do not know what is happening thought feeling and apparent sensory impressions can be precisely manipulated and controlled riots and demonstrations to order for example they use old anti-semitic recordings against the chinese in indonesia run shop and get rich and always give the business to another tiddly wink pretty familiar suppose you want to bring down the area go in and record all the ugliest stupidest dialogue the most discordant sound track you can find and keep playing it back which will occasion more ugly stupid dialogue recorded and played back on and on always selecting the ugliest material possibilities are unlimited you want to start a riot put your machines in the street with riot recordings move fast enough you can stay just ahead of the riot surf boarding we call it no margin for error recollect poor old burns caught out in a persian market riot recordings hid under his jellaba and they skinned him alive raw peeled thing writhing there in the noon sun and we got the picture

do you get the picture

the techniques and experiments described here have been used and are being used by agencies official and non official without your awareness and very much to your disadvantage any number can play wittgenstein said no proposition can contain itself as an argument the only thing not prerecorded on a prerecorded set is the prerecording itself that is any recording in which a random factor operates any street recording you can prerecord your future you can hear and see what you want to hear and see the experiments described here were explained and demonstrated to me by ian sommerville of london in this article i am writing as his ghost

look around you look at a control machine programmed to select the ugliest stupidest most vulgar and degraded sounds for recording and playback which provokes uglier stupider more vulgar and degraded sounds to be recorded and play back inexorable degradation look forward to dead end look forward to ugly vulgar playback tomorrow and tomorrow and tomorrow what are newspapers doing but selecting the ugliest sounds for playback by and large if its ugly its news and if that isn't enough i quote from the editorial page of the new york daily news we can take care of china and if russia intervenes we can take care of that nation too the only good communist is a dead communist let's take care of slave driver castro next what are we waiting for let's bomb china now and let's stay armed to the teeth for centuries this ugly vulgar bray put out for mass playback you want to spread hysteria record and play back the most stupid and hysterical reactions

marijuana marijuana why that's deadlier than cocaine

it will turn a man into a homicidal maniac he said steadily his eyes cold as he thought of the vampires who suck riches from the vile traffic in pot quite literally swollen with human blood he reflected grimly and his jaw set pushers should be pushed into the electric chair

strip the bastards naked

all right let's see your arms

or in the mortal words of harry j anslinger the laws must reflect society's disapproval of the addict

an uglier reflection than society's disapproval would be hard to find the mean cold eyes of decent american women tight lips and no thank you from the shop keeper snarling cops pale nigger killing eyes reflecting society's disapproval fucking queers i say shoot them if on the other hand you select calm sensible reactions for recordings and playback you will spread calmness and good sense

is this being done

obviously it is not only way to break the inexorable down spiral of ugly uglier ugliest recording and playback is with counterrecording and playback the first step is to isolate and cut association lines of the control machine carry a tape recorder with you and record all the ugliest stupidest things cut your ugly tapes in together speed up slow down play backwards inch the tape you will hear one ugly voice and see one ugly spirit is made of ugly old prerecordings the more you run the tapes through and cut them up the less power they will have cut the prerecordings into air into thin air

PART THREE

All in All Is
All We Are

This is gonna be the end of the Cold War and the beginning of the hot one. We're gonna kick some ass. First off, we're gonna invade Hawaii, send in the Red Army and make us a little offshore holiday home. Then, we're gonna nuke our home town, 'cos the place is kind of a drag and we got hassled there when we were kids for wearing our hair long and playing our music loud.

—Krist Novoselic after Nirvana was elected President of the Soviet Socialist Republics within the pages of *Melody Maker*

It's your crossword puzzle.

—Kurt Cobain on Nirvana's lyrics, from *Live! Tonight! Sold Out!*

In August of 1992, *Vanity Fair* published an article by Lynn Hirschberg called "Strange Love." It was supposed to be an exposé of the wife of one of the biggest rock stars in the world. It turned out to be "evidence" used by the Los Angeles County Children's Services Department to take away their child, Frances Bean. This was the single greatest injustice inflicted on Kurt Cobain and Courtney Love by the media frenzy surrounding them, and they talk about it with Everett True in the interview below.

Following this interview with the parents of Frances Bean is an interview Cobain did with Kevin Allman for the gay and lesbian periodical, *The Advocate*. It too describes the effect of the *Vanity Fair* article, and it also demonstrates Cobain's commitment to gay rights. Nirvana consistently championed social causes from gay rights to relief for Bosnian war victims. In "Cobain't That Peculiar," Everett True talks with Cobain backstage during the benefit Nirvana headlined for Bosnian refugees at the Cow Palace in San Francisco.

Deborah Russell describes Krist Novoselic's political organizing in his home state of Washington and Jon Pareles ascends the Space Needle with the band to talk about their music and the pressures of fame.

In "Verse Chorus Verse: The Recording History of Nirvana," Gillian G. Gaar provides the most comprehensive and detailed account of Nirvana's recorded music ever published. Gaar gives us a history of the band from the perspective of the only thing that matters—the music. Gaar's article is an exhaustive discography as well as a passionate reading of Nirvana's legacy.

The book ends with the ending of Nirvana. In an elegiac essay, David Fricke describes Nirvana's *MTV Unplugged* performance and the loss from which rock will never recover. Everett True describes Courtney Love taking the stage soon after Cobain's death—it is a brave way of saying good-bye.

Priscian moves there along the wearisome
  sad way, and Francesco d'Accorso, and also there,
  if you had any longing for such scum,
you might have seen that one the Servant of Servants
  sent from the Arno to the Bacchiglione
  where he left his unnatural organ wrapped in cerements.

      —Dante, *The Inferno* (trans. By John Ciardi)

It was as if he were an autodidact possessed of a huge vocabulary of
odors that enabled him to form at will great numbers of smelled sen-
tences. . . . Perhaps the closest analogy to his talent is the musical wun-
derkind, who has heard his way inside melodies and harmonies to the
alphabet of individual tones and now composes completely new
melodies and harmonies all on his own.

      —Patrick Süskind, *Perfume* (trans. by John E. Woods)

Jason took hold of her hand and squeezed it forcefully, attracting her
attention. He had never understood her dislike of fans; to him they were
the lifeblood of his public existence, his role as worldwide entertainer,
was existence itself, period. "You shouldn't be an entertainer," he said to
Heather, "feeling the way you do. Get out of the business. Become a
social worker in a forced labor camp." "There're people there, too,"
Heather said grimly.

      —Philip K. Dick, *Flow My Tears, the Policeman Said*

Women must write through their bodies, they must invent the impregnable language that will wreck partitions, classes, and rhetorics, regulations and codes, they must submerge, cut through, get beyond the ultimate reserve-discourse, including the one that laughs at the very idea of pronouncing the word "silence."

—Hélène Cixous, "The Laugh of the Medusa" (trans. By Keith and Paula Cohen)

There is no need for a note here on Courtney Love—she is a woman who does not need an introduction. And yet her importance for considering the music and legacy of Nirvana necessitates putting her in perspective. As the following interview with Love and Cobain demonstrates, their fates were bound up together in emotional and aesthetic knots. These were the knots that were severed in 1994, and we saw it all on TV. She grieved in front of the world. Say what you will about her, but there is one thing no one can take from Love: she is an incredibly brave person. She also has had a significant impact on popular culture through her music and her overt embrace of feminism. But to understand this we must look at her beginnings.

Courtney Love's father, Hank Harrison, was an early business manager of the Grateful Dead (it's rumored that the Dead's Phil Lesh is her godfather). As a good American, Love rejected the music of her parents and embraced punk. She played in an early incarnation of Babes in Toyland, then began her own band, Hole, in 1989. (The name for the band came from Euripedes' *Medea:* "There is a hole burning deep inside me.") She then moved from Los Angeles to Seattle. Hole released their first LP, *Pretty on the Inside* (coproduced by Kim Gordon), in 1991. Hole's early recordings and performances were direct influences on the Riot Grrrl movement—a movement that gave bands such as Bikini Kill the basis for their attack on the phallocentrism embodied in rock.

In 1992, when *Nevermind* was tearing apart the charts, Love and Cobain married. Frances Bean Cobain was born in August of the same year. As the following articles describe it, Nirvana's uncontrollable fame precipitated a media frenzy which, in the form of a single article in *Vanity Fair,* almost tore Love's family apart.

Hole released their second LP called *Live Through This* in 1994. It was a deeply ironic title, but, as Everett True shows us in "Love Hangover," Courtney Love is a survivor. Her music does nothing less than depict this.

ALL YOU NEED IS LOVE: FACE TO FACE
WITH KURT AND COURTNEY[1]

Melody Maker, 1992

1

"This is the hardest job I've ever had," the reluctant star begins. "I can't believe it . . ."

He pauses.

"I like it, though!" he exclaims. "I'm thoroughly enjoying myself. It's just a lot more demanding than I expected."

He pauses again.

"You know, she can fart as loud as I can . . ."

"Oh Kurt!" his wife interrupts, offended.

"And burp as loud as I can," he finishes unabashed, smiling his mischievous little smile.

"Keep it down," his wife scolds him. "It's not feminine."

But she's a baby. Babies are allowed to fart.

"Oh, okay," the protective mother says, mollified, looking proudly at the wide-eyed sproglet by her side.

Does having a baby make you see life in a different way?

"Definitely," replies Courtney. "Yeah . . ."

She stops, distracted by the look in her husband's eyes. He's rolling 'em.

"Stop it! Why do you do this?" she shouts.

"Do what?" he asks, innocently, as Frances Bean reaches out for his hand.

"Switch off when the tape recorder switches on."

"I've pretty much exhausted the baby opinions," Kurt Cobain—America's most successful "punk rock" star—says, defensively. "I just don't have anything important to say. I mean, duh, it's fun, it's great, it's the best thing in my life."

---

1. This piece was originally published as two separate articles in *Melody Maker*: "All You Need Is Love" appeared on December 19, 1992; "Kurt and Courtney" on January 2, 1993. —*Ed.*

Silence falls over the bedroom. We go back to watching the latest *Ren and Stimpy* cartoon, the new cult favourites of young America. Frances Bean Cobain's nanny appears, ready to take the little 'un—a bouncing, almost nauseatingly healthy, blue-eyed child (Kurt's eyes, Courtney's nose)—downstairs for her nap.

Silence. Courtney takes a sip of lukewarm strawberry tea, I take a gulp of vodka. Kurt belches.

We all have to keep up appearances.

Kurt and Courtney's new apartment is prime L.A.: near the top of a hill overlooking West Hollywood, surrounded by palm trees and winding pathways lined with foliage and security fences. You need an elevator—with a private key—to reach it.

Inside, one room is set aside for Kurt's paintings—strange, disturbing collages and images (he used to paint headless babies when his wife was pregnant, now he paints angels and dolls). There's a large, old-fashioned kitchen with a mirror running along the length of its outside wall, sundry guest rooms up top. Upstairs, Courtney's wardrobe is crammed with antique "baby doll" dresses. It's larger than some flats I've lived in. (Well, *almost*.)

Pizza crusts and half-full doughnut containers litter the spacious main room. There's a telescope, guitars, old rock books, clipped photos, baby things scattered everywhere—prime space is given over to a tasteful pink crib, bedecked in ribbons. A stereo in one corner blares out Mavis Staples. The place has an air of being only half-lived in, as do most L.A. residences.

As I arrive, the couple are lying in the double bed in the master bedroom with Frances Bean ("Frances! Say hello to you Uncle Everett!"—Courtney). She: wearing a nightie. He: in pyjama bottoms and the ubiquitous scruffy cardigan and tee-shirt. On the TV screen, three huggy male rock musicians in dresses surreally smash instruments, regardless of the backing track. It's the new Nirvana video for "In Bloom."

Courtney's sifting through a coloured box-load of Nirvana letters, sent to Kurt by *just one girl*. There are about 30 or 40 of them, all painstakingly hand-coloured, hand-lettered, with audio tape accompaniment.

"Look, Kurt!" Courtney picks on one particularly lurid specimen. "She's spelt out your name over these envelopes . . . oh, here's a picture of her (pause) . . . oh, she's got a muscular wasting disease . . . we have to write her back! We've got to! She's an outsider, just like me!"

Kurt grunts affirmation. We pour over her scribblings with renewed interest, grateful that we've never been thus afflicted. Someone puts her name down on the Christmas Card list.

Kurt decides he wants to tell us about his high school days, but then dries up.

"That's because you're a stoned retard," Courtney teases him. (It's well known that Kurt spent a fair few hours at school partaking of the demon weed.)

"Go on!" Courtney urges her husband. "I always talk! I'm sick of it."

Another pause. Frances gurgles slightly, a happy thought obviously striking the Bean. There's no sign of the "Diet Grrrl" graffiti her father had wickedly drawn on her stomach earlier. Kurt sighs.

Kurt 'n' Courtney (or "Kurtney," as they're collectively known) have only ever given two joint interviews before this—both to American publications. They wanted to speak to the [*Melody*] *Maker* to clear up certain matters—mostly arising from a profile of Courtney which appeared in the September issue of *Vanity Fair,* an up-market fashion magazine.

Clearly, we'll have to tread carefully.

Courtney mumbles something from where she's sitting, behind the bed by the ghetto blaster. Sorry?

"You were wrong," she says. "I should have been sullen and demure."

What?

"When I asked you that question a couple of years ago," she explains. "In a bar. In L.A."

You can't hide your personality—well, maybe *you* can.

"I wouldn't have minded," she whimpers. "I used to be sullen and demure."

She's referring to when she first met me, last year, when she asked me how she should behave in relation to the press.

"I used to be really loud and obnoxious," Kurt interrupts. "And then I stopped hanging out with people."

Why?

The singer shifts from where he's lying, sprawled out on the mattress. Courtney moves to switch the TV off.

"Because I was tired of pretending that I was someone else just to get along with people, just for the sake of having friendships," he replies. "I was tired of wearing flannel shirts and chewing tobacco, and so I became a monk in my room for years. And I forgot what it was like to socialise."

But didn't you drink.

"Yeah, I drank," he agrees. "And I was obnoxious when I drank too much. Then there was a period during the last two years of high school when I didn't have any friends, and I didn't drink or do any drugs at all, and I sat in my room and played guitar."

Then, when you formed Nirvana, you started drinking and hanging out with people, and you were back to where you were a few years before. . . .

"Not really," responds Kurt, stretching. "I still have the same best friends I had a few years ago. The scale of social activity that I have is so fucking minimal—nothing, my entire life—so the little bit of socialising I did at parties when I was loud wasn't much more than when I started socialising again in Seattle.

"I started hanging out with people like Mudhoney," he continues. "Mainly they were just other people in bands. I wasn't really part of a thriving Seattle social scene. Both Chris and I thought of ourselves as outsiders—we wrote that song, 'School,' about the crazy Seattle scene, how it reminded us of high school.

"It hasn't got any different. I just . . ."

He pauses, choosing his words carefully.

"I guess living in L.A. makes me more reclusive," he says, "because I don't like L.A. at all. I can't find anything to do here. It's pointless going out and trying to make friends, because I don't have these tattoos and I don't like death rock."

"Axl wants to be your friend," Courtney reminds him, sitting back down again. "Axl thinks that if I wasn't around, you and him could be backstage at arena rock shows fucking self-hating little girls."

"Well, that was always my goal," replies Kurt, sarcastically. "To come down to Hollywood and ride motorcycles with Axl on the Strip—and then you came along and ruined it all."

"That's what Axl says," Courtney explains. "Did you hear about that show where he got on stage and started saying something like, 'Nirvana's too good to play with us. Kurt would rather be home with his ugly bitch . . .'?"

Well, it's true, isn't it. (Not the "ugly" part.) Kurt *would* rather be home with you, bathing Frances Bean, wandering around in your nightie, than out bonding with Axl and the boys. Why should he act any differently? It's weird how some famous people seem to want to hang out with other famous people, just 'cos they're all famous.

Do you like it here in Hollywood, Courtney, or are you fed up with running? From what I know of your past life—as much as anyone can know—it seems to me you've been running for a very long time.

"I just always ended up back here," she muses. "Jennifer [L7] lives here, and she's always been a pretty good friend. I'd call her and say, 'This town didn't work out!' And she'd go, 'Oh, come back to L.A.!' It's so big, it can just absorb you. People here are so . . ."

She pauses, struggling to find the right words.

"We thought it might be easy to live here because people are trained to deal with fame," she says. "The thing is, however, it's not really like that. They don't stare, but they know who you are and the second you leave the store, they're on the phone to friends . . ."

She pauses again.

"It's not even that," she corrects herself. "I wouldn't have got nearly as much trouble if I hadn't chosen to live here. I just thought it would be interesting to go into the mainstream and fuck things up because people always say they're going to, but no one ever does—and I didn't have any choice really. It's weird here: nurses calling Cowboy Capers [a Hollywood delivery firm] for their valium subscriptions. It's scary, because everybody wants the fame. They all want fame."

"Fame is more of a reality here," her husband agrees.

"See, here's where it started, too," she adds, "before I became the prisoner of my husband, before I occupied this position I'm now in. But until we started going out, I never realised that's how people in L.A. really are."

Do you feel poisoned by Courtney, Kurt?

"By Courtney, or by Courtney's stigma" he replies. "Poisoned by . . . the whole fucked-up misconception of our relationship. Everyone seems to think that we couldn't possibly love each other, because we're thought of as cartoon characters, because we're public domain. So the feelings that we have for each other are thought of as superficial."

"It's not everybody that thinks that, though," Courtney adds. "It's a couple of has-been, pontificating, male rock stars and, mostly, women who work in the American music industry. I think that's because, in the early Eighties, if you were a woman and you wanted to play music, there was a real slim chance you would succeed. So a lot of women who wanted to empower themselves within rock without being self-loathing joined the music industry—and these are some of the most vicious women I know.

"I've heard industry women talking about how horrible L7 are, I've heard industry women talking about how unattractive PJ Harvey is, which is ridiculous. . . . I just think these powerful women have this real competitive, jealous nature which manifests itself like this. And when I married Kurt, they went into overload.

"It's insane, this real complex issue . . . It's an attempt to create something out of nothing—the whole superstar thing. They at least try to take away my intellect, and take away my ethics, and create . . ."

She pauses again, jumbled.

The thoughts are pouring out of her too fast for coherent speech now. Spend even five minutes in Courtney's company, and you'll be overwhelmed by the sheer torrent of words and ideas that pour from her. Courtney is rumoured to spend 12 hours a day on the phone. To her, to think is to be.

You must find it annoying, Kurt, that people perceive you to be this stupid henpecked husband, because that's implied in the whole image of Courtney Love's devious and evil nature.

"Yeah, there've been quite a few articles like that," he growls. "I don't know how to explain what happens to me when I do an interview, because I usually shut myself off. It's really hard to explain. I just don't like to get intimate. I don't want anyone to know what I feel and what I think, and if they can't get some kind of idea of what sort of person I am through my music, then that's too bad.

"I don't see how people can get the idea that I'm stupid," he continues, "because I know my music's semi-intelligent. I know it takes a bit of creativity to write the kind of music I do, it's not just a wall of noise. I know there's a formula to it, and I've worked really hard at it.

"I've always been the kind of person that if I think someone thinks of me a certain way—like I'm stupid—then I'll act stupid in front of them. I've never felt the need to prove myself. If someone already has a misconception about me, then fine, let them have it all the more. I'll be happy to massage that."

Jackie, Frances Bean's nanny, shouts from downstairs that Kurt is wanted on the phone. Kurt tells her to tell whoever it is to call back later. I take another gulp of vodka and continue.

Here's a question that's been bothering me for a while. How subversive are Nirvana? For a number of reasons, not the least of which is her sassiness and the way she gets up the establishment's noses, Courtney is subversive.

But Nirvana?

"We aren't," replies Kurt, tartly. "It's impossible to be subversive in the commercial world because they'll crucify you for it. You can't get away with it. We've tried, and we've been almost ruined by it."

"There have been things that have happened to us that are so . . ." Courtney trails off, momentarily wordless.

"Like, after the baby was born," she continues, "a social worker walked into my room with a picture from *Vanity Fair,* trying to take our baby away. Having to get lawyers just to the hospital, just having crazy, crazy shit. Having friends' mothers horrified, because one person lied! It's okay to say that I'm obnoxious, because I am. . . ."

Her anger overcomes her.

"It's amazing what damage that one article has done!" Kurt snarls. It certainly painted Courtney in a very bad light, as the "bad girl" of American rock—a gold-digging parasite, a mother who took drugs while she was pregnant, a "Yoko" who tried to break up Nirvana, a malcontent who argued bitterly with her "best friend" Kat Bjelland, a fraud, an obsessive, a heroin addict. It conveniently overlooked the fact that she used to be—and presumably will continue to be in the future—a highly respected artist in her own right. Especially if the new single is anything to go by.

"Kurt didn't want to play the [MTV] *Video Awards,* for instance," his wife continues. "Never mind that if he didn't play the *Video Awards,* they'd never show clips of his or my band again. That wasn't it . . ."

"Also," says Kurt, "they wouldn't have played any Gold Mountain [Kurtney's management company] acts, like Sonic Youth, Beastie Boys . . ."

Yeah, I heard about that from Thurston. They threatened your management with a boycott of all their acts if Nirvana didn't toe the line. You can be as subversive and radical as you like, but they only really bother with you once you're big enough to be a threat.

"So all the political nastiness that I've heard of for years from independent record people is true," Kurt snarls. "A lot of people, especially people like Bruce Pavitt and Calvin Johnson—people who have been pretty successful throughout the years with introducing underground, independent music and creating a community feel within their environment and just exercising the whole DiY ethic—have known a lot of people who have experienced the major label fuck-overs. . . ."

Calvin Johnson runs Olympia's fiercely partisan, independent K records (Olympia being where Kurt moved after leaving Aberdeen and forming Nirvana). Calvin used to help Bruce (Sub Pop) Pavitt run a fanzine in the early Eighties.

Olympia is a small liberal college town an hour's drive away from Seattle, which, in 1991, hosted the International Pop Underground Convention—thus providing the initial impetus for Riot Grrrl. Nirvana even contributed a track to the convention's *Kill Rock Stars* compilation LP, before being (apparently) ostracised for signing to a major label.

Kurt continues his rant.

"I know that some of these people I used to look up to—people who have put out magazines or who've had a record label for years—these people have had the real inside dirt on what a major label is like, but they never told me. . . ."

He sounds oddly betrayed.

"I never paid any attention to mainstream press, either," Kurt continues. "I never understood the mechanics of it, how it works. I never read a major record label rock 'n' roll interview, except when I was a kid in *Creem* magazine and that was always so tongue-in-cheek. I've never read a *Rolling Stone* article that I can think of—just skimmed through a couple of the political ones."

From below, we can hear the sound of Frances Bean crying. Kurt half-rises to go downstairs, but changes his mind.

"Now that it's happened, I still can't help laughing about it," he adds. "But it went overboard. It went just a little bit too far to take in good humour. . . ."

"A little bit?" Courtney interrupts him, angrier than ever. "Social workers coming to take your baby because of something you didn't do and you didn't say is not judicial, and it's not justice . . .

"That article," she spits. "The whole drug thing . . ."

She's floundered because she's so riled.

"We did drugs and it was really fun, and now it's over. Anybody who knows me knows I'm way too paranoid to get wasted all the time. . . ."

She pauses again, searching for the right words.

"It's just so insane," she cries, "what it's done and who it's hurt because of one woman's vendetta. When you look at it, Everett, I think the end of rock is pretty damn near when Madonna is trying to buy Pavement for a million dollars and put out Xerox fanzines. When Madonna thinks that I am the cutting edge—that's how you can judge how out of it she is."

Vanity Fair also dwelt shortly and harshly in Courtney's claims that Madonna was vampiric, ready to take from Courtney what she wanted and leave the rest of her for dead.

"Who," Madonna was quoted as saying, "is Courtney Love?"

She should know. It was Madonna who asked her manager to sign Courtney's band to her label last year. It was Madonna herself who phoned Courtney to arrange a meeting. Wanna know why I'm so sure? I spoke to Courtney immediately after the call—and *nobody* makes shit like that up.

"I wish I'd never come in her eye-line," Courtney cries. "Isn't there any punk rock value in the fact that I turned her down and she then sent one of her toadies to execute me? The *Vanity Fair* piece would never have happened if I hadn't turned her down."

"It's twice as bad for Courtney," explains Kurt, "because she hasn't even had the chance to prove herself like I did. It's one thing for me to be subversive at this point, because I can afford to be. I can pretty much get away with ripping up a picture of the Pope on television and it wouldn't create so much of a stink as someone commercial like Sinead—or Courtney, who doesn't have the security of having sold lots of records. . . ."

The baby cries. Courtney interrupts her husband, excited.

"How did it go so fast," she asks, sounding genuinely bewildered, "from having a record of the year in the *Village Voice* and being perceived as an artist, to being Nancy Spungen in three months?"

There's something I'd like to get down on tape now. I'd forgotten that Hole were one of the initial inspirations for Riot Grrrl. When Cathi of Bikini Kill saw Hole, it was pretty much what inspired her to form a band.

"Cathi wrote me a letter saying she wanted to start a band and what should she do," recalls Courtney. "And I wrote back and said she should find the biggest slut-bitches in her town that everybody hates. I thought if there were three people who were like the town bitch in one band, that would be fucking amazing. I don't know if that really happened, but it turned out to be . . ."

(Cathi actually recounted this event in her fanzine, *Bikini Kill*, about the formation of her band, adding that when she saw Courtney, it was like, "the guitar went into flames—almost a religious experience.")

"I'm very supportive of them, on a personal level," she adds.

She then moves on to talking about Julian Cope, stung by the adverts for his tour which were then running in the music press, where he—among other stupid and provocative statements—wrote, "Free us [the rock 'n' roll fans] from Nancy Spungen–fixated heroin a-holes who cling to our greatest rock groups and suck out their brains. . . ."

"He's one of these people who actually knows me," she says, hurt. "Not well, but he does know me, and who was somebody—for all his horns and back-up singers—when I was younger, really affected me and charmed me and made me feel, 'Wow, for an English person he's pretty original and cool.'

"And for him to be slagging me off in his poem in his ad, it's like . . ."

She pauses, struck by another thought.

"Wait, where do people get this fucking Nancy Spungen thing from?" she demands. "I'm sorry I ever dyed my hair. Is it that superficial? Is it just because I'm blonde?"

Well, it's partly because you joked about it in a couple of interviews.

"It's this Nirvana/Sex Pistols thing, too," she corrects me.

But Your Jo(e) Average Person On the Street never seems to realise that people in power can joke about what are perceived to be serious matters. Perhaps they aren't allowed to. Maybe it's just because Your Jo(e) Average Punter is obtuse, but I doubt if it's even that. It's probably more that it's always been the case that people take whatever they want from what they read.

"Right," Courtney agrees. "But the fact of this, too, is how women, unless they totally desexualise themselves, have no intellect subscribed to them. . . ."

"That's totally true," murmurs Kurt.

"If I were subscribed intellect, nobody would ever think that I was Nancy Spungen, because Nancy Spungen is not an intellectual," she finishes. "It's because I've chosen to negotiate the world on the world's terms—I've said, 'Okay, I'm going to have this experiment,' after having spent most of my life being plain and un-decorative. So I decided to lose some weight and wear some lipstick and see what fucking happens—be a little dangerous, more subversive."

"It's a lot fucking easier," her husband says.

"It was for me," she agrees, "but, at the same time, now what's happened is that we are married and these people are trying to take away my livelihood and they're trying to take away the thing that matters the most to me, other than my family. And now they're even trying to take away my family.

"So me and Kurt get married and we're peers—his band were always ahead, but they started before us—then, suddenly, his band get real successful and we're not peers anymore. He's involved in free trade in America and I'm not making much of a dent. It's really amazing to see."

She pauses.

(And so for the moment, do we.)

2

The story so far . . .

Courtney Love is still livid about the profile of her that appeared last September in the American magazine, *Vanity Fair*. No fucking wonder. It alleged that she'd taken drugs during her pregnancy, thus endangering the life of her unborn child. The implication was that she was dangerous and irresponsible, unfit to be a mother. Call her paranoid, but Courtney is convinced that the hostility of the profile had something to do with Madonna, who had wanted to sign her to her fledging Maverick label, and been unceremoniously rebuffed.

Kurt Cobain, meanwhile, is increasingly incensed with being cast as the "unwilling dupe" in their relationship, easily manipulated by the devious Courtney because he's dumb and can't see what she's doing to his life and career.

As you join us, Courtney has just been wondering how her fall from grace—from having a record of the year in the *Village Voice* to being the Nineties equivalent of Nancy Spungen—came about so fast.

Frances Bean Cobain went to bed half-an-hour ago.

"One thing that's pleased me," Courtney says, drawing on a cigarette, "that I've been really surprised by and learnt a lot from, is the psychic protection I've got from so many girls and women. . . ."

She pauses. I'm not sure what point she's trying to make.

"I mean, it's really fucking obvious, unless you're stupid," she goes on. "Like, I walk around and say, 'Oh, he should have married a model, but he married me,' with a straight face."

This is more familiar territory. This is, in fact, the line Courtney usually takes when she's trying to wind up the people who think Kurt's marriage to her was ill-advised. Her argument is something like, well, who should he have married then? A model? The point being . . . *Kurt's not like that.*

"There were like 60 sarcastic things I told *Vanity Fair,*" she goes on, "that they quoted straight because they're so stupid. Their whole attitude was like, 'Let's go and be condescending to these wacky punk rock kids and make allusions to how, in their world, success is bad. Aren't they cute."

But Kurt, you never said success was bad, did you?

"What kind of success?" he sighs. "Success in general? Financial success? Popularity in a rock band? Most people think success is being extremely popular on a commercial level, selling a lot of records and making a whole bunch of money. Being in the public eye.

"I think of myself as a success because I still haven't compromised my music," he continues, "but that's just speaking on an artistic level. Obviously, all the other parts that belong with success are driving me insane—God! I want to kill myself half the time."

But people still don't get it. Nirvana catch a lot of flak from people I know because (a) Kurt Cobain whines a lot, and (b) Nirvana slag off corporate rock bands, even though they're one themselves.

"Oh, take it back from him, the ungrateful little brat!" mocks Courtney.

"What I really can't stand about being successful is when people confront me and say, 'Oh, you should just mellow out and enjoy it,'" explains her husband, interrupting her. "I don't know how may times I have to fucking say this. *I never wanted it in the first place.*

"But I guess I do enjoy the money," he relents. "It's at least a sense of security. I know that my child's going to grow up and be able to eat. That's a really nice feeling, that's fine, but you know . . ."

But Frances will only be treated nice to her face: people will kiss her butt and stab her in the back at the same time.

"Yeah, but she'll know about it, because she'll come from us and she'll be cynical by kindergarten," Courtney answers, looking fondly at the empty crib. "She's cynical already."

"I don't mean to whine so much," continues Kurt. "There are just so many things that I'm not capable of explaining in detail."

"I am!" Courtney interjects.

"But people have no idea of what is going on," her husband complains. "The sickening politics that are involved with being a successful rock band are really aggravating. No one has any idea."

"It doesn't matter though," Courtney almost shouts. "The whole thing with you is that you've got your success, but I've been victimised by it and, at the same time, I still haven't proven myself to myself.

"I remember last year Kat came up to Chicago and we went to this bar and they started playing *Nevermind*—this was just when it was starting to get really big. So we sat there and drank and drank, and got really mad. Because we realised no girl could have done that. I want to write a really good record and I haven't done it yet."

This is where I disagree with you, Courtney. *Nevermind* was a great record. But so was "Teenage Whore." *Nevermind* was made by a bunch of blokes. Why should it have been made by a bunch of girls?

"No girl could have come from the underground and done that," she argues. "It's just the fact that somebody did it. It happened."

But Hole were an astonishing band, particularly live. I can't think of many artists who've come across so powerfully and fatally magnetic on stage as you. I mean it.

"Yeah, but Everett, not many people remember that," whispers Courtney, touched.

But what I'm saying is that you're judging yourself on your husband's terms, and that's ridiculous. You don't write songs like Kurt writes songs—why should you? You're completely different people. If the commercial market refuses to accept your music, then it's a failing of the business, not with your music.

Another couple of things: your marriage and pregnancy means that your own career has been on hold this last year. You haven't written many new songs, you haven't had a record out, you haven't played live. Which means that people who only know about you through Kurt have nothing to judge you on but your very public "bad girl" image.

The bottom line is, you have to get back out there and perform, if you want to regain the respect for your music you once had.

No amount of hedging will alter that.

"The fact I judge myself on Kurt's terms is part of me subscribing to the whole male rock ethic, too," Courtney explains. "You know, Kim Gordon—like every woman I respected—told me this marriage was going to be a disaster for me. They told me that I'm more important than Kurt because I have this lyric thing going and I'm more culturally significant; and they all predicted exactly what was going to happen.

"I said 'No, that's not going to happen,'" she recalls, bitterly. "Everyone knows I have a band, everybody knows about my band, I can do this—my marriage is not going to be more important than my band."

She pauses, then explodes.

"But not only has my marriage become more important than my fucking band, but our relationship had been violated," she cries. "If we weren't doing this interview together, no male rock journalist would dare ask Kurt if he loved his wife. 'Do you love your wife? Do you guys fuck? Who's on top?' . . . I'm not saying you would, Everett.

"They wouldn't ask him to explain his relationship with me, because he's a man and men are men and they're not responsible for any emotional decisions they make."

She's shaking with emotion now.

"Men are men!" she exclaims. "They do the work of men! They do men's things! If they have bad taste in women . . . whatever! All of a sudden Axl and Julian Cope and Madonna decide I'm bad taste in women and it's the curse of my life and tough shit. What can I say?

"I never experienced sexism before," she says, excitedly. "I really didn't experience it in any major way in connection with my band until this year, and now I have. The attitude is that Kurt's more important than me, because he sells more records. Well, fuck you! Suck my dick!"

There's a brief silence. Courtney's just taking a breather before going for the kill.

"You wouldn't look good in leather," Courtney says to Kurt, looking fondly at him. "Kurt and Julian Cope and Axl Rose and Danny Partridge riding around in a limousine, fucking women that are idiotic and self-hating that want to fuck them to get some attention for themselves, instead of grabbing their guitars and going, 'Fuck you, I could do this better, with integrity and with more ethics than you, and with revolution and—fuck you!' I created this rock thing in the first place for my own amusement and I'm going to take it back.

"I always have lofty ideals about it and yet I deserve it." She's resorting to sarcasm now, she's so worked up. "I deserve to get raped by a crowd if I stagedive in a dress, I deserve to get raped if I go to a bar and I'm wearing a bikini, I deserve to get raped because I did all these things I said before—nipping a hot young rock star in the bud, having a baby, having been a stripper, having used drugs . . .

"And then to be perceived as a child abuser!" she exclaims, anguished, off on another exclamatory track. "Two of the last people on earth that would ever hurt a child or a harmless person. *Ever.* I've never picked on harmless people. I've always picked on people that I felt were corrupt or more corrupt than me."

Silence.

"Alright," she adds, gently. "I'm done now."

From far off comes the sound of a baby crying.

"I didn't think in those terms, when I was doing my record," Kurt says, stirring. "Although, at the end, I did allow the record to be produced cleaner and more commercial than I wanted it to be. I don't know what the reasoning for that was, besides just being dead tired of hearing the same songs. We'd tried remixing it three times and we rang this professional mixologist to do it and, by that point, I was so tired of hearing those songs, I said, 'Go ahead, do whatever you want.'"

"You say you didn't think in those terms, 'cos you're more punk than me?" Courtney asks him, annoyed.

"No, I'm not saying I'm more punk than you," snaps Kurt. "Actually, I'm wondering right now if I wasn't subconsciously thinking that I did want success, because I did. . . ."

"Is it such a sin to say that you wanted to be in *Billboard*?" she asks him. "That you knew you were going to be popular, or that you were going to be rock stars?"

"I knew we were going to be popular, but I didn't know we were going to be this popular," he says. "I'm so tired of saying this. I'm so tired of saying, 'Oh, we thought we were going to be as big as Sonic Youth,' and all that shit. It's so fucking boring at this point."

"But isn't there another part of you, that personality who wrote 'Aero Zeppelin' that . . ." starts Courtney.

"Right!" her husband exclaims. "There is. And maybe, because I allowed the record to be mixed commercially enough that any song could get on the radio, maybe I was thinking it would be kinda funny, really hilarious to see how far we could push it, how popular we could get."

"Well, that was my excuse until this marriage thing happened," Courtney shrugs, "that it would be really funny and kinda hilarious, and now I don't think it's either of those things. Yet the desire is still there. And I'm not the Yoko Ono of Nirvana—I'm the one who lost two band members, not Kurt."

"You didn't lose any band members over this," Kurt shoots back, annoyed.

"Not over this," Courtney replies. "But my band lost two band members. You can make what you want of it, and say that you were running my life. Where's the theory that you're the one wearing the pants? That you're running me into the ground? Nobody's come up with that theory. You haven't been victimised with the whole macho guy persona."

"I'd rather be in your position than be thought of as a fucking idiot," complains Kurt, "a puppet on a string, being manipulated 24 hours a day. You didn't lose your band members over anything connected with this marriage, or by being associated with me at all . . ."

"I'm not saying I did . . ."

"I've lost more drummers than you have," Kurt points out.

It's interesting that Courtney should raise this point about the imbalance in your relationship. Someone remarked to me once recently that they think Kurt Cobain is one of the biggest sexists in America.

Kurt becomes seriously upset.

"That's not true," Courtney says, leaping to his defence. "No. I've looked for it, but not at all."

"A comment like that is just such a pathetic last attempt at having some kind of opinion . . ." starts a riled Kurt, before I cut him off.

No, hold on. I think what they're referring to is your relationship—the way it's so effectively castrated Courtney's art (especially when Courtney was such a strong female role model before her marriage). The comment wasn't meant to be a reflection on you, just on the way people perceive your marriage.

"Right," says Kurt. "I don't understand why that happens."

"The whole thing of the media theorising on two people's relation-ships," says Courtney, "is my fault for allowing journalists into my home. I see now why people say, 'I'm not going to talk about my famous hus-band.' I understand now. We've become these two cartoon characters you can theorise about . . ."

She stops, and starts on a different tack.

"You can't please everybody," she says. "I don't care if I get criticised. I don't give a shit if I get a bad review. I don't care if people say I'm a bitch or I'm obnoxious, 'cos I am those things. Or that thing of being a witch, or that Paul Lester guy saying I'm ugly and Debbie Gibson's pretty. . . . I fucking think that shit's funny. It's this crazy lying. *Do you understand?*"

She's starting to rail again now.

"It's my life," she says, almost spelling the words out.

"A social worker coming to my hospital, trying to take my baby from me, *trying to take my baby away from me*. Spending hundreds of thou-sands of dollars on lawyers—all of Kurt's money went to lawyers because of fucking Madonna, because I turned down Maverick. Whatever. I know this sounds crazy . . ."

She pauses, takes another breath.

"The *Vanity Fair* article put quotes in my mouth, there were things I was supposed to have said about Madonna that I never said," she contin-ues. "They twisted things around.

"I didn't do heroin during pregnancy. And even if I did, even if I shot coke every night and took acid every day, it's my own motherfucking busi-ness. If I'm immoral, I'm immoral. It's not your goddamn business if I'm immoral or not."

She pauses, trying to sort her words out.

"A photographer for *Vanity Fair* caught me smoking a cigarette. It was my birthday. I smoked something like four cigarettes in six hours. I was smoking a cigarette in one of the pictures. And the line around the block for magazines that wants that picture is so big that this mother-fucker has charged me $50,000 to get the pictures back. It's blackmail, pure and simple. And if I don't get them, they'll keep after her [Frances Bean]."

In some states in America, these photographs would be enough to prove that Courtney is "unfit to mother," thus giving the state legal rights to remove the child into their custody.

"They filed a legal report on me based on *Vanity Fair* and nothing else, no other fucking evidence, that I was an unfit mother," she continues. "That I smoked during my pregnancy. Fuck you, everybody smokes during their pregnancy—who gives a shit? And it's because I married Kurt, because he's hot, young and cute.

"And I certainly don't buy people worrying about the baby," she adds. "If you want to ask about my drug problem, go ask my big fat smart 10-pound daughter, she'll answer any questions you have about it."

"I just want to get back to the Kurt-complaining-about-his-success thing," says Kurt, interrupting his wife's flow of invective. "How many questions in every article are placed on my success? People are so obsessed with it, that's all I ever get a chance to talk about. Ten different variations on the same question every interview."

" 'You funny little boy!' " Courtney squeals, mocking his tormentors. " 'You didn't set out to be successful! What an angle! Cinderella!' "

"It's a fine scam, it's a fine image," he says, sarcastically. "I'm getting really fucking bored with it."

"Why don't we switch?" Courtney says, bringing the interview round full circle. "I'll be demure and sullen and you'll be loud and obnoxious."

Then you'd be Axl Rose.

"No, then I'd be his cod-piece," she corrects me. "Fuck me Kurt, fuck me Julian, fuck me Julian's drum tech, make me feel my worth! It's ridiculous. And, for $50,000 I have to buy this image of a really pregnant woman with a garland in her hair smoking a cigarette, this whole fertility image with a cigarette. As if I did it deliberately, as if I did it to provoke!"

She's off again.

"Someone called up my manager after the *Vanity Fair* article, saying, 'Does Courtney think she's being that whole Seventies cool shock rock thing?'—as if I had planted this whole drug, cigarette sensationalism!

"Ask Kurt," she continues. "I didn't want to talk to *Vanity Fair*, because I knew it was based on the Madonna thing and our marriage. They don't even do rock people—I sell 60,000 records, what the fuck do they want with me? But I did it anyway, because I was sick of industry women talking and saying terrible things about me.

"I thought, if I was in *Vanity Fair*, it would shut their fucking mouths and they'd leave me in peace," she laments. "But that was my mistake and I just shouldn't have done it. I should have known more about the mainstream press and how they operate.

"Also, the whole thing where it made me seem to be so competitive with Kat [Bjelland: Babes in Toyland] is just like . . . I was totally provoked. I was mad with Kat about something, and I got provoked into gossiping about something off the record."

According to *Vanity Fair,* Kat and Courtney were embroiled in a bit-ter argument over who first started wearing the "baby doll" kinderwhore dress both are famous for: Kat was quoted as saying, "Last night, I had a dream that I killed her [Courtney]. I was really happy."

"And then she provoked Kat into saying things about me, by telling her what I said," Courtney continues. "If you notice, Kat hasn't gone on record as saying anything shitty about me, and I certainly didn't mean to go on record saying anything shitty about her. We're not best friends any-more, but we don't hate each other. It's ridiculous that it's been turned into something where you have to choose between one of us. We're different. We write differently.

"But that's why it's so competitive," she adds. That's why this whole foxcore/Riot Grrrl thing is so competitive. It's like rap music. There's a void, and there's only room for one of you in the void."

The tape switches off.

Courtney decides that she's said enough. Kurt nods in agreement. Time to view the new Nirvana video once more, and discuss whether to go out tonight (Therapy? are playing the Whiskey).

Courtney decides to accompany me—the first time she's been out in L.A. since giving birth.

Kurt prefers to stay in, and mind the baby.

KEVIN ALLMAN

THE DARK SIDE OF KURT COBAIN

The Advocate, February 9, 1993

It's 4 o'clock on a cold Seattle afternoon, and Kurt Cobain, the lyricist–guitarist–lead singer of Nirvana, is sitting in a downtown hotel room, playing with his 5-month-old daughter, Frances, while his wife, Courtney Love—lead singer of her own band, Hole—applies makeup. At the moment, the Cobains (including baby) are on the cover of *Spin* maga-zine—which has named Nirvana as Artist of the Year—and the band's new album, *Incesticide,* is due out within the week. The Nirvana media machine should be in high gear.

But, no.

What's surprising is what's not in the Cobains' room: no entourage, no groupies, no publicists, and no signs of the high life—in any sense of the term. Cobain, in fact, is wearing a pair of fuzzy green pajamas. And he and Love are in Seattle for the sole reason of trying to speed the deal on a modest house they've been trying to buy. The only concession to Cobain's being what he mockingly calls "a rock icon" is the pseudonym under which he registered, Simon Ritchie.

It's a joke—Ritchie was the real name of Sid Vicious, the Sex Pistol who died from a heroin overdose—and it shows that the Cobains have a sense of humor about being tagged by the press as a modern-day Sid and Nancy. If the Cobains are being reluctant these days, they explain, it's not because they're strung out but because they feel they've been strung up— by the media, which they feel have painted them as a pair of junkies without a cause. "Everyone thinks we're on drugs again, even people we work with," says Cobain resignedly as Love paints on a perfect baby-doll mouth. "I guess I'll have to get used to that for the rest of my life."

While Cobain, 24, is quiet and thoughtful, Love is tailor-made for media attention, blessed and cursed with what seems an almost genetic inability to censor herself. Within the first five minutes of *The Advocate*'s arrival, she is spinning a story about an ex-flame and his lingerie fetish: "He had to wear nylons to have sex—not just any nylons but flesh-colored nylons. And he couldn't buy them, he had to *find* them." Listening, Cobain smiles, holding Frances by her arms, walking her across his lap. He is—at least for the moment—not feeling beaten up.

Getting beaten up, though, is a recurring theme in Cobain's life. In his hometown of Aberdeen in rural Washington, he was branded a "faggot" from an early age. It was a title he eventually embraced and threw back in his tormentors' faces—just for the hell of it. In 1985 he was even arrested when he and friend Chris Novoselic spray-painted HOMOSEXUAL SEX RULES on the side of a bank.

Four years later, Cobain, Novoselic, and drummer Dave Grohl released the first Nirvana album, *Bleach,* on a small Seattle label, Sub Pop Records.[1] Recorded for $605.15, it was a blast of pure punk rock that earned them a reputation in Seattle and drew the interest of several major labels. Their major-label debut, *Nevermind,* was released by DGC in September 1991—and by the end of the year, *Nevermind* (fueled by the inescapably catchy "Smells Like Teen Spirit") had come from far left field to sell 3 million copies and top rock critics' best-of-the-year lists. Last January cellular phones all over the record industry were crackling when Nirvana hit number one—toppling U2, Metallica, and Michael Jackson

---

1. Dave Grohl did *not* play on *Bleach*. Chad Channing was the drummer on the first Nirvana album.—*Ed.*

from the top of the charts. Punk rock was suddenly a commodity, and the term *grunge,* denoting flannel shirts, ripped jeans, dirty hair, and especially anything Seattle-based, entered the lexicon. Soon record executives were spending weekends in Seattle, trying to find the "next Nirvana," and models cropped up on Paris runways sporting haute grungewear.

But even as Nirvana went from playing club dates to selling out 40,000 seat arenas, the band still didn't play by the rules. They spurned an offer to tour with Guns N' Roses, further fueling the rumors that Cobain and his then pregnant wife had a big problem with heroin. Last April, when *Rolling Stone* put the band on its cover, Cobain showed up for the photo session in a T-shirt that read CORPORATE MAGAZINES STILL SUCK. And an unflattering profile of the Cobains in September's *Vanity Fair* dropped the two into the world of glossy journalism with a jolt when Love confirmed to writer Lynn Hirschberg that she and Cobain were indeed using heroin in the early stages of her pregnancy.

While not denying the heroin use, both Cobain and Love insist that they have been misquoted and misunderstood. They maintain that the interview was given early in the year, and at the time the article appeared (the same month Love gave birth to Frances), both had been clean for months. "When I first talked to her [Hirschberg], I had just found out I was pregnant, and I had done some drugs in the beginning of my pregnancy, and that's what I told her," says Love.

Equally misunderstood, to Cobain, is Nirvana itself—particularly the fact that the band appeals to many of the same hard rock fans who pack Guns N' Roses concerts. But while Axl Rose sang derisively about "immigrants and faggots" in his song "One in a Million," Cobain closed his song "Stay Away" by howling "God is gay!" and Nirvana defiantly cavorted in dresses in the video of their hit single "In Bloom." Last year Nirvana traveled to Oregon to perform at a benefit opposing Measure 9, a statewide ordinance that would have amended the state constitution to prohibit protections for gays and lesbians. And when they appeared in *Saturday Night Live,* Cobain and Novoselic made a point of kissing on-camera.

In person, Cobain is the antithesis of a preening guitar cocksman: He's small, pale, soft-spoken, and articulate. Prejudice infuriates him; he spits out the words "homophobe" and "sexist" with the same venom he reserves for the word "spandex." Particularly upsetting to him was an incident last year in Reno, when two men raped a woman while chanting a Nirvana song. On the liner notes for *Incesticide,* he vented his frustration in a blunt statement to Nirvana fans: "If any of you in any way hate homosexuals, people of different color, or women, please do this one favor for us—leave us the fuck alone! Don't come to our shows and don't buy our records."

Despite Cobain's wish that people "leave us the fuck alone," both he and Love seem determined not to surround themselves with a glass bubble of security precautions and stereotypical rock-star trappings. Before this interview—the only one the band's leader singer says he plans to do for *Incesticide*—Cobain set down no conditions regarding the questions that could be asked, nor did he bother to notify his record company the interview would be taking place. (Love, in fact, insisted that the mutual friend who arranged the meeting put *The Advocate* in direct contact with the couple: "Gay people can have our phone number!")

Back in the hotel room, Love goes out and leaves Cobain to his interview, but she's wary enough to come back twice: "I'm worried about what they're going to write," she finally blurts. Still, her need to trust overwhelms her protectiveness. When she leaves for the third time, she says, "It's a gay publication, Kurt, so don't forget to tell them about the time you stole your tights out of your mother's drawer." Cobain smiles; she laughs and sighs. "I guess I have that effect on men. Bye." And then she's gone for good, pushing Frances's stroller out the door.

Kevin: You two don't seem like Sid and Nancy.

Kurt: It's just amazing that at this point in rock-and-roll history, people are still expecting their rock icons to live out these classic rock stereotypes, like Sid and Nancy. To assume that we're just the same because we came from the underground and we did heroin for a while—it's pretty offensive to be expected to be like that.

Kevin: Does it hurt worse when they say bad things about Courtney?

Kurt: Oh, absolutely. What they say about me is not half as strange as what they've said about her. She doesn't deserve that. She sold 60,000 records, and all of a sudden she's found herself as commercially popular as me, and she's just in a punk rock band. Just because she married me, she's subjected to being as popular as an actress or something.

Kevin: Who do you trust now?

Kurt: Uh—no one? [*Laughs*] I've always kind of kept myself purposely naive and optimistic, and now I've been forced to be really paranoid. Judgmental. Really defensive all the time. It's been hard for me to change my attitude.

Kevin: You're here in this hotel room. Can you go out?

Kurt: Yeah. The other night we went shopping at a second-hand store and bought some fuzzy sweaters and some grungewear.

Kevin: Real grungewear, not the designer kind?

Kurt: Not Perry Ellis. [*Laughs*] We were driving around in our Volvo, after buying some grungewear, and we realized that we're not necessarily as big as Guns N' Roses, but we're as popular as them, and we still don't have bodyguards. We still go shopping; we still go to movies and carry on with our lives.

I've always been a paranoid person by nature anyhow, and now I have these people so concerned with what I say and what I do at all time that it's really hard for me to deal with that. I'm dealing with it a lot better than I would have expected. If I could have predicted what was going to happen to me a few years ago, I definitely wouldn't have opted for this kind of life-style.

Kevin: Would it be cooler to have stayed in Seattle and not been on the cover of Rolling Stone?

Kurt: Yeah. Well, I chose to do that—although it was a hell of a fight. We were on tour in Australia and I had completely forgotten that I had promised to do the *Rolling Stone* piece. And that day, they called and said, "Are you ready to do the photo shoot?" And it was like, "No, I really don't want to do this." I had so much pressure from my management and the band members—they wanted to do it and I just agreed. On my way there I just decided, "I'm going to write something on my shirt that's offensive enough to stop getting our picture on the cover." This way I could say that I actually played along with it and still didn't get picked to be on the cover. I wasn't necessarily challenging *Rolling Stone*, saying "You suck" and "We don't want to have anything to do with you, but we'll still use you for our exposure."

Rolling Stone sucks, has always sucked, and still sucks just because they have a hip band on the cover. We're not as cool and hip as everyone thinks. Having us on the cover isn't going to make *Rolling Stone* any cooler. Ever since this band has been popular, I've always thought of us as just a '90s version of Cheap Trick or the Knack. They had the two sides of appeal that made them kind of a cool band—a commercial side and kind of a new-wave side. We have that.

Kevin: Everything you do seems to get analyzed. You can't even say or do anything off-the-cuff.

Kurt: Yeah. I still have the same views I've always had. When I used to say things to my friends, I didn't expect to be taken so seriously. Now I have to detour my thoughts and what I say in order to stop someone from saying I'm a hypocrite. That was the *Rolling Stone* debate: "Corporate magazines suck, but you're still on the cover." Well, of course! It's a joke. Get over it.

People should take things rock stars say with a grain of salt because there's no one in rock and roll right now who's a relevant example or a spokesperson for anything. They do have an influence on people, and I think there's a new consciousness that's really positive among rock stars, like Rock the Vote. They're trying to make people aware, but I really can't think of anyone who's really schooled enough to be political to the point that would be required for a rock star. If Jello Biafra [former lead singer of the Dead Kennedys] was a big international star, it would be really cool. But he's not on a major label, and he doesn't write commercial enough music to use that as a tool.

Kevin: Does it make you laugh when people take apart all your songs and try to figure out what you're saying?

Kurt: Oh, yeah. At the time I was writing those songs, I really didn't know what I was trying to say. There's no point in my even trying to analyze or explain it. That used to be the biggest subject in an interview: "What are your lyrics about?" [*Laughs*] I haven't written any new lyrics, that's for sure. We have about 12 songs for the new album we're scheduled to record in February, and I don't have any lyrics at all. Within the past year, notebooks and poetry books I've had lying around have either been destroyed or stolen. So I don't have anything to go back on at all. It sucks.

This past year I haven't been very prolific at all. A few months ago we went on tour to Europe and before we went I took two of my favorite guitars and all my poetry books and writings and two tapes that had guitar parts I was going to use for the next record, and I put all this really important stuff in our shower, because we've never really used our shower before. And the roommates upstairs had a plumbing problem, so when we came back, everything was destroyed. I don't have anything to go back on at all. It's pretty scary.

Kevin: I read the liner notes you wrote on Incesticide. *I've never seen somebody on a major label say, "If you're a racist, a sexist, a homophobe, we don't want you to buy our records."*

Kurt: That's been the biggest problem that I've had being in this band. I know there are those people out in the audience, and there's not much I can do about it. I can talk about those issues in interviews— I think it's pretty obvious that we're against the homophobes and the sexists and the racists, but when "Teen Spirit" first came out, mainstream audiences were under the assumption that we were just like Guns N' Roses.

Then our opinions started showing up in interviews. And then things like Chris and I kissing on Saturday Night Live. We weren't trying to be subversive or punk rock; we were just doing something insane and stupid at the last minute. I think now that our opinions are out in the open, a lot of kids who bought our record regret knowing anything about us. [*Laughs*]

There is a war now in the high schools now between Nirvana kids and Guns N' Roses kids. It's really cool. I'm really proud to be a part of that, because when I was in high school, I dressed like a punk rocker and people would scream "Devo!" at me—because Devo infiltrated the mainstream. Out of all the bands who came from the underground and actually made it in the mainstream, Devo is the most subversive and challenging of all. They're just awesome. I love them.

Kevin: Maybe there'll be a Devo revival soon, like the Village Revival.

Kurt: I saw the Village People years ago in Seattle! They were so cool. They still have the same costumes.

Kevin: Is there anything about Guns N' Roses' music you like?

Kurt: I can't think of a damn thing. I can't even waste my time on that band, because they're obviously pathetic and untalented. I used to think that everything in the mainstream pop world was crap, but now that some underground bands have been signed to majors, I take Guns N' Roses as more of an offense. I have to look into it more: They're really talentless people, and they write crap music, and they're the most popular rock band on earth right now. I can't believe it.

Kevin: Didn't Axl Rose say something nasty to you at the MTV Video Music Awards in September?

Kurt: They actually tried to beat us up. Courtney and I were with the baby in the eating area backstage, and Axl walked by. So Courtney yelled, "Axl! Axl, come over here!" We just wanted to say something to him—we think he's a joke, but we just wanted to say something to him. So I said, "Will you be the godfather of our child?" I don't know what had happened before that to piss him off, but he took his aggressions out on us and began screaming bloody murder.

These were his words: "You shut your bitch up, or I'm taking you down to the pavement." [*Laughs*] Everyone around us just burst out into tears of laughter. She wasn't even saying anything mean, you know? So I turned to Courtney and said, "Shut up, bitch!" And everyone laughed, and he left. So I guess I did what he wanted me to do— be a man. [*Laughs*]

Kevin: Does he remind you of guys you went to high school with?

Kurt: Absolutely. Really confused, fucked up guys. There's not much hope for them.

Kevin: When he was singing about "immigrants and faggots," people were excusing it by saying, "Well, he's from Indiana—"

Kurt: Oh, well. that's OK then. [*Laughs*] Insane. Later, after we played our show and were walking back to our trailer, the Guns N' Roses entourage came walking toward us. They have at least 50 bodyguards apiece: huge, gigantic brain-dead oafs ready to kill for Axl at all times. [*Laughs*] They didn't see me, but they surrounded Chris, and Duff [McKagen of Guns N' Roses] wanted to beat Chris up, and the bodyguards started pushing Chris around. He finally escaped, but throughout the rest of the evening, there was a big threat of either Guns N' Roses themselves or their goons beating us up. We had to hide out.

Since then, every time Axl has played a show he's said some comment about me and Courtney. When he was in Seattle, he said, "Nirvana would rather stay home and shoot drugs with their bitch wives than tour with us." [*Laughs*] That's why there's this big feud in most of the high schools. It's hilarious. He is insane, though. I was scared. I couldn't possibly beat him up, I know he would beat me up if he had the chance.

Kevin: *How do you feel about Guns N' Roses fans coming to see you?*

Kurt: Well, when we played that No on 9 benefit in Portland, I said something about Guns N' Roses. Nothing real nasty—I think I said: "And now, for our next song, 'Sweet Child o' Mine.'" But some kid jumped onstage and said, "Hey, man, Guns N' Roses plays awesome music, and Nirvana plays awesome music. Let's just get along and work this out, man!"

And I just couldn't help but say, "No, kid, you're really wrong. Those people are total sexist jerks, and the reason we're playing this show is to fight homophobia in a real small way. The guy is a fucking sexist and a racist and a homophobe, and you can't be on his side and be on our side: I'm sorry that I have to divide this up like this, but it's something you can't ignore. And besides, they can't write good music." [*Laughs*]

Kevin: *You know, you were probably taking money from people who were voting yes on 9—but they really wanted to see Nirvana.*

Kurt: [*Laughs*] Right! Chris went to a Guns N' Roses concert when they played here with Metallica a couple of months ago, and he went backstage, and there were these two bimbo girls who looked like they walked out of a Warrant video. They were sitting on the couch in hopes of sucking Axl's dick or something, and one of them said, "Chris, we saw you at that No on 9 benefit! We're voting yes on 9! You kissed Kurt on the lips! That was disgusting!" [*Laughs*] To know that we affect people like that—it's kind of funny. The sad thing is that there's no penetrating them. After all that, after all the things those girls had seen us do, that was the one thing that sticks in their mind.

Kevin: *You used to push people's buttons like that in high school, didn't you?*

Kurt: Oh, absolutely. I used to pretend I was gay just to fuck with people. I've had the reputation of being a homosexual ever since I was 14. It was really cool, because I found a couple of gay friends in Aberdeen—which is almost impossible. How I could ever come across a gay person in Aberdeen is amazing! But I had some really good friends that way. I got beat up a lot, of course, because of my association with them.

People just thought I was weird at first, just some fucked-up kid. But once I got the gay tag, it gave me the freedom to be able to be a freak and let people know that they should just stay away from me. Instead of having to explain to someone that they should just stay the fuck away from me—I'm gay, so I can't even be touched. It made for quite a few scary experiences in alleys walking home from school, though.

Kevin: *You actually got beat up?*

Kurt: Oh, yeah. Quite a few times.

Kevin: *And you used to spray-paint* God is Gay *on people's trucks?*

Kurt: That was a lot of fun. The funniest thing about that was not actually the act but the next morning. I'd get up early in the morning to walk through the neighborhood that I'd terrorized to see the aftermath. That was the worst thing I could have spray-painted on their cars. Nothing would have been more effective.

Aberdeen was depressing and there were a lot of negative things about it, but it was really fun to fuck with people all the time. I loved to go to parties—jock keggers—and just run around drunk and obnoxious, smoking cigars and spitting on the backs of these big redneck jocks and them not realizing it. By the end of the evening, usually I'd end up offending a girl, and she'd get her boyfriend to come and beat me up. [*Laughs*]

Kevin: *Because people thought you were gay and you had gay friends, did you ever wonder if you might be gay?*

Kurt: Yeah, absolutely. See, I've always wanted male friends that I could be real intimate with and talk about things with and be as affectionate with that person as I could be with a girl. Throughout my life I've always been really close with girls and made friends with girls. And I've always been a really sickly, feminine person anyhow, so I thought I was gay for a while because I didn't find any of the girls in my high school attractive at all. They had really awful haircuts and fucked-up attitudes. So I thought I would try to be gay for a while, but I'm just more sexually attracted to women. But I'm really glad that I found a few gay friends, because it totally saved me from becoming a monk or something.

I mean, I'm definitely gay in spirit, and I probably could be bisexual. But I'm married, and I'm more attracted to Courtney than I ever have been toward a person, so there's no point in my trying to sow my oats at this point. [*Laughs*] If I wouldn't have found Courtney, I probably would have carried on a bisexual life-style. But I just find her totally attractive in all ways.

Kevin: She has been described as a fag hag—

Kurt: Oh, she is. That was all she did for about five or six years of her life—hang out in gay clubs. She learned everything about perfume and fashion from her friends.

Kevin: Now that you've got a baby, how are you going to teach her about sexism and homophobia and things like that?

Kurt: I think that just growing up with Courtney and I will be a good enough example that, hopefully, she won't be prejudiced. You have to admit that most of the reasons a person grows up hating the isms is because their parents taught them. She might get confused, but I'm not worried at all.

Kevin: With the state the world is in, do you ever feel scared for her?

Kurt: Well, I have apocalyptic dreams all the time. Two years ago, I wouldn't even have considered having a child. I used to say that a person who would bring a child into this life now is selfish. But I try to be optimistic, and things do look like they're getting a little bit better—just the way communication has progressed in the past ten years. MTV, whether they're the evil corporate ogre or not, has played a part in raising consciousness.

It seems tacky almost, but rock and roll and our generation are not going to put up with the same Reaganite bullshit we were subjected to when we were younger. I was helpless when I was 12, when Reagan got elected, and there was nothing I could do about that. But now this generation is growing up, and they're in their mid 20s; they're not putting up with it.

I know there's still Republicans all over the place, but don't you feel that it's getting a little bit better? Not just because Clinton's in office now—look at the first thing he did. He tried to take away the ban on gays in the military, and I think that's a pretty positive thing. I don't expect a lot of change, but I think in the last five years our generation's gotten a lot more positive. I know that by reading *Sassy* magazine, you know? As tacky and stupid as that seems, I can tell that the average 14-year-old kid is a lot more sensitive—or trying to be—than they were ten years ago.

Kevin: Are you pro Clinton?

Kurt: Oh, yeah. I voted for him. I would have rather had Jerry Brown. I contributed my hundred dollars. But I'm definitely happy Clinton's in.

Kevin: Would you play at the White House if they asked you to?

Kurt: [*Laughs*] If we could have some kind of influence on something, yeah. I know that Chelsea likes us a lot, so maybe Chelsea could say, "Dad, do this and do that! Nirvana says so!" [*Laughs*] Sure, I'd play for the president. And Chelsea seems like a pretty neat person—Birkenstock-wearing kid. Amy Carter's pretty cool too, from what I've heard. She's been seen at Butthole Surfers concerts!

Kevin: You guys aren't preachy about your opinions. It's a sensible approach.

Kurt: Gee. That's pretty flattering, but out of all the people I know, I'm about the least qualified to be talking politically. I hope I come across more personal than political. About a year ago, when we realized the impact that we have, we thought it was a great opportunity to have some kind of influence on people. I've been called a hypocrite and an idiot and unqualified, but I can't help it. It's just my nature. I have to talk about things that piss me off, and if that's negative or that's preachy, then that's too bad. No one's gonna shut me up. I'm still the same person I was. Actually, I used to be way more of a radical than I am now.

Kevin: In thought or deed?

Kurt: Both, really. Mostly in deed; I can't really go around vandalizing anymore. But I have—actually, I just did a while ago.

Kevin: What?

Kurt: I can't say! [*Laughs*] I can't even say! I have people checking up on me all the time—especially because of the heroin rumors. That's been blown out of proportion so severely that I'm constantly harassed at airports and immigration all the time. And the cops—I get pulled over whenever they recognize me, and they search my car.

It all started with just one fucking article in Bam magazine. This guy—I wasn't even high that night, and he just assumed I was and wrote a piece on how sunken in my cheeks were and how pinholed my eyes were and that I wasn't able to cope with success and everything that was going on with the band. It was very embarrassing. It didn't bother me at first, but then once one article is written about a person that's negative, it just spreads like wildfire, and everyone just assumes it's true.

Kevin: You're talking about Lynn Hirschberg's profile of Courtney in Vanity Fair.

Kurt: I've never read an article that was more convincing yet more ridiculous in my life. Everybody from our record label to our management to our closest friends believed that shit.

She [Hirschberg] did a really good job of taking a piece of what Courtney had said and turning it into something completely different. I've seen that happen before—it's happened with me a lot of times—but this was such an extreme and done so well that I have to give her credit. She's a master at being catty.

Kevin: What about the drug use?

Kurt: Courtney was honest about the heroin excursion we went on for a few months. Then Courtney found herself pregnant, realized she was pregnant and had a drug problem, and got off of drugs. It's as simple as that. But it made it look like eight months after the fact, Courtney was nine-months pregnant and still doing drugs and everyone was really concerned. Like there was some awful den of iniquity going on in our apartment. I looked really skinny. Well, I am a skinny person, and I gain ten pounds every time I'm photographed, so people assume I'm this chunky, normal-weight person.

I'm just so tired of thinking about this. We have to live with the results of this one article every fucking day. It's something we have to deal with all the time.

Kevin: How did you feel when you read it?

Kurt: I was totally pissed off. My first thoughts were to have her fucking snuffed out. I wanted to personally beat the shit out of her, and I've never wanted to do that to anybody, especially a woman. But I just had so much anger in me. It was done so well. We were just helpless to combat something like that. We've had to do fluff pieces to try to fight this thing. It's embarrassing to have to do that: to pose with your family on the cover of a magazine, to hope that some people at least question the validity of [*Vanity Fair*].

Kevin: You're talking about posing for the December Spin *cover?*

Kurt: Yeah, and we've done a couple of other things. It pissed me off to the point of . . . not even wanting to hate that much. We could have filed a lawsuit with Condé Nast, but they have so many millions of dollars, they could have filibustered for ten years, and we wouldn't have come up with anything except losing most of our money.

Kevin: What's the funniest thing you've ever seen written about you?

Kurt: Practically all of it. [*Laughs*] Most of the time I come across as just this redneck little rocker kid who basically can't put a sentence together, you know? I come across a lot of times as just a stupid rock-and-roll kid.

Kevin: Courtney comes across in the press as the Nancy Reagan of this relationship.

Kurt: It's just sick. God! I don't want to say something like "Well, if anything, I wear the pants in the house." It's completely divided. We have influence on each other. It's totally 50–50. Courtney insists on this: She has a tab when she borrows money from me that she has to pay back. She's only up to $6,000. We're millionaires, and she goes to Jet Rag [a Los Angeles vintage-clothing shop] and buys clothes—$5 dresses. Big deal! I'll gladly buy her some $5 dresses. We don't require much at all.

Our personal expenses over the last year—we made a million dollars, of which $380,000 went to taxes, $300,000 went to a house, the rest went to doctors and lawyers, and our personal expenses were like $80,000. That's including car rentals, food, everything. That's not very much; that's definitely not what Axl spends a year. She insisted on a prenuptial agreement; no one knows that. So there's definitely not manipulation going on in this relationship at all.

It really sickens me to think that everyone assumes this. It makes me feel even stupider. I'm not the most secure person in the world, and I don't need to know that every time I go outside and someone recognizes me, they think of me as this defenseless little rocker idiot that's being manipulated by his wife. It's a little bit more complex than that.

Courtney's had misconceptions about herself all her life. I talk to people who knew Courtney five years ago, and she was way more of a volatile, fucked-up person than she is now. She was insane at parties just begging for attention. I never could have predicted a successful marriage with this person a few years ago. It just couldn't have happened.

Kevin: How does all this affect the other members of Nirvana?

Kurt: Definitely not as severe as everyone thinks or what has been written. There was an article in the [British music magazine] *NME* that was nothing but an "exposé" on Courtney fucking up Nirvana and making us come close to breaking up. It's pretty frightening to find that an article like that can be written by a friend of yours. It makes it hard to trust anybody.

Chris and Dave liked Courtney before I even liked Courtney. During that time, I knew that I liked her a lot, but I wouldn't admit it. She and Dave were really good friends—I shouldn't say this, but they almost wanted to get together for a time. When we were on tour in Europe, some of our shows collided with Hole shows, and Courtney would hang out on the bus with us, and Chris and Courtney were really good friends. And it hasn't changed at all. There hasn't been any bad blood except after the *Vanity Fair* piece.

For a few days, even Chris was convinced that Courtney had said those things. Courtney had said, "Why don't you kick Chris out of the band?" She said that, but it was a total joke. That's the biggest problem with articles—context. The word *sarcastic* needs to be in parentheses 90% of the time in an interview with us. Dave and Chris are dealing with this fine, and they're defending us as much as they can, but we can't expect them to go on a defense crusade, because it doesn't affect them like if affects us.

Kevin: Have there been times in the last year when you've just wanted to quit?

Kurt: Oh, yeah. The other night. I called up Chris late at night; I was really drunk, and I said, "I don't want to be in this anymore. I'll call you tomorrow." I was dead serious. For a couple of hours. [*Laughs*]

Kevin: How is it dealing with a big label?

Kurt: We haven't had any complications. In our contract we have 100% artistic control. What that means in fine print, I don't know. All the evil corporateness that I've heard about since I've been into underground rock probably is true with other bands, but we have a good lawyer and a great contract. And we sell a lot of records for them, so we have the upper hand.

Kevin: Courtney's band got a good contract too?

Kurt: It's actually better than ours. This is the first decade major labels have even dealt with a contract like this. They're so used to having bands that don't even know what they want to do that they have to be in control. There are a lot of bands that don't have any artistic direction at all, so they need to dress up in spandex.

Kevin: So you can turn on mainstream radio and hear some music you like these days.

Kurt: That's part of the reason I'm a little bit more optimistic this year—Clinton and because the Screaming Trees are on heavy rotation right now. It's commercial, but it's good music. I don't like Pearl Jam's music at all, but at least they have good attitudes; they're not another Van Halen, who totally refuse to address anything.

The only sad thing about it is that the innocence of underground music has been lumped in with the corporate idea of what underground is. There are no boundaries. Pearl Jam's a good example. I don't mean to harp on them; I'm tired of talking shit about them, but they're a real commercial rock band.

Kevin: What do you do when you're not playing music?

Kurt: Well, I'm reading *Perfume* for the second time. It's about a perfume apprentice in the 1700s. And I really like Camille Paglia a lot; it's really entertaining, even though I don't necessarily agree with what she says. I still paint once in a while—I painted the cover of *Incesticide*.

And I make dolls. I like the style of things from the 1700s and 1800s from Yugoslavia and that area. I copy from these doll-collector magazines. They're clay. I bake them, and then I make them look really old and put old clothes on them. They look like I actually came across a real antique, because I don't know where to find dolls that are in those magazines. I could go to a doll-collectors show, but they're so expensive. I don't want to indulge in things like that—"Now that I'm a rock star, I buy antiques," you know? [*Laughs*] Some of those things are, like, $50,000.

I can't find anything I want. I go shopping, and I buy food, and that's about it. Now that I have all this money, I just can't spend it on anything. Everything that I appreciate is old but not necessarily an antique, so I can get it really cheap.

Kevin: So you're not falling into the trap of spending money on things just because you can?

Kurt: Sometimes I wish I could. I've noticed there are specialty shops for the rich and famous that have basically the same things you can find at Kmart, but they have a ridiculous price tag, and people buy it just because they don't have anything else to do with their money. There are a lot of things like that on Rodeo Drive. We went into Gucci just to see what a Gucci bag cost. [*Laughs*] Just this leather bag, and because it had a Gucci name on it, it was like, $10,000!

Kevin: Do you like L.A.?

Kurt: I *hate* L.A. I love the weather, but I can't stand being there. I absolutely hate it. A lot of it has to do with having the responsibility of driving around with the baby. People are so rude there. I'm not that bad a driver, and I get in a wreck almost every day.

We were there for the riots. That decision was the most asinine thing I'd ever seen. If they were going to riot, I just wish they could have rioted in the middle of Beverly Hills. Got all the Gucci bags. [*Laughs*]

Kevin: *Now's your chance to say anything you'd like to say.*

Kurt: I always clam up when that question is asked. Maybe I'll just fumble and stutter and end up saying, "Don't believe everything you read." I always knew to question things. All my life I never believed most things I read in history books and a lot of things I learned in school. But now I've found I don't have the right to make a judgment on someone based on something I read. I don't have the right to judge anything. That's the lesson I've learned.

A NOTE ON FRANCES FARMER

Her downfall brought forth little compassion in the Glamour Town which had exploited her. She had been a difficult "troublemaker"; they were glad to be rid of her. (William Wyler once went on record as saying, "The nicest thing I can say about Frances Farmer is that she is unbearable.") And to boot, she had been a pinko.

—Kenneth Anger, *Hollywood Babylon*

The title tells it all: "Frances Farmer Will Have Her Revenge on Seattle." The inclusion of this song on *In Utero* was an obvious reference to the media persecution Cobain, Love, and (to a lesser extent) the other members of Nirvana were forced to endure. Cobain was particularly fascinated by the story of Farmer's life, and he even made an effort to contact her biographer. (Frances Bean Cobain was named after Frances McKee of the Vaselines, but Cobain told Michael Azerrad in *Come As You Are* that he wished she had been named after Farmer.) But to see how Farmer became a patron saint of the persecuted we must turn to her life before she was known as the "New Garbo."

Frances Farmer was Frances Farmer before she ever left Seattle. Born there in 1914, she also attended the University of Washington to study acting. While still in school she entered an essay contest in a communist periodical and won a trip to the Soviet Union (she later said it was a great way to get to New York). The essay and her trip would have been enough to have her blackballed during the "Red" hunts of the 1950s. But by then her star had been pulled from the sky.

Farmer had one quality that doomed her in the Hollywood of the 1930s: a sensitive, quick, and independent mind. She got sucked into the Hollywood movie machine, but what always mattered to her most was the work she did for the stage; she acted for a time with the Group Theatre in New York and worked with Elia Kazan and Clifford Odets. She was committed to serious acting but the glamour monster pushed her into insipid films like *Rhythm on the Range* with Bing Crosby. When Hollywood could not completely control her, it did away with her, and no one in her home town of Seattle raised a finger to help her.

Farmer's downfall began on the night of October 19, 1942. She was pulled over for a minor traffic violation and ended up in jail for being drunk and acting up with a cop. From here on things went from bad to hellish. She began to drink heavily (she later told a judge, "I drink everything I can get, including benzedrine"). She was arrested again after an altercation in a hotel bar. Her appearance in court was highlighted by her asking the judge: "Have you ever had a broken heart?" She then threw an inkpot at him. When she was refused the right to make a phone call, she swung at a policeman and was hauled off to a cell in a straitjacket.

She was in desperate need of help but no help came—no help from the studio she worked for, no help from the Seattle community that had been once so proud of her "making it" in Hollywood. Then the person she least needed stepped in: her mother appeared and had her committed to a sanitarium. She spent the next five years in mental hospitals and was forced to take insulin shock treatment. She was reportedly also gang raped and given a partial lobotomy.

Farmer was never the same. She made a brief come-back on television and died in 1970.

JON PARELES

NIRVANA, THE BAND THAT HATES TO BE LOVED

The New York Times, November 14, 1993

Nirvana rolls into New York City tonight [11/14/93] as the great alternative-rock success story. Its first album for a major label, *Nevermind* has sold nearly nine million copies since late 1991; its new one, *In Utero*, zoomed directly to No. 1 when it was released in September. Nirvana's concert tonight at the 7,000-seat New York Coliseum sold out immediately.

But if ever a band was ambivalent about reaching a mass audience, it is Nirvana. In a song from the new album, "Radio Friendly Unit Shifter"—music-business jargon for a recording that gets played on radio stations and sells well—Kurt Cobain snarls, "I do not want what I have got" and agonizes, "What is wrong with me?"

What's wrong with him is that he writes songs all sorts of people can like. And ever since *Nevermind* lodged in the Top 10, Nirvana has been trying to remain a band of punk underdogs rather than a pop commodity. Ask Mr. Cobain about *In Utero* hitting No. 1 on release (it has since slipped a few notches) and he says: "I don't have high hopes of staying up in the charts. Meat Loaf is so obviously more talented than I am." In fact, prosperity and its discontents nearly tore apart the band.

On a sunny late-summer afternoon in Seattle, Mr. Cobain, Chris Novoselic and Dave Grohl—the guitarist, bassist, and drummer of Nirvana—were reluctantly doing advance promotion for *In Utero*. Dressed in thrift-shop shirts, fraying jeans and sneakers, the three musicians didn't act like limo-level rock stars. Lunch was microwaved burritos at a 7-Eleven. Eventually, the band members decided to take the visitor to the city's emblematic Space Needle.

On line for the express elevator, a teenager approached, lugging a large video camera. "Uh, um, is it O.K. if I take your picture?" he asked Mr. Cobain. The guitarist scowled, his blue eyes narrowed. "I'll kill you," he said; the teen-ager cowered. Then Mr. Cobain's face relaxed into a broad smile. "Sure, go ahead," he said.

That teen-ager with the camera is both Nirvana's livelihood and its nightmare. The band had hoped to reach a market of intelligent iconoclasts, people who distrust bands that are too popular because if so, they must be too easy to take. "When the album first started getting heavy play, I think we were mostly concerned with losing those college kids," Mr. Cobain said of *Nevermind*. "For some reason, that didn't happen to us."

Looking back, he now thinks *Nevermind* sounds too "clean." "Ugh," he said. "I'll never do that again. It already paid off, so why try to duplicate that? And just trying to sell that many records again, there's no point in it." In July, Nirvana confirmed its allegiance to the college crowd with its first New York show since 1991. The band played Roseland Ballroom as part of the New Music Seminar, the annual convention and showcase where the rock underground meets the business. To start the set, Mr. Novoselic intoned, "Alternative rock, the sound that's sweeping the nation!" The concert ended with Mr. Cobain alone on stage, kneeling with his guitar by an amplifier, creating a torrential squall of feedback.

The new album, too, is drenched in guitar noise and sounds much rawer than *Nevermind*. To produce *In Utero*, Nirvana chose Steve Albini, known for the low-budget blasts of bands like the Pixies and Big Black. Mr. Albini, who had once dismissed Nirvana as "unremarkable," asked for only a $100,000 fee—not a percentage of royalties, like most other producers—but refused to allow any Geffen Records staff to visit the sessions. All the vocals, Mr. Cobain said, were recorded in a single seven-hour marathon; *Nevermind* took days.

The songs on *In Utero* alternatively lash out—"Go away, get away, get away," Mr. Cobain howls in "Scentless Apprentice," based on the Patrick Süskind novel *Perfume*—and tear at themselves.

Mr. Cobain does not like explaining lyrics, which he says he assembles from spiral-bound notebooks of bed-time jottings. "It's just thumbing through my poetry books going, 'Oh, there's a line,' and writing it down. That's all I do.

"None of my poems are coherent at all," he continued. "They're not based on anything. It's just a bunch of gibberish. I mean, I try to have relations to some of the lines, and there's a lot of double meanings, and in certain senses, they do relate to something, but it's always changing. But when I say 'I' in a song, it's not me, 90 percent of the time."

Yet when pressed, the songwriter admits he can be found in his songs. Mr. Cobain, 26, and Mr. Novoselic, 28, both grew up in Aberdeen, Wash., a logging town of 16,800 on the western end of the Olympic Peninsula.

To his family, Mr. Cobain was a dead-end kid. A verse in "Serve the Servants" from *In Utero* says: "I tried hard to have a father / But instead I had a Dad / I just want you to know that I / Don't hate you any more." Behind it, he acknowledged, is his own story.

His parents, Don and Wendy Cobain, were divorced when Kurt was 7 years old. He frequently skipped school, smoking marijuana and often heading for the town library. After reading through the local selection, he started using the state's inter-library loan system. "The library never kicked me out, though they knew I was under age," he said. "It was the only place I could hide."

Both he and Mr. Novoselic recall getting "swats" in school: corporal punishment with a paddle. At the urging of the principal, Mr. Cobain dropped out, played guitar, hung out. "When I was 17, I got kicked out of my mom's house," he said. "I was living on the streets and I called my dad, and he said I could come back to stay for a few days, on a trial basis. When I did, he had me take the test for the Navy, and he had me pawn my guitar. He had the recruiter come to the house two nights in a row.

"I was really trying to better myself and do what my parents wanted me to do. But I smoked some pot and magically came to this realization that I don't belong here—especially not in the Navy. So I just packed up my stuff and left, walking past the recruiting officer, and I said, 'See ya.'"

In person, as in his songs, Mr. Cobain ricochets between opposites. He is wary and unguarded, sincere and sarcastic, thin-skinned and insensitive, aware of his popularity and trying to ignore it. Before agreeing to do an interview, he had demanded clippings by the interviewer, particularly on music by "women and minorities," said a Geffen Records staffer. But he's not exactly politically correct; he owns, he said, "an M-16, a few revolvers and one Beretta."

By mixing punk, heavy metal and good pop tunes, Nirvana altered the pop-music landscape with *Nevermind*. "There is a pre-Nirvana and post-Nirvana record business," says Gary Gersh, now president of Capitol Records, who signed the band to Geffen. "*Nevermind* showed that this wasn't some alternative thing happening off in a corner, and then back to reality. This is reality."

But in 1992, the band nearly self-destructed. According to Michael Azerrad's exhaustive biography, *Come As You Are: The Story of Nirvana*, Mr. Cobain started using heroin regularly in late 1991—at first, he has said, to relieve debilitating stomach pain.

He had also begun a romance with Courtney Love, the brash lead singer of a Los Angeles band called Hole. They were both injecting heroin at the end of 1991 when Ms. Love became pregnant; they were married in February 1992. But she kicked the habit, she has said, soon after she found out. He continued on and off until August 1992, when their child Frances Bean Cobain was born.

An article in *Vanity Fair* implied that Ms. Love had taken heroin well into her pregnancy. Two weeks after the baby was born, using the article as evidence, the Los Angeles Department of Children's Services forced the couple to surrender the child to Ms. Love's sister. Although the Cobains soon regained custody, county officials continued to monitor them until March 1993.

Still, Mr. Cobain said, the title of *In Utero* doesn't refer to the allegations of Ms. Love's drug use during pregnancy. "I just liked the way it sounded," he said. The album's tone is by turns wrathful and miserable, the lyrics full of images of sickness and decay. The album's back cover, a collage of rubber fetus dolls, orchids and models of bodily organs, suggests the aftermath of a massacre.

When *In Utero* was released, the national Wal-Mart chain refused to sell it, apparently due to that image (although the chain's spokesman claimed it was for lack of consumer interest). So did Kmart, which stated that the record "didn't fit within our merchandise mix."

"One of the main reasons I signed to a major label was so people could buy our records at Kmart," Mr. Cobain said. "In some small towns, Kmart is the only place that kids can buy records."

Clearly, Nirvana still makes some people uncomfortable. But can a band remain an underdog with millions of fans? "I think we look ridiculous already," he said. "I don't want to have a long career if I have to put up with the same stuff that I'm putting up with. I'm trying it one last time, and if it's a more pleasant year for us, then fine, we'll have a career. But I'm not going to subject myself to being stuck in an apartment building for the next 10 years and being afraid to go outside of my house. It's not worth it. I would gladly give up music for my life. It's more important."

Mr. Novoselic added: "We were fools. But on the other hand, look where we are."

EVERETT TRUE

COBAIN'T THAT PECULIAR

Melody Maker, April 24, 1993

This article started off as a belated attempt to create some "new" Nirvana literature. It has since mutated radically. The comments in bold type are Kurt Cobain's. The comments in normal type are the journalist's.

Kurt: "So this is where I'm supposed to describe how I feel after a major show, right? Okay, I remember this one time I went to see Sammy Hagar when I was in Seventh Grade. Everyone was passing round pot, and I got really high and I lit myself on fire. I had a Bic lighter in my sweatshirt pocket and I was watching Sammy, swinging upside-down from the rafters, mocking everyone else who was holding their lighters above their heads. I looked down, and petrol had spilt out everywhere, and my shirt was on fire. It went well with the piss-stained pants.

"I got those before the show, when we drank a case of beer and got stuck in a traffic jam. There was nowhere to go, so I peed my pants in the back of the car. What else do I remember about the show? Wanting desperately to leave. Did you ever go to a big concert?"

Yeah, sometimes. Hold on. Let me think. It was the other night—hey, you were there right? A benefit for Bosnian refugees. A real big event; 14,000 sun-kissed Californians, come to show their solidarity, or was it just to get their fucking MTV rocks off? Who cares, right? As long as the money benefits a worthy cause.

Chris Novoselic, who put the concert together, rendezvoused with the Tvesnjevka Women's Group in Zagreb in January this year, contacted all the bands . . . well, his wife was at the door leafleting people as they came in, trying to make 'em stop and think a second, participate. Some hope! These kids were here 'cos MTV told 'em to be. Still, it's far better to attempt than accept. Plus, MTV got Clinton in with their "Rock the Vote" campaign, however much you scorn them.

Anyway. So there I was, sitting up among the pigeons with Kim and Jo from the Breeders and some other guy, looking down upon you, so fragile, so vulnerable, one speck of humanity against a whole generation of curiosity seekers, fans, the cynical, the bored and a whole buncha lame cheerleaders—no tattoos—in butt-hugging slacks.

You were singing that damn fine line from the achingly poignant "All Apologies" about "All in all / Is all we are." No, I didn't have any popcorn. Tears were prickling behind my eyelids like from before, when you sang "Francis Farmer," that slow and melancholic one from Reading, dedicated to Courtney and Frances Bean, or anytime you've played the ironic "In Bloom," and I fell to wondering . . .

Look, when I see U2 or Rush or Prince or Iggy Pop or whoever, I feel lost, traumatised by this singular, fascistic vision of rock. When I see Nirvana, I feel all those emotions, but bewildered, too—bewildered that this music should reach me and the *untrained* simultaneously. When I see Hiphoprisy, I feel warm inside, glowing all over. When I hear the Breeders, I feel delirious.

And when I see L7? I wanna laugh with pleasure. It's been proven that if you expose an eight-year-old to the most off-the-wall music, they'll take it on board, place it next to their favorites, *as long as they've heard it in the correct context. Sassy* magazine, too, constantly proves this in their musical coverage for cool U.S. teenage girls. It's only later people start shutting down. Okay, I'm burbling.

So I saw Rush at Wembly once, and it was nothing like the Cow Palace. No leaflets about abortion rights, no cool supports, no crushing melodies, either. Just a whole buncha multi-coloured lights and . . .

Kurt: "Right. The only other major arena rock concert I went to was Iron Maiden on the Fourth of July. People were shooting bottle rockets and throwing M-80s into the crowd all night, until they had to stop because the roof caught fire. It was entertaining, I suppose, but I felt alienated. You may as well throw in the bathroom thing right now."

What bathroom thing? Your show was so neat. Sorry if I'm sounding like I write for *Hit It Or Quit It*, or some cool U.S. girlzine or something. But it was. Especially when you toppled into Dave's drum kit in slow motion at the crescendo to "Endless, Nameless" for old time's sake, and he emerged, face all black and bruised. At least, that's what we wanted to imagine from our vantage point, perched among the rafters.

The new songs shone: as blue and battered as anything from the devastating, forthcoming debut album by Madder Rose; as raw and trembling as any Daniel Johnson live tape (although, I guess, you'd have to add the adjective "assured" here); as mighty and pounding as any waves washing up on a beach where the shingle has backed up too high to ever be overwhelmed, but still the waves try, dammit, still they try.

Hey, you like my new metaphor? Yeah, lame, isn't it? So "Penny Royaltea," the one I woke up singing two days later in San Francisco as the sun blistered and the sound of the Melvins pounded into my skull, nearly shuddered to a halt several times, but each time it shuddered, it emerged sounding more triumphant than ever. Whatever trials and pressures you and Chris and Dave have suffered, surely they were worth it for this?

Er, what was that about a bathroom?

Kurt: "Right. Listen. At Sammy Hagar's, in the bathroom, there was a passed-out, drunken Seventh Grader lying in the piss trough. People relieved themselves on him throughout the concert, not even caring. There were these two girls cutting lines of coke on a small mirror when, all of a sudden, a drunken man fell behind their chairs and vomited all over the two girls' laps, ruining their lines of coke. The two girls had their boyfriends beat up the drunken coke killer.

"Look, when you type this up, can you fix it so the words end in mid-letter, at the end of each line. That looks far more punk rock."

I doubt it, Kurt. I'm as much owned by a large corporation as you are. More, probably. It would be false. Anyway. So that was at Hagar's, right? Most of the concerts I've seen over the past decade in London were simply a matter of scared wannabe punk rock indie boys wearing spectacles and clutching carrier bags, wishing there were some cute girls to eye up in the crowd. That's why metal is so popular, I guess—those girls shakes their tushes. Am I allowed to say that? Fuck it.

These kids would've been terrified at the Cow Palace, watching how well their precious Breeders communicated, perhaps a little shocked at the massive glaring differences between new Breeders material and the (unsurprisingly) mediocre Frank Black album. God, Kurt, I know folk like us have been saying this for years—but just *who was the main creative force behind the Pixies*?

Breeders songs shuffle and shatter, stumble and shudder just as much as old Pixies (*Surfer Rosa*, say) ever did, but now they have an added vulnerability, the sweetest, most caustic vocals. Charles lost something a long time back. Anyhow, how many fucking songs about serial killers and space rockets can one critic take? The trick where they drop all their instruments one by one, until there's just Jo's surfin' bass flaunting, or Kelley's harsh guitar squalling, is a mighty fine one. And, God, that new drummer can fucking hit those drums!

Did I tell you Kurt, about how some kids came and badgered me while the Breeders were on? They asked me if they were L7, nodded appreciatively when I mentioned the name Pixies, invited me down the "pit" with them. I declined, of course, on grounds of age and alcohol. They tried to hit on me for tabs. I shook the young punks off and went to buy a commemorative tee-shirt. You wanna say something here?

Kurt: "Yeah. That reminds me. One night, we decided to hire two Manchester Mafia goons to fend off tee-shirt bootleggers. I got very drunk during Eugenius's set, who, at the time, were called Captain America, I exited out the side door with drink in hand to urinate. The two goons didn't recognise me as being their employer and decided to rough me up a bit for pissing. I threw a rock star fit, threw my glass of vodka in their faces, and darted back in through the exit door. They chased me round inside the hall among the dancing fans until I was rescued by my Scottish tour manager."

The last 10 shows I got completely fucked up were Nirvana shows. Once, I drank a bottle of vodka and ended up pushing the "star" out in front of 60,000 "fans" in a fucking wheelchair. All I remember was backstage, racing around with Kurt in the chair, chasing those crazy L7 girls, getting faster and faster, and the security and organisers and managers and everyone going near crazy 'cos they figured I might push him off the stage and, bang! there go a million lawsuits.

I wasn't drunk at the Cow Palace, but L7 were still there, proud and strident and manly as ever. Soon, they're gonna be capable of an album as good as the Runaways' *Live in Japan*. That's not meant as an insult. I used to fucking love the Runaways—and how much cooler it would have been if only they'd been in control. Joan Jett still kicks fucking ass, and pretty much most of the U.S. rock stars I know agree.

I didn't take too much notice of L7 or Hiphoprisy, which was unfair, I know. I was too busy talking with Mrs. Novoselic about the new surge of optimism in America, that doctor guy who just got murdered by the very scary and quite insane pro-"lifers," the Rodney King sideshow, the confusion in tonight's punters' faces when they asked her just who are the good and who are the bad guys in Bosnia and she told them it isn't as simple as that. Hmm. Reagan's legacy is lasting, right?

But L7 proved their worth, amply. They rocked as good as any man, and got the the meatheads moshing to cool, fucked up songs. That's a victory. You wanna add something, Kurt?

Kurt: "I was in Dallas, I had the flu. A doctor came to my hotel room and gave me unnamed antibiotic shots in the ass. Drunk again, and feeling the results of the antibiotics and heavy booze, I stumbled onstage and played four songs. In the middle of the fourth song, I took my guitar to the monitor board, smashing it to bits as the crowd cheered 'bullshit, bullshit.'

"The bouncer, who was also the owner of the monitor board, didn't appreciate what I'd done. For the next five songs, he paced back and forth, punching me in the ribs. I jumped into the crowd with my guitar. He pretended to save me from the vicious crowd, yet he grabbed my hair and punched me in the ribs a few times. I swung the butt end of my guitar into his face. He bled, and proceeded to beat the shit out of me. Once again, I was saved by my Scottish tour manager.

"After the show, Chris and I got into a cab in front of the club, only to be greeted by the bloody bouncer and 10 of his heavy metal vomit friends with Iron Maiden and Sammy Hagar tee-shirts. The bloody bouncer smashed his hand through the side of the cab and choked me senseless. We couldn't move because we were stuck in the traffic. After 20 minutes of cat and mouse, we fled away into the night."

So what relevance does all this have to the Cow Palace, or to whether L7 kicked ass? Does it tell us if Hiphoprisy had a new guitarist and a whole cavalcade of new songs, which were slightly less focused, slightly more encompassing than before (I'm talking topic-wise here)? We haven't even mentioned Hiphoprisy's enthusiastic reception, their PC-checking of the "Stop Using Women's Bodies as a Battleground" scene, their still fiery renditions of "California" and "Television."

We were discussing the show, right? You think you're a major league star, you think you can get away with telling us any bogus "boy" story, right?

Kurt: "Hey, you fucking asked me. I didn't even see most of the show, okay? Fuck you."

Okay. The hack hears he might be stepping into the realm of fiction. It's time to bring this whole "concept" crashing down round its ears. Kurt, say something, and we'll call a halt to this. Agreed?

Silence. The star is on the phone. His wife is at the table, reading up on books on cool feminist thought. I thought I'd give you names, but you're too lazy to listen. A log fire cracks. In the distance, a lake glistens under a dim night sky. God, don't you just love having stars to envy?

The first time I saw Nirvana, I was so hyped up by the guys over at Sub Pop, I expected some fucking punk band who'd come along and change the fucking world. They didn't suck exactly, but I'm sure glad they got rid of that extra guitarist.

DEBORAH RUSSELL
NIRVANA BASSIST FORMS ARTIST, FAN ACTION LEAGUE IN SEATTLE

Billboard, February 18, 1995

Los Angeles—Nirvana bassist Krist Novoselic is fronting a new group of industry activists that is stepping up the political fight to defend the rights of artists and their fans.

Novoselic is president of the Seattle-based Joint Artists' and Music Promotions political action committee, which was unveiled in Seattle on

Feb. 7 [1995]. The PAC is affiliated with the Washington Music Industry Coalition.

JAMPAC will stage a rally on the steps of the capital building in Olympia, Wash., on Wednesday. The primary focus of the rally will be to fight new lyric bills introduced in the state legislature in January.

JAMPAC's members agree that more proactive, aggressive lobbying efforts are required to keep the state's lawmakers from authoring and introducing such bills.

"Conventional politics are influenced by campaign contributions and relationships with representatives," says Novoselic. "We're going to start playing American politics the way they are played."

Early financial supporters of JAMPAC include members of Pearl Jam, who have already contributed $2,500 to the group's efforts. Additional JAMPAC pledges include Susan Silver Management, Soundgarden, Sky Cries Mary, Monqui Presents, A&M Records, Capitol Records, Gold Mountain Entertainment, MCA Concerts, and the Recording Industry Assn. of America.

JAMPAC's message to politicians is that the Seattle music scene, community, and industry has an economic base and an international profile that benefits the state and the nation, says Novoselic.

"We are an economic force and we create jobs nationally," he says. "These people are obstructing commerce with these laws. While other growth industries are encouraged in Washington state, we're being discouraged."

One of Novoselic's main priorities for JAMPAC is to launch an impact study to gauge the significance of the music industry's contribution to the state's economy. But the organization's immediate goal is to raise funds necessary to influence the political process at the state, regional, and local levels, says Novoselic.

Forthcoming fundraisers likely will take the form of concerts, with several local and nationally recognized acts contributing proceeds to the PAC, he says.

Seattle city government elections, scheduled for June, also are a major priority for the coalition. Five seats on the city council will be open; JAMPAC has yet to endorse any candidates. The coalition's concerns focus on a proposed teen-dance ordinance, anti-postering laws, and noise ordinances, which it perceives as threatening to the local music scene.

Washington has been a hotbed of lyrics-legislation proposals in recent years. In 1992, an "erotic music" statue was passed banning the distribution, sale, or display of sound recordings deemed "obscene." That law was found to be unconstitutional by King County Superior Court Judge Mary W. Brucker (*Billboard,* Nov. 4, 1992).

In April 1994, the state legislature passed a new version of the state's "harmful to minors" statute that would make it unlawful to display or sell material, including recordings and live performances, "appealing to the prurient interest of minors" or depicting "ultimate sexual acts," "violent or destructive acts," or "sexually explicit nudity" (*Billboard,* March 26, 1994).

The nonprofit WMIC was successful in lobbying governor Mike Lowry to veto the bill. A senator and representative are now seeking to override the veto, and the WMIC is lobbying to block that override. Meanwhile, new bills were introduced in the House and Senate in January that are virtually the same as the vetoed statue, although the Senate version exempts libraries, schools, and museums.

"These [politicians] are relentless," says Novoselic. "They have a social agenda and they're going to just keep throwing stuff against the wall until something sticks."

JAMPAC's board of directors includes VP Richard White, executive director of the WMIC. Its temporary treasurer is Robert Taylor-Manning, who also serves as president of the WMIC.

GILLIAN G. GAAR
VERSE CHORUS VERSE: THE RECORDING HISTORY OF NIRVANA

Goldmine, 1997

Nearly three years after Kurt Cobain's death in April 1994, interest in his group, Nirvana, remains strong. The band's latest album, *From the Muddy Banks of the Wishkah,* released this past October, became their fourth #1 album, and their third to enter the charts at #1. *Wishkah* remained in the Top 40 for six weeks, and though its stay in the Top 40 was relatively brief, its initial high placement is an indication that future releases from the band will certainly follow.

Though Nirvana has officially issued six albums, the number of non-album B-sides, compilation tracks, and other rarities the group has released is enough to comprise at least two additional albums; only a fraction of these songs appeared on the band's "odds and sods" collection,

1992's *Incesticide*. The release of *Wishkah* has sparked further conjecture about tracks that may still be left in the vaults. This article will chart the band's recording history, examining the unreleased material that is out there, in addition to looking at the market of Nirvana collectibles.

Nirvana's story has been previously covered in *Goldmine* (December 10, '93 and May 13, '94). But it's worth going back in order to take a closer look at the band's work in the studio. Cobain was born February 20, 1967 in Aberdeen, Washington, though he spent the first six months of his life living in the neighboring town of Hoquiam. The family then moved to Aberdeen, a block away from the North Aberdeen bridge, which crosses the Wishkah river—the same river that gave Nirvana's latest album its name.

Cobain's interest in art and music was evident from a young age. Cobain's aunt, Mari Earl (then Fradenburg, the sister of Kurt's mother Wendy), recalls, "He was singing from the time he was two. He would sing Beatles songs like 'Hey Jude.' He would do anything. You could just say, 'Hey Kurt, sing this!' and he would sing it. He had a lot of charisma from a very young age" (the family taped some of these impromptu performances). Earl, a musician herself, was also the first one to put a guitar in Cobain's hand, at the age of two. "I put it in his hand, and he turned it around the other way, 'cause he was left handed," she says. "We had kind of a bond because of music."

Until his early teens, Cobain's artistic interests were primarily channelled into visual art, including an attempt at claymation. Not much of this early work has been seen, though a few illustrations appeared in Northwest newspapers after Cobain's death. But he maintained his interest by playing drums in the school band, and visiting Earl in order to use her musical equipment. Earl regularly performed in area nightclubs, and explains, "In between gigs I always set up the equipment in a corner of the dining room so I could rehearse. Kurt was probably about ten years old when he first started asking if he could turn on the equipment, play my guitar and sit behind the microphone. I don't have any vivid memory of what he sounded like, but I remember him being very careful not to damage the equipment. He respected it." As his interest in music accelerated, Cobain was given a guitar—a Lindell—for his fourteenth birthday by his uncle, Chuck Fradenburg, who also worked as a musician.

By this time, Cobain's musical influences ranged from '60s pop groups like the Beatles and Monkees to classic '70s rock acts like Led Zeppelin, Queen, and Black Sabbath. As he learned to play guitar in the early '80s, his musical tastes widened again, after meeting Matt Lukin and Buzz

Osborne at Montesano High School (Montesano being another neighboring town in the area). Both Lukin and Osborne played in a local band called the Melvins (Lukin would go on to play in Mudhoney), and through Osborne, Cobain learned about the burgeoning hardcore scene and such bands as Black Flag and Flipper. Back at Aberdeen High, Cobain met Chris Novoselic, born in California in 1965, who'd moved to Aberdeen with his family in 1979. The two hung out at the Melvins' practice space, largely because of the lack of anything else to do in Aberdeen.

During this period, Cobain made what may be his first recorded effort, again at Earl's house, who had married and moved to Seattle (two hours drive from Aberdeen). While visiting over Christmas vacation in 1982, Cobain brought along his electric guitar, and made a tape, also using Earl's bass, and drumming on an empty suitcase with wooden spoons. "Most of what I remember about the songs was a lot of distortion on guitar, really heavy bass, and the clucky sound of the wooden spoons. And his voice, sounding like he was mumbling under a big fluffy comforter, with some passionate screams once in awhile. Musically, it was very repetitious. He called the recording *Organized Confusion*." Cobain would continue to make home recordings on a regular basis, both before and during the Nirvana years, up to the last weeks of his life. It's not known how much of this material has survived, or what the quality is—or if tracks said to be "Kurt's home recordings" on the innumerable bootlegs on the market are indeed what they claim to be.

"Kurt enjoyed coming up here," Earl adds. "He always was very very careful; whenever he ran into any problems, he would always ask me, 'Aunt Mari, could you help me with this?'" But though she was a musician herself, Earl says Cobain rarely discussed the specifics of his work with her. "As far as really sharing his music with me, and saying, 'What do you think of this?' or whatever, he really didn't do that," she says. "Kurt was very sensitive about the stuff that he wrote and he was very careful about who he let hear it. 'cause he didn't really like someone just poking fun at it. And being a songwriter myself, I can understand that."

As he grew more proficient, Cobain developed a strong desire to get a band together. But he wouldn't be in a regularly performing group for some time; he had already auditioned for the Melvins, and failed. Osborne, in Michael Azerrad's Nirvana biography *Come As You Are*, remembers another tape of original songs Cobain made around this time, accompanying himself on electric guitar.

Dropping out of high school in 1985 left Cobain with even more spare time to work on music. By the end of the year, he had formed a band called Fecal Matter with Melvins drummer Dale Crover (who played bass in the band), and Greg Hokanson on drums. Hokanson only lasted a few gigs, so it was Cobain and Crover who performed on the band's demo, recorded at Earl's Seattle home on a four-track TEAC, with Crover on drums.

"They set up in my music room and they'd just crank it up!" Earl remembers. "It was loud. They would put down the music tracks first, then he'd put the headphones on and all you could hear was Kurt Cobain's voice screaming through the house! It was pretty wild. My husband and I, we'd just look at each other and smile and go, 'You think we should close the window so the neighbors don't hear? So they don't think we're beating him or something!'"

Earl says the session lasted a few days. "I don't recall any of the songs being early versions of anything he did with Nirvana," she says. "It just resembled the Nirvana sound. The drums were strong and forceful and Kurt was playing some pretty good bass by this time. The guitar riffs were fast and furious, with a powerful hook. The lyrical content was rebellious and angry. Mostly slams against society in general. Kurt didn't like the social ladder in school. Kids thinking they were cool because they wore the 'right' clothes or were handsome or pretty, or had money. His songs back then reflected his opinions about these things." The final tape consisted of seven songs, including an early instrumental version of "Downer," which would appear on Nirvana's first album.

For the next few years, Cobain played in a variety of short-lived bands. In 1986 he fronted a one-off group featuring Crover on drums and Osborne on bass, performing under the name Brown Cow—the original name, Brown Towel had been misspelled on a poster—in Olympia, the Washington state capitol, an hour's drive from Aberdeen. It was at this performance that Cobain met Dylan Carlson, who became a longtime friend; Cobain would later record with Carlson's band Earth. He also played in a number of bands with Novoselic: one with Cobain on guitar, Novoselic on bass, and Bob McFadden on drums; another with Novoselic on guitar, Steve Newman on bass, and Cobain on drums. Both also played in the Stiff Woodies, which featured Osborne, Crover, Lukin, and Gary Cole. Novoselic played in another band with Osborne and original Melvins drummer Mike Dillard, and a Mentors cover band.

In 1987, Cobain and Novoselic teamed up once again, determined to keep this new band together at all costs. With Cobain on guitar and Novoselic on bass, the first in a long line of drummers was Aaron Burckhard. Their first performance by the then-unnamed band was at a house party at nearby Raymond. The band was soon playing in venues as far away as Tacoma (about an hour and a half drive from Aberdeen), and had run through a number of names, including Skid Row, Bliss, Pen Cap Chew (also the name of one of the band's songs), Ted Ed Fred, Throat Oyster, and Windowpane, before finally choosing the name that would stick, Nirvana.

The band's first recording was a nine song performance recorded live in the studio at KAOS, the radio station at Olympia's Evergreen State College in April '87. According to Steve Fisk, a producer who later worked with Nirvana, the band's appearance came about through the efforts of another local band, Danger Mouse, when two of the band's members, John Goodmanson and Donna Dresch, heard Nirvana and brought them up to KAOS to record. Six of the songs—"Spank Thru," "Love Buzz," "Floyd the Barber," "Downer," "Mexican Seafood," and "Hairspray Queen"—would be re-recorded nine months later, when the group recorded in a professional studio for the first time, Reciprocal Recording, in Seattle.

Reciprocal had started in 1986, in order to record the new crop of bands springing up in Seattle in the mid-'80s who were mixing punk and metal into a new style of music that would come to be called "grunge." Jack Endino, one of Reciprocal's engineers (and who also played in the band Skin Yard), had already ready recorded such groups as Green River (who would later split into Mudhoney and Mother Love Bone, the latter becoming Pearl Jam) and Soundgarden when he took a call from "Kurt Kovain" (as he wrote Cobain's name down in the studio's session log). "Kurt called up out of the blue," Endino remembers. "And said, 'We just want to record some songs really fast.' And so we did."

At this point, Cobain and Novoselic were no longer working with Burckhard, with whom they were dissatisfied. In October '87, they had gone so far as to place an ad in *The Rocket,* a Seattle-based music paper: "SERIOUS DRUMMER WANTED. Underground attitude, Black Flag, Melvins, Zeppelin, Scratch Acid, Ethel Merman. Versatile as heck. Kurdt 352–0992" (the number of Cobain's home in Olympia, where he was now living). Finally, they brought Dale Crover as their drummer when they showed up at Reciprocal on January 23, 1988 to record what Endino calls the *Dale Demo*. Endino adds that the group didn't appear to have a name yet; "The word 'Nirvana' was never mentioned until long after that. Months later. It was just Kurt Cobain and some friends. And they didn't even tell me how to spell his name!

"So they just came up and whipped out these ten songs in this one afternoon. And we mixed them right then. It wasn't a very serious mix.

And they took it home with them." The ten songs were, in order, "If You Must," "Downer," "Floyd the Barber," "Paper Cuts," "Spank Thru," "Hairspray Queen," "Aero Zeppelin," "Beeswax," "Mexican Seafood," and "Pen Cap Chew," which was given a fade-out ending as the tape was running out. Of the ten songs, "If You Must," "Spank Thru," and "Pen Cap Chew" remain officially unreleased. The entire session, including mixing, lasted six hours, from noon to six, though Endino only charged them for five, for a total of $152.44.

Endino had never seen the band before, and was particularly impressed with Cobain's voice. "His singing stood out because he was really pretty impassioned. And some of the songs were pretty good; it sounded as good as any of the Seattle bands that were getting hype at that point." Endino was so impressed he also made his own mix of the session after the band had left, so there are two mixes of the session in existence; Endino's rough one-hour mix (which the band took with them) and his own personal "after-hours" mix. It was this latter mix that Endino would pass on to Sub Pop co-founder Jonathan Poneman. Both mixes of the session have also made their way to the collector's circuit. And though the band didn't have a record out yet, "Floyd the Barber" was soon in regular rotation at KCMU, the college radio station at the University of Washington in Seattle.

A bootleg that exists from a Tacoma show around this period is said to be from December 1987, but Endino speculates that it might have been recorded the same day as the demo. "When we did the *Dale Demo*, they told me that day they were going to play a show down at [Tacoma's] Community World Theater. I think this is that same show, because they play the same songs from the demo, all ten, in the exact same order! Obviously fresh in their minds! I finally got to hear the actual ending of 'Pen Cap Chew' after all these years!" (the song was faded out on the demo, as the tape was running out). A slight reshuffling of the order became necessary during the set when a bass string breaks during "Hairspray"; the band returned to the song after going through the other demo tracks. They also performed two songs not recorded, or even played at the demo session—or at any other session that Endino worked on. It's worth mentioning that Nirvana played around ten original songs live that were never recorded in a studio.

A few months after being given a copy of *Dale Demo* by Endino, Poneman contacted Nirvana about recording for Sub Pop. The band had spent the early part of the year going through a series of drummers; Crover had moved with the Melvins to San Francisco, and was replaced by Dave Foster. It was this line-up that played Nirvana's first show in

Seattle at the Vogue, on April 24, '88, as part of the "Sub Pop Sunday" series. Among those in the audience was photographer Charles Peterson, who was doing work for the fledgling record label. "Bruce [Pavitt, Sub Pop's other co-founder] and Jon said, 'There's this band, Nirvana, they're going to be playing tonight, from Aberdeen, we think they're going to be the next big thing.' And I went and saw them and I thought they were atrocious! I had my camera there and I didn't bother to take pictures. I just thought, 'This is a joke. This is not going to go anywhere.'" Despite Peterson's initial impression, his photos of the group would be used on nearly every Nirvana release.

Foster's tenure with Nirvana was short-lived when, following a fight, he lost his driver's license. The band then worked with Burckhard again until he was arrested for drunk driving. They also placed another ad in *The Rocket* that ran in the magazine's March '88 issue: "DRUMMER WANTED. Play hard, sometimes light, underground, versatile, fast, medium slow, versatile, serious, heavy, versatile, dorky, nirvana, hungry. Kurdt 352–0992." Finally, Chad Channing, whom Cobain and Novoselic had first met when they played a show on the same bill with Channing's band, Tick-Dolly-Row, joined the band. Channing would remain with the group for next two years.

Shortly after Channing joined, Nirvana returned to Reciprocal to record their first single, once again working with Endino. There were a total of four sessions; June 11 (five hours), June 30 (five hours), July 16 (three hours) and September 27 (two hours). Four complete songs were recorded: a cover of Shocking Blue's "Love Buzz," and the originals "Big Cheese," "Blandest," and a re-recording of "Spank Thru" (with Endino on backing vocals). Endino says the third and fourth sessions were probably used to re-record the vocal for "Love Buzz," and mixing.

Cobain also brought along a 30-second sound collage he'd recorded on cassette at home that he wanted to use as the intro for "Love Buzz." It was shortened to around ten seconds for the single, and eliminated entirely on *Bleach*. The single is also a different mix, and another sound collage was dubbed into the instrumental break. "It's just barely audible underneath the guitar noise," says Endino. "And we had to do it live when we mixed because we had used up all eight tracks. So when we were mixing we had to have this cassette going through the mixing board along with the eight tracks from the eight track machine. And when we got to the middle part of the song, he had to reach over and press play on the cassette deck right at the right time, every time I went through the mix. So we had a sort of virtual ninth track! And when we went to remix the song for the album version, he had forgotten the cassette. So no sound collage, no nothing in the middle."

"Blandest" is the first true Nirvana outtake—a complete song recorded at an "official" recording session, as opposed to a demo session. "Blandest" has never been officially unreleased, and survived only because it made its way to the bootleg circuit. "It's basically lost," says Endino. "The only versions that exist are on bootlegs. They recorded this song, we did a rough mix of it, and then they decided they hated it. And they told me to erase it. Because they had no money, they were paying for the tapes. They said, 'Erase it and we'll do a better version of it later.' So we erased it and they never got around to recording it again.

"Chris asked me years later, 'You remember "Blandest"?'" Endino continues. "'Yeah, I remember "Blandest."' 'Do you have a tape of it anywhere?' 'No, I don't have a tape of it. You guys told me to erase it!' And then later I'm talking to some collector who informed me that he had a bootleg with 'Blandest' on it. I said, 'Oh my God, it can't be the one I'm thinking of, send me a copy.' And he sent me a copy and it was the song. It was a terrible rough mix with the drums way too loud, and it's been widely bootlegged now, and it's obviously from a cassette that went to the band. Because the only place where cassettes went was the band themselves and possibly Sub Pop. And whether anyone at Sub Pop got a hold of this song I don't remember. I don't think so though, because it was a rough mix and the band didn't like it, and they were pretty particular about not giving anything to Sub Pop unless they liked it. So all I can assume is that somebody stole some tapes from the band. I think that's where a lot of these bootlegs came from."

As the date for the single's release came closer, Sub Pop contacted photographer Alice Wheeler to take pictures for the cover sleeve. Wheeler had met Pavitt when she was living in Olympia, attending Evergreen State College, where Pavitt had also been a student. "He was always around talking about taking over the world and stuff," she says. "I'm always a person for that kind of thing!" Wheeler had also helped run the GESSCO hall in Olympia, where Cobain and an early version of Nirvana had played; she was also friends with Tracy Marander, Cobain's girlfriend at the time.

The "Love Buzz" photo session, Wheeler's first session for Sub Pop, was held in August or September. "We just went down to Tacoma," she says. "They wanted to go out to Never Never Land—a public park near the Tacoma Narrows Bridge—and so off we went. I was having technical difficulties; I didn't have a very good camera at the time. The pictures are infra-red so they're kind of fuzzy. One of them's really under-exposed and the other one's really over-exposed!" Wheeler thinks she was paid $25 for the session, during which she used around eight rolls of film.

"Love Buzz"/"Big Cheese" was finally released in November, launching the "Sub Pop Singles Club." The club had been conceived as a way to bring in a steady cash flow; for a one year subscription ($35 at the time), members would receive a limited-edition single through the mail. The singles were ostensibly only available through the club, but early singles in the series, including Nirvana's, were available through mail order, for a mere $3.50 (including postage). "Love Buzz" was packaged in a hand-numbered, fold-over sleeve (the number written in red), in a run of 1000. *Record Collector* also claims that a few jukebox singles were manufactured, in plain sleeves. The sleeve was the first to use an alternate spelling of Cobain's name, crediting him as "Kurdt Kobain." Cobain used this spelling of his name up to the release of *Nevermind,* and occasionally after—such as on November 26, 1993, when he signed a guitar after a show in Jacksonville, Florida, in this way.

As the release was near the holiday season, Cobain gave copies of his first single to members of his immediate family that Christmas. "I was really excited for him and proud of him," Mari Earl says. "As I was putting it back into the jacket, I laughed as I read 'Why don't you trade those guitars for shovels?' etched in the vinyl on the 'Love Buzz' side." Though both songs would later be available on the *Bleach* CD, the original single is now one of the group's most valuable releases. After Nirvana's break-through in 1992, the single's value jumped to $100; since Cobain's death, it has continued to increase, with at least one dealer offering it at the rather excessive price of $1000. As a result, counterfeit copies have been made in the U.S. and U.K.; the U.K. counterfeits are easier to spot, as the sleeves are not numbered.

In December '88, the re-recorded version of "Spank Thru" appeared on the box set *Sub Pop 200*. The set, issued in a run of 5000, was made up of three 12-inch EPs, and a booklet, and was packaged in a plain black box; other groups on the set included Soundgarden, Mudhoney, and the late poet Jesse Bernstein. The set later appeared on a single CD; in 1989, a "condensed" version of the set, entitled *Sub Pop Rock City,* was released in Europe on Glitterhouse.

The photo of Nirvana that appeared in the *Sub Pop 200* booklet came from Charles Peterson's first "formal"—as opposed to live—session with the group. Peterson thinks the session took place in the late spring or early summer of '88, and was as casual as Wheeler's first session of the group.

They decided to take the ferry over to Bainbridge Island, where Channing lived, and, Peterson remembers, "We drove all over the countryside with Shocking Blue playing on the cassette. It was really fun. The setting kind of fit more who they were at the time, 'cause they really weren't much of an urban band at all. They were hicks from the sticks."

Peterson's subsequent sessions with Nirvana proved to be equally informal. "I'd be like, 'Well what would you guys like to do?' 'I don't know.' 'Okay, well, it's a sunny day, let's just go down to the waterfront.' When I photograph a band posed, and Nirvana particularly, I just wanted to make it as comfortable and natural as possible. English rock photographers always try and do something really clever with the band. And I was just always more interested in composition and lighting, no matter what they're doing."

December '88 also marked the beginning of the recording sessions for the band's first album, *Bleach*. There were a total of six sessions; December 24 (five hours), December 29 (five hours), December 30 (five hours), December 31 (four and a half hours), January 14, 1989 (five hours), and January 24, 1989 (five and a half hours). Songs recorded included "Blew," "About a Girl," "School," "Negative Creep," "Scoff," "Swap Meet," "Mr. Moustache," and "Sifting," all of which appeared on *Bleach*. The song "Big Long Now" was also recorded during these sessions, but was ultimately cut from album's line-up; "At the last minute Kurt decided that there was already enough slow, heavy stuff on *Bleach*, and he didn't want that song to go out," Endino explains.

Endino also says that at least one session, probably December 24, was used for a bit of experimentation. "The band came in and said, 'We're going to tune our instruments way down, really low and we're going to try recording all these songs this way,'" he remembers. "I think Kurt was having trouble singing and wanted to make it a little easier for himself. Well, of course they were way out of tune, and didn't sound too good. So they ended up hating it, and then came back another day and re-recorded all of it! I think the only one we kept in that tuning was 'Blew.' And all the rest of it was erased!" Or almost all; early versions of at least "Sifting," "Blew," and "Mr. Moustache" recorded at the time have turned up on bootlegs. But the general practice, says Endino: "If it wasn't good, we just erased over it and did a better version."

Though the bulk of the album was rooted in the grunge vein, there was a nod to the band's budding pop sensibility already exhibited on "Love Buzz" and "Spank Thru" with "About a Girl," which opened with the gentle strumming of a guitar instead of a thudding drumbeat or howling scream. "I think Kurt felt nervous about putting 'About a Girl' on there," Endino says. "But he was very insistent on it. He said, 'I've got a song that's totally different from the others, Jack, you've gotta just humor me here, 'cause we're gonna do this real pop tune.' I was like, 'Great, fine, whatever.' I think the question was raised at some point, gee, I wonder if Sub Pop's going to like this, and we decided, 'Who cared?' It's your album; put it on. And Sub Pop said nothing. In fact, I think they liked it a lot. Jonathan is a total pop head. And Bruce actually didn't like *Bleach* that much anyway, because I think he thought it was a little too heavy metal."

Though *Bleach* provided Nirvana with a powerful base from which to grow, Endino admits he'd have liked to have worked with the group when they had more time and money to spend. "It's nice doing a record quickly, but then, it's nice to not be in a hurry," he says. "To be able to step back and go, 'Wait a minute. Let's get a different drum sound on this song. Why don't we play with a different guitar amplifier?' That's the sort of thing you can't do when you've got a day to do an album. You just have to set up the mikes and go. Which is why *Bleach* pretty much has the same guitar sound from beginning to end 'cause we had one guitar amp, one day to record it. We recorded on 8-track, but we didn't even use all of them—we used six or seven, usually. You basically just roll tape. And that's what's fun about indie rock, but that's also what limits it sometimes."

After the recording of *Bleach,* Jason Everman joined the band as a second guitarist in time for a short West Coast tour. Everman was another friend of Dylan Carlson's, had previously played in high school bands with Channing, and had also lived in Aberdeen as a child. Though he didn't play on the record, Everman paid the recording bill ($606.17), and was credited with playing guitar; he was also pictured on the album cover shot and on the limited edition poster included with some copies of the album.

Everman ended up only playing on one session with the band that spring at Evergreen State College, when Nirvana recorded "Do You Love Me" for a Kiss covers compilation Seattle indie label C/Z was planning to put out (the session also yielded an early version of "Dive"). The idea for the album had originated with Australian-based indie label Waterfront Records, who distributed C/Z's records in Australia (C/Z returned the favor by distributing Waterfront's records in the U.S.). "We struck a deal where I would help to get a number of bands and make the product more of an international thing," says Daniel House, C/Z's owner. "And in turn, if Sub Pop wasn't interested in licensing the record domestically, he was going to give it to me. And Sub Pop passed; they thought it was too gimmicky and weren't interested. And I was totally interested." The album was released the following year.

Bleach was finally released on June 15. Sub Pop's one-page catalogue boasted "Hypnotic and righteous heaviness from these Olympia pop stars [though actually Cobain was the only member living in Olympia]. They're young, they own their own van, and they're going to make us rich!" The first 1000 copies appeared on white vinyl, the next 2000 came with a poster. In the U.K., the album was released on the Tupelo label in August, with the first 300 on white vinyl, the next 2000 on green; there have been subsequent reissues in different colors. In Australia, the album was released on Waterfront, with the first 500 on blue vinyl; the words "Nirvana" and "Bleach" on the cover were in blue and yellow. Subsequent issues were again in different colors.

Choosing a cover shot for the album was somewhat problematic. A session was done with Alice Wheeler, but the results were unsatisfactory. "Nirvana came over to my house in the afternoon," she says, "and we went up the street and took some pictures and they weren't that great. It was kind of funny, because Jason was like Mr. Glamboy compared to Kurt; Kurt looks pretty washed in most of those pictures, I don't like them very much. And the band didn't like them. And I don't want someone to have pictures they don't like of themselves for their record. Bruce loved 'em. But of course he liked the idea of the scary hick from Aberdeen. And I think that kind of hurt Kurt's feelings.

"But Tracy's picture ended up on the cover, and I thought that was really nice," she adds. Marander's picture was a live shot of the group performing at the Reko/Muse gallery in Olympia; the poster shot, taken by Charles Peterson, is from a show at the HUB Ballroom at the University of Washington, February 25, 1989.

The U.S. and U.K. albums differed in that the U.S. version featured "Love Buzz," while the U.K. version had "Big Cheese" instead. The U.S. CD issue featured both tracks, along with another cut from the *Dale Demo,* "Downer." In the U.K., the *Bleach* CD initially mirrored its vinyl counterpart; a later issue contained both "Love Buzz" and "Downer." Remastered versions of both the CD and cassette were issued in 1992. The CD used another of Peterson's shots from the February '89 show in the insert, in addition to a shot from a February 15, 1990 show at Raji's, Los Angeles on the back inner sleeve.

The *Dale Demo* versions of "Floyd" and "Paper Cuts" were used on the album "because they weren't happy with the way Chad was playing," Endino says. "Dale had pretty much written the drum part for those two songs; he played them the best. And Chad was good on the stuff that they had written with him. That's the way it is with drummers. So Chad did all the new stuff, and then those two songs they pretty much wanted to use the *Dale* version." Both songs were remixed for the album, with backing vocals added to "Paper Cuts"; Endino doesn't remember if "Downer" was remixed when it was added to the CD.

Endino also says the album's original sequence was different. "The band phoned it to me; they said, 'Here's the list,'" he says. "And then Pavitt listened to it and he didn't like it. So he said, 'Let's change the sequence, let's put "Blew" first, and put this second and put this third.' So then they called me up and said, 'Bruce wants us to resequence it, so here's the new order.' So then I had to go back and resplice the whole thing again." All Endino can remember of the original line-up is that "Floyd the Barber" may have been the first track.

Back in Aberdeen, Cobain's family was keeping up with his band's progress. "When *Bleach* came out, I remember going down to visit Kurt's mom," says Mari Earl. "She was playing the album really loud on her stereo. Having it up that loud just about drove me crazy, so I don't remember much more about that particular visit!"

It was during this year that Nirvana also signed a contract with Sub Pop. At the time, most agreements with indie labels in the Northwest were sealed by verbal commitments or handshakes. Jesse Bernstein was the first Sub Pop artist who demanded a record contract, and Nirvana was soon to follow. The contract was for one year, January 1 to December 31, 1989, with two further one year options. The band was to turn in three album master tapes during this period, and would receive $600 from the label for the first year, $12,000 for the second, and $24,000 for the third. The contract was signed by all four members of the band.

As the band was on their first U.S. tour that summer, the first side-project involving a member of the group was released in July. Cobain joined Olympia's Go Team on their one-sided single "Scratch It Out"/"Bikini Twilight" released on K Records (both songs on one side). The Go Team had a revolving membership, based around core member Calvin Johnson, K's founder, and Tobi Vail (spelled "Vale" on the sleeve), later Cobain's girlfriend, and also a founding member of Bikini Kill. Cobain (again spelled "Kurdt Kobain") is credited with guitar.

The Go Team had actually planned to release a single every month in 1989. "It was just a grand idea we had where we would release one every month," explains K's Candice Pederson. "But we fell behind. And then the core of the Go Team broke up while they were on tour, and so it went as far as August. We also had the grand plan that we were going to package them, in a bag, with a label on top, kind of like cheap candy. But after the first month—I mean, my God, we were hand-stapling them, and stuffing them and pressing the bags and I was just like, 'This is really a nice concept but it's not going to work for 12 months!' It was just a very laborious project. But ideally we would have 12 of those singles and I think it would have made a nice package. But we had nine which is really good."

After the U.S. tour, Cobain planned another side-project with Mark Lanegan, lead singer of Screaming Trees. "Mark and Kurt got together," remembers Endino. "I think they got drunk together, or really stoned, and wrote a bunch of songs, and got all excited and told Jonathan, 'Hey we want to do an album together! And we've got a name for it—we're going to call it the Jury.' And so Jonathan said, 'Okay, okay, get in with Jack and record.' And then finally they show up at the studio, and they go 'Well, we forgot all the songs, 'cause we didn't tape any of them! And I lost my lyric book.'"

As a result, all that came out of the the Jury sessions (August 20, six hours; August 28, three and a half hours) were two Leadbelly songs; "Where Did You Sleep Last Night?" and "Ain't It a Shame." Lanegan sang lead on "Where Did You Sleep . . .", with Cobain on guitar and Novoselic on bass; Cobain took over on lead on "Ain't It a Shame," and Mark Pickerel of the Screaming Trees played drums. "That was going to be the Jury single," says Endino. "But nothing ever came of it. And ultimately Lanegan came in and did his solo album [*The Winding Sheet*] and ended up putting 'Where Did You Sleep Last Night?' on his album. And 'Ain't It a Shame,' ended up in the vaults somewhere. That one, as far as I know, has never been bootlegged. Maybe Sub Pop will put it out someday."

In addition to "Where Did You Sleep . . ." (which was remixed for the album) Cobain contributed background vocals to another track on *The Winding Sheet,* "Down in the Dark." Though it's not known which day Cobain recorded his vocals, dates for the Lanegan sessions were: December 10–11 (nine hours both days), December 14, 16 (seven hours both days), December 18 (ten hours), December 20 (eight hours), and January 1, 1990 (nine hours).

The U.S. tour resulted in Everman's departure from the group; Cobain and Novoselic said he was fired, Everman claimed he quit. So when the band next entered the studio, they were back to being a three piece, much to producer Steve Fisk's surprise. "I was excited about doing a four piece thing, but they explained Jason wasn't going to be part of the session," he says. "Jason was in the Sub Pop office telling people he was still in the band, but he was not."

The sessions, held at Seattle's Music Source studio, were for the purpose of recording material for an EP to promote the band's upcoming European tour, though as it turned out, the record wasn't released until after the tour was completed. Fisk remembers the sessions as lasting two evenings. "The Music Source didn't do rock stuff in the daytime except on the weekends," he explains. "So the rock stuff started at 6 PM. I think it was booked for three evenings and we may have done it in two. We recorded all the basics, and then I think we got back the next week and did the vocals and the mixes and the guitar parts. The mixes may have gone on a third night, but it was a very cheap, quickie session."

Though the band had not yet toured extensively, their habit of regularly trashing their instruments during shows meant their equipment was not in the best shape. "Their gear was falling about," Fisk remembers. "The fiberglass drums were cracked and held together with tape. The bass amp and the speakers were blown up and rumbling. It was a lot like recording some dodgy band with broken-up gear where you realize, 'Things would sound a lot better if we had this or this or this, but this is what we have.' And so you sort of equalize around that.

"Chris was really bummed out because he'd been in Olympia all day, running around trying to get his bass tweaked," Fisk continues. "And apparently got it better but not fixed! So the big amplifier sound was shit. And the drums were kind of classless in the first place; that's the point of fiberglass drums. They all sound the same. And Chris had been doing this trick where he'd been using the bass like a hatchet to split the kick drum, and there was tons and tons and tons of duct tape all around the drum holding it together."

The group worked on five songs; "Been a Son," "Stain," "Even in His Youth," "Polly," and "Token Eastern Song." "The songs were together," says Fisk. "They didn't record 'em quick; they did a lot of trying it again. There was a little sort of medium tension, talking to each other in between takes. I just tried to help; I didn't really have any great ideas. Though if I would've explained that not saying 'fuck' so much in 'Stain,' that song could've been a hit! But I just didn't have the forethought then as a record producer to say, 'Kurt, you can't say "fuck" that many times. It just won't fly on the radio.' It was hard to really have the scope back then.

"'Been a Son,' I've been told by several people, is the most commonly bootlegged Nirvana track," Fisk continues. "In every bootleg you get, it's like the first thing people do, is they take this beautifully recorded CD and just make a copy of it! The signature with that one is the huge bass solo in the middle. Instead of a guitar solo, it's a bass solo that's like twice as loud as the song, so when it stops the band sounds kind of wimpy and stupid. That's actually where a lot of the work was. They were just trying to figure out how big they could make things, and how small they could make things. So I did a lot of following orders and changing shit around. And that was really fun."

The session was a clear demonstration of how Nirvana was progressing toward even more of a pop sound. "I got them thinking about Top 40 radio, and their drum sound, and how that relates to Top 40 radio," says Fisk. "After I'd been working on the mix all evening, in a soft, considered voice we were talking about making the snare bigger. I was playing with early '80s ideas with mid-'80s toys. We were turning the three-part guitar thing all the way down; it's three tracks, exactly the same guitar part, with exactly the same EQ, one in the middle, one on the left, one on the right! And we were turning those down and turning those up, and Kurt got all excited about it, because it was a good Top 40 drum sound."

"Been a Son" and "Stain" were finished and appeared on the *Blew* EP. The other three songs were unfinished. "I think the idea was to finish two and we were supposed to finish the other ones at a later date, and we just never got around to it," says Fisk. "They were talking to me about maybe working on their new record for Sub Pop. But that was a long way away. Jonathan was offering them ten, twelve-thousand to spend on their next record and they hadn't even figured out what they were going to do."

The uncompleted songs have scratch vocals, and Fisk doubts there are any other outtakes or alternate versions. "There's five songs on one reel," he says. "There probably is not a lot of multiples. There might be bits and pieces. There was no money. It was recorded on some used tape that we had lying around. Sub Pop was broke. And they wanted to do everything as cheap as possible, so any corner we could cut, we would cut. That was how it was back then."

Fisk also remembers Nirvana's more playful side in the studio. "When 'Been a Son' was done, Kurt and Chris asked, 'Can we dance on the tables?'" he says. "And I said, 'Okay.' So they jumped up on one table and they rocked, and I jumped up on another and rocked. Me and Chris were almost up to the ceiling and Chad was in the other room watching TV or something. And as we listened to the song, we rocked. Ah! That's cool! That's fucking cool. Not a lot of people ever got to do that. I got to nail the mix and jump up on the furniture and rock with Nirvana."

In October, Nirvana went on their first European tour, with TAD. While on tour, they recorded a session for John Peel's radio show in London, performing "Love Buzz," "About a Girl," "Polly" (then still unreleased), and "Spank Thru." In Hilversum, Holland, they recorded another session for radio station VPRO, performing "About a Girl," and "Dive," the latter also unreleased at that point.

In November, the first Nirvana track to not appear on Sub Pop was released, when "Mexican Seafood," a track from the *Dale Demo*, appeared on the compilation EP *Teriyaki Asthma, Vol. 1* (the first in a series of ten EPs), released on C/Z. Daniel House had been interested in Nirvana ever since Endino had played him the *Dale Demo* [both Endino and House were in Skin Yard]. "Jack was in the studio going 'Dude, you gotta hear this. You're not going to believe this. This band's amazing!'" House remembers. "So within a week of their recording that first demo, I'd heard of them, had received a tape and had fallen in love with their music!"

Some of Nirvana's early Seattle shows also saw them sharing the bill with Skin Yard. "They were very very timid, very gawky, awkward looking," says House. "This big tall lanky bass player who didn't look comfortable in his own body, and you had this timid frail guy who seemed to be afraid of getting too close to the mike, but the music was still really powerful." House would have offered Nirvana a deal with C/Z, "but Jonathan jumped on them so fast," he says. Nonetheless, he arranged to have the group contribute a track to C/Z's upcoming Kiss tribute album, and asked to use "Mexican Seafood" on *Teriyaki Asthma*. The other artists on the 7-inch EP were Coffin Break, Helios Creed, and Yeast. The EP was probably issued in a limited edition run of 1000; House thinks it may have been as many 1500 copies, and adds, "We must've done some on colored vinyl I'm sure!"

The *Blew* EP was the next Nirvana record to be released, in December in the U.K. only, as both a 12-inch and CD, on Tupelo. The songs were "Blew," "Love Buzz," "Been a Son," and "Stain," with the cover photos again shot by Tracy Marander. That same month, Novoselic married his longtime girlfriend on December 30.

As 1990 dawned, Nirvana spent January 2 and 3 working with Endino at Reciprocal, for seven hours and three hours, respectively. "This was when they came in and just did one song, 'Sappy,'" he says. "That was first time I knew that Kurt was fallible, because everything he'd done had been brilliant to me up to then. And then there was this song which just didn't seem that interesting. And he was determined to get it. And I was like 'No, write some more songs, Kurt!'"

In fact, Cobain was working on a number of new songs, which would be recorded that spring, when the band began work on what they believed would be their second album for Sub Pop. One of the new songs was previewed when the group shot four videos over spring break at Evergreen State College with a crew of three, including Alex Kostelnik, who wrote about the experience in an unpublished manuscript. "I showed Kurt how to edit the stuff he taped off TV to use for background footage in the videos. Our payment? Forty dollars and some pizza." The four songs were "School," the new song "Lithium," "Big Cheese," and "Floyd the Barber." The videos are essentially performance videos, the "background" footage consisting, among other things, of shots of Shaun Cassidy. They have never been officially released, though they have appeared on the collector's circuit.

The band had gone on a short West Coast tour in February, and in April began another U.S. tour. Prior to the tour, the band spent the first week in April in Madison, Wisconsin, recording at Smart Studios with Butch Vig. Vig had previously worked with a number of Sub Pop bands, and though he was aware of Nirvana, he admits, "I wasn't totally crazy about *Bleach* the first time I heard it. Except I really loved 'About a Girl.' The funny thing was, I remember Jonathan Poneman saying, 'If you saw Nirvana here in Seattle, it's like Beatlemania. And they're going to be as big as the Beatles!' And I'm thinking to myself, 'Yeah, right.' Now all I hear is, 'This band's going to be the next Nirvana!' "

As far as Vig and the band knew, the sessions were for the purpose of recording Nirvana's second Sub Pop album. "When they showed up, they were actually very funny and charming, particularly Chris," Vig remembers. "Kurt was always an enigma. He was very charming when he came, and then he would get really moody and sit in the corner and not talk for 45 minutes. I didn't really have to do too much fine tuning in terms of what they were doing. They had been playing most of the songs, the arrangements were pretty solid. I could tell that Kurt wasn't too pleased with Chad's drumming, because he kept going and getting behind the kit showing him how to play things."

The band ended up recording at least seven songs: "Dive," "In Bloom," "Polly," "Pay to Play," "Lithium," "Immodium," and "Sappy," most of them having been in the band's repertoire for the last six months. As usual, the emphasis was on recording quickly. "Most of the Sub Pop records I made we'd do in a week," Vig says. "Record, track over two or three days, and then overdub a couple days, and finish the vocals or whatever, and then mix two or three days. But Kurt was having problems with his voice. Basically he'd be able to get through one or two takes, except for something like 'Polly' which was soft. All the other stuff he was singing, he'd get through one or two takes and wouldn't be able to sing anymore. I remember we had to take one day off in the middle of recording."

The songs themselves were undeniably the strongest material Nirvana had come up with to date. "I thought they were totally amazing," says Vig. "The songs were much more focused in terms of melody. They still had the punk attitude, but they were really really hooky songs. 'In Bloom' was an amazingly hooky song when that chorus comes in. And Kurt's lyric writing was becoming even more enigmatic. You weren't quite sure what he was singing about, but you knew it was really intense. I thought that his songwriting was just amazing. He'd really developed. I also realized a lot of the stuff, a lot of the hooks in the songs, Chris was writing on bass. And I think that Kurt basically let him come up with his own parts. They're great hooks."

Vig also says that the band recorded a cover of the Velvet Underground's "Here She Comes Now" at Smart, and it's possibly this version that turned up later that year later on *Heaven and Hell Vol. 1*. But he doesn't think there were any other songs, or outtakes saved. "If a take wasn't a keeper, we'd just erase it and do another one," he says. "I sent the tapes to Sub Pop; there may be something else on them. And I don't know if Kurt had any other songs finished or not, 'cause he didn't play me anything else at the time."

The band had to go out on tour before being able to complete the album. "Initially, I think they were planning on coming back and doing some more stuff, or they had talked about me going to Seattle," says Vig. "But it was all fairly up in the air at that point. Very shortly after that is when they started talking to Geffen." In fact, the proposed album for Sub Pop now became a demo the band sent to major labels in hopes of a new deal. Other friends received copies of the tape as well; Endino remembers being given one with the request "Don't tell Jonathan I gave you this!" He was also amused at the reappearance of "Sappy." "It's just not a memorable tune," he contends. "There's four versions of that song; there's the one I did, there's the one they did with Butch Vig, there's the one that's on that CD [*No Alternative*, with the song retitled "Verse Chorus Verse"], and there's an acoustic version floating around on bootlegs. I mean, Kurt just could not give up on that song!"

While on tour, the band made another video, of the Smart Studios version of "In Bloom." The video later appeared on the *Sub Pop Video Network Program 1*, released in 1991 (and the only official release of this version of "In Bloom"), by which time Channing was no longer in the band, and the band was no longer with Sub Pop. After the spring U.S.

tour, Channing was fired, though like Everman, he says he quit. In assessing the situation, Endino observes, "All I can think, is the reason they got rid of Chad was more personality-wise. I always thought Dale was a brilliant drummer, and it was pretty hard for anybody to come up and fill his shoes. And when Chad first joined the band, he had to sweat it a little bit; it took Chad a while to get into the groove of it. When I recorded the 'Love Buzz' single, I didn't think he was very good. He wasn't hitting very hard; it was hard to record him. That's why the drum sound on 'Love Buzz' is really not that great, because I had to do horrible things with it to try and make it sound good at all. Because he was barely touching the drums.

"By the time they did *Bleach* he was playing much better," Endino continues, "and by the time they did those demos with Butch Vig, I thought he was playing very very well indeed. And then they got Dave. You'll notice if you play the Chad demos for the *Nevermind* stuff, and compare them to *Nevermind*, they're exactly the same drum part. The guy was getting pretty good when they got rid of him. But Dave is obviously an amazing drummer himself, so what are you going to do? He was a much harder hitter than almost anybody."

May '90 saw the release of Mark Lanegan's *The Winding Sheet* on Sub Pop, the first 1000 copies on red vinyl. Nirvana brought Dale Crover back in as drummer for a West Coast tour in August, but used Dan Peters, Mudhoney's drummer, in their next trip to the studio. With plans for a second album still on hold, Sub Pop at least wanted to put out another Nirvana single. "Dive" was chosen from the Vig sessions, and the A-side, "Sliver," was recorded at Reciprocal on July 11.

Endino already had a session with TAD that day. "Jonathan called up and was begging, 'We want Nirvana to cut this one song really fast while they're in town. And is there any way they can use Tad's equipment?' And Tad was like, 'This is our time, we're trying to record something here.' He was kind of testy about it. And I was like, 'Well, you guys go and eat dinner. I'm sure we can do this in an hour.' And Nirvana just came in and used their bass and guitar and drum set and did it. There were two takes of 'Sliver.' Only one of them was finished. And they're almost identical. And then we spent an entire day [July 24] re-doing the vocals and maybe some guitar and mixing it."

In August, Nirvana's second track for C/Z, "Do You Love Me," appeared with the release of the Kiss tribute album *Hard to Believe*. The album has several variations. The U.S. release was a single album, initially in a gatefold sleeve, then a single sleeve. It was later released on CD and cassette. The U.S. version also has four tracks (by Skin Yard, Coffin Break, Hullabaloo, and the Melvins) not found on any other version. The U.K. release (on Southern) and European release were also single albums, while the Australian release, on Waterfront, was a double album.

There are also two different issues of the CD and cassette. "Gene Simmons was getting ready to do *Kiss My Ass,* and he decided it was time to eliminate the competition on the playing field, and decided to call Waterfront and say 'Cease and Desist,'" says Daniel House. "And what he cited as the reason for doing this was unauthorized use of the Kiss logo, and 'You have used paintings of us and we have not given you permission to use our likenesses!' Waterfront panicked and freaked-out. So we faced with possibility of a suit. So we repackaged it before we 'ceased.'" The second cover has no logo, no pictures, and the "i" in the word Kiss is replaced by a pair of lips—actually the lip prints of *The Rocket* magazine's receptionist at the time, C/Z then based in an office down the hall. On the inside is the request "Love you, Gene baby. Please don't sue us." There was also a reshuffling of the lineup, with two tracks removed and a Treepeople track added. The album is now out of print.

Dan Peters was also Nirvana's drummer on September 22, when the band played the Motor Sports International Garage in Seattle. The space was not a music club at all, but a real garage, since torn down and replaced by an open-air parking lot. The other bands on the bill were The Derelicts, The Dwarves, and The Melvins. A color shot by Charles Peterson from the show appears on the back inside cover of *Incesticide*. Alice Wheeler was also present. "I was out in the audience and Dylan Carlson and found me and brought me backstage," she says. "Kurt had told him to come and find me, and told me to take pictures!"

Also in attendance at the show was Dave Grohl, who had flown up to audition as Nirvana's new drummer. Though only 21 at the time, Grohl already had an impressive musical background. Born in Warren, Ohio, in 1969, Grohl grew up in Springfield, Virginia, and began playing guitar around age 10. He soon formed a duo, the H. G. Hancock Band, with his friend Larry Hinkle and began making tapes. He received his first electric guitar at Christmas when he was 12, and in the summer of 1984, at age 15, he joined his first band, Freak Baby.

It was at this time that Grohl met Barrett Jones, when Freak Baby recorded a cassette at Jones's Laundry Room Studios in Arlington, Virginia—so named because the studio was originally in the laundry room of Jones's parents house. The cassette was sold locally, and Grohl and Jones established a firm friendship. "I pretty much recorded every other band that he was in!" says Jones. "We were always doing music together, when he wasn't touring or something like that." At one point, Grohl even played drums in Jones's band Churn.

A line-up change in Freak Baby saw Grohl moving from guitar to drums, after which the band changed their name to Mission Impossible. The band broke up in the summer of 1985, their sole recorded output a split single with Lunchmeat. Grohl then formed the band Dain Bramage, who recorded one album, *I Scream Not Coming Down*. "None of this stuff was ever really released in anything more than 500 or 1000 copies total, and it never really got distributed," says Jones.

By the spring of 1987, Grohl joined Washington D.C. hardcore band Scream. Grohl played on the band's fourth album, *No More Censorship*, released in 1988 on RAS. In 1989, the band released *Live at Van Hall in Amsterdam* on Konkurrel. The band also released a self-titled live album on the Your Choice Live Series label, and the single "Mardi Gras"/"Land Torn Down" before disbanding in 1990. Throughout this period, Grohl continued recording solo material at the Laundry Room, eventually building up a huge backlog of material; "There's an awful lot of that stuff!" says Jones.

Cobain and Novoselic had admired Grohl's drumming in Scream, and he was readily welcomed into Nirvana. After a short stay with Novoselic in Tacoma, Grohl moved in with Cobain, who was still living in Olympia. During an appearance on KAOS a week after the Motorsports show, Cobain announced that Grohl was the band's new drummer, even though Peters had not yet been told he was out of the band. Cobain also performed a few acoustic songs on air, including "Lithium" and "Opinion," the latter a song never released by Nirvana.

"Sliver"/"Dive" was released in September, the first 3000 on blue vinyl. "Sliver" is the only Nirvana single on Sub Pop still in print, and it's been reissued in a number of colors; original copies are in fold-over sleeves, while reissues are in solid sleeves. In January '91, "Sliver" was released in the U.K. in a variety of formats. The rarest is the orignal 7-inch, packaged in a gatefold sleeve, the first 2000 on green vinyl. The 12-inch single added a live version of "About a Girl" (in a twist, it's the orignal, black vinyl version of the single that's more valuable; the blue vinyl is a reissue), and the CD had live versions of both "About a Girl" and "Spank Thru" (misspelled "Through"). The cover featured another of Charles Peterson's shots from the Raji's gig in February '90. The A-side also features a telephone conversation between Jonathan Poneman and an inebriated Novoselic at the end of the song, recorded on Novoselic's answering machine.

Another Nirvana track appeared in October, when "Here She Comes Now" was officially released on the Velvet Underground tribute *Heaven and Hell Vol. 1,* released in the U.K. on Imaginary Records, on vinyl, cassette, and CD. The album was released in the U.S. the following year on Communion, and the Nirvana track was released by the same label as a split single with the Melvins, released in seven different colors of vinyl. Imaginary reissued the CD in the U.K. in 1994, retitled *Fifteen Minutes: A Tribute to the Velvet Underground.*

That fall, Nirvana toured the U.K. for the second time, their first time with Grohl. They recorded another session for John Peel, particularly of interest as the entire set consisted of covers: the Wipers' "D-7," Devo's "Turnaround," and the Vaselines' "Molly's Lips," and "Son of a Gun." The band was back at The Music Source on January 1, 1991, recording their first new material with Grohl, "Aneurysm" (which featured one of Cobain's most bloodcurdling screams) and a re-recording of "Even in His Youth."

In November '90, Nirvana had signed with the management company Gold Mountain, and was preparing to sign to DGC. But since their contract with DGC wouldn't be signed until April 30, '91, Nirvana was still technically signed to Sub Pop at the time of January '91 session. Even so, the Music Source session was a private endeavor. "This was not for Sub Pop or anything," Steve Fisk confirms. "This was something Nirvana was doing with Craig [Montgomery], their soundman, who was friends with this other guy, Brian, that worked at The Music Source. Remember how much money Sub Pop owed everybody then? So Nirvana figured their own way in."

In addition to the two completed tracks, Fisk thinks there may have been other material recorded. "There were a lot of things with scratch vocals that Kurt was just playing with," he says. "I was talking with Brian, and he said there was a lot of *In Utero* stuff. I was really surprised. But maybe I heard him wrong. Sorry, dear readers! I think some of the Nirvana tapes got lost in the shuffle. I helped rescue the session I did for Sub Pop, but that was way before the studio was closed down. And I think there was one quarter inch that Brian found, and there was another one that I thought I saw that was untraceable. I think it was a really quick session; it might have been a weekend or one day on a weekend."

In addition to receiving a buyout fee of $75,000 from DGC, a percentage of Nirvana's first two albums (*Incesticide* was later added to the deal), and their logo on the DGC albums, Sub Pop was able to squeeze out one more Nirvana single, albeit a split single with The Fluid. Like their first single for the label, "Molly's Lips" (b/w The Fluid's "Candy") was another Singles Club release; it was issued in January '91. The first 4000 copies were on green vinyl, the rest of the run, 3500, on black, and the foldover sleeve folded horizontally, not vertically. The sleeve featured another Charles Peterson shot, from his last formal session with Chad Channing—an appropriate choice, given that "Molly's Lips" was a live version recorded in Portland in the spring of '90 when Channing was still in the band. The single also has the word "Later" etched in the run-out groove.

While waiting for formal details with DGC to be completed, Nirvana prepared to record their major label debut, which would be called *Nevermind*. Their first choice of producer was Butch Vig, then working with the Smashing Pumpkins on Gish. Though Vig was aware of their interest, he says "I wasn't really sure if I was going to do the record, 'cause I was so very unknown that I think the label thought it would be smarter for them to work with a more experienced producer. It sounded like Don Dixon was going to produce, and I was just going to engineer it. But I think they felt comfortable working with me and they liked some of the sounds that I had got on the earlier recordings. And at the eleventh hour the band just decided that they wanted me to do it. Literally it was about a week before we started, I got a call that said, 'Can you leave next week?' And I had a couple things scheduled, but I just moved 'em around. I was excited about doing this. It was my first major label album."

The band planned to re-record most of the songs from the Smart Studios sessions: "In Bloom," "Lithium," "Pay to Play" (now rewritten and retitled "Stay Away"), and "Immodium" (now retitled "Breed"). "Polly" would be taken straight from the Smart sessions, and remixed. The band was also working on new material, including the song that would be their break-through single, "Smells Like Teen Spirit." The band first played the song in public in one of their last small scale shows in Seattle, April 17 at the O.K. Hotel. To a packed house, Cobain introduced the band by proclaiming, "Hello, we're major label corporate rock sell-outs," the crowd cheering in response. "Teen Spirit" was still obviously a work-in-progress; the melody was worked out, but the only part of the lyrics that would survive was the chorus.

A week before recording started, Vig received a demo tape from the band, "a really really raw boombox cassette recording," he says. "It distorted so badly that you could barely make out what they're playing. I still have that cassette somewhere." Recording began in May at Sound City Studios in Van Nuys, California. It was the first time Vig had worked with

Grohl. "Kurt had called me up and said, 'I have the best drummer in the world now. He plays louder and harder than anybody I've ever met.' And I'm like, 'Yeah, right.' But they were totally right on the first day they set up in the rehearsal room. Kurt's guitar was super loud and the bass was super loud, but the drums, there were no mics on them in this room and they were just as loud acoustically as the amps. And also Dave turned out to be so cool; really easy to work with, and full of energy, and really brought a lot of life and fun to the sessions. He kept it real light."

Rehearsals were kept short. "I didn't want them to play too much 'cause I didn't want them to burn out on the songs," Vig explains. "But I remember after hearing 'Teen Spirit,' I was so into the song I had them play it as much as possible! The song was amazing." Recording soon began at Sound City, and continued into June. The studio was chosen, Vig says, because the band "wanted to work in a live tracking room that was cost effective. It also had a Neve board, and so that fit the bill. And they'd done a lot of classic records there in the '70s and the '80s, like Tom Petty, the Jacksons, Rick Springfield and Fleetwood Mac. A lot of big records were done there. It was a pretty simple studio. It was fairly bare bones. But they did have really good mics."

It was a learning experience for both the band and producer, each working for a major label for the first time. "I got the band to do some things I think they didn't necessarily want to do," says Vig. "The first recording [at Smart] was very very simple and had very few overdubs. Now I got to work more on the production, and got them to do more vocal overdubs, and more guitar overdubs, and basically tried to make the record a lot more fuller sounding. They sounded so amazing live, to me, that in order to get that kind of sound on record you had to use more production work in the studio; doubling guitars, using multiple mics on things and splitting them left and right, just trying to make it sound larger than life 'cause that's how they sounded when they played live.

"The songs were basically in really in good shape, but I did do more arranging with them," Vig continues. " 'Teen Spirit' was longer and the little ad-libs after the chorus were actually at the end of the song. I suggested putting those in at the end of each chorus as a bridge into the next verse. And I remember Kurt sitting down with the acoustic and he had a couple variations of the melody and the verse he was singing and we picked the one that was best. But most of the songs were fairly finished. I don't know whether they played them live a lot, but I know that they did practice a lot. It wasn't like, 'What are you playing here?' They knew. Chris had figured out his bass lines, and the drum patterns for the most part were worked out, and Kurt had a pretty good idea of what he wanted to do. But he had a couple lines in some songs that he was still working on."

Unlike the band's previous recordings, songs for the new album were frequently compiled from a number of different takes. "Kurt would do vocal takes and I'd try to get him to do three or four," Vig explains. "I liked to go through and pick the best bits. That's typically how I like to work with a vocalist. And on some of the songs he did sing some different lines. Sometimes he'd do a take and then come in and listen to it and go, 'I don't like that verse, I'm going to use this one instead.' Kurt would sing so amazing. That's one reason he would blow his voice out, he was singing hard. He would sing the verse a certain way and usually come to the chorus and if he was singing really hard he would totally blow his voice out every time.

"Then after we cut stuff, we would go back," Vig continues. "I had Chris re-do some of the bass tracks 'cause I wanted them to be really locked with the drums. And every now and then work on the parts a little bit, see if we could come up with something better. And the same with Kurt. We kept the live guitar, and went back and overdubbed more guitar, and experimented with tones and different mics and amps and guitars. Kurt in particular did not really want to do that. But I somehow was able to push him farther than he wanted. I think he really wanted to kind of stay with the punk aesthetic, that everything is one take and that's all. But also, he knew if he didn't have a good performance, and he wanted it to be good."

But for the most part, Vig says the sessions were fairly relaxed. "The band was really loose. They were going out all night and partying. I think that they had a certain sense of 'We can do whatever we want!' Typically, I would go in before them, like around noon or one, and they would get in mid-afternoon, 3 or 4 o'clock and we'd work until 11 o'clock or midnight. And they'd leave and I'd usually work a little longer." The sessions lasted into June, for a total cost of around $130,000.

There has been a lot of speculation about what extra material the group may have recorded during the *Nevermind* sessions. "They had about 15 songs that they were working on," says Vig. "And I thought we were going to at least try and record all of them. There were a couple that we recorded that Kurt never finished the lyrics on. One was called 'Song in D'; it was really catchy. I was hoping he would finish the lyrics 'cause it would have been another amazing song. It had kind of an R.E.M. feel to it. And one was more of a punk thing. He had one other one he was playing on acoustic; it was kind of bluesy. I asked, 'You want to try and put that down on tape?' And he said, 'No, it's not really done.' And one of the songs I think Kurt may have given part of the chord progression to Courtney for one of the Hole songs, or at least there's a little bit of a nod from it. 'Old Age,' I think."

Vig adds that no early versions of *In Utero* songs were recorded. As for any additional outtakes, "I'm pretty sure that they'd be in the Geffen vaults," he says. "We kept more stuff, and obviously with a bigger budget there were more reels of tape. And also I knew at that point, whenever I could, I wanted to keep stuff. So any of those extra tracks, they're sitting in the vaults somewhere at Geffen."

Once the record was completed, Vig planned to mix it. "I think we mixed about half the songs," he says. "And the band was mixing them with me, and they really weren't turning out that well. It didn't really work having the band there, 'cause Kurt would come up and go, 'Turn all the treble off all the channels and turn the bass up full; I want to hear it really heavy.' It's just not really being realistic in terms of trying to make everything balance in the track! And also, at a lot of points, he was trying to bury his vocal. And I would argue with him; 'Your voice is the most intense thing about the songs and the band, and it deserves to be right up there in your face as well as the music!'"

Ultimately, Andy Wallace was chosen to mix the album, largely because the band liked his work with Slayer. Vig still has cassette copies of his own original mixes. "The mixes that I like best were the rough mixes that I did that were straight off the Neve board," he says. "With very little on them; no processing at all. Just real simple. I remember we finished the record, and I would just play 'Teen Spirit' over and over in the car. It just sounded so amazing; everything was just coming straight out of the speakers at you.

"I think Andy's mixes sound great," Vig adds. "He didn't add too much polish to the songs, but got really good separation between the instruments and vocals, mostly through EQ. He also kept Kurt's vocals in the front of the mix." Though Cobain was later critical of the album's sound (telling Azerrad, "Looking back on the production of *Nevermind,* I'm embarrassed by it now"), Vig says "I know for a fact that Kurt loved the album when it was finished. But over a period of time I think all artists become critical of their work. And as a punk, it's not cool to endorse an album that sells in the millions. When Kurt talked to me about working on the first Hole record with Courtney, he told me he wasn't happy with *In Utero* either."

After the band finished their album, they played a few West Coast dates, and in August headed back to Europe. Aside from the occasional few weeks off, they would stay on the road until the end of February '92, playing the U.S., England, Europe, Australia, New Zealand, and Japan. Prior to leaving for Europe, the band filmed their video for "Teen Spirit," chosen as *Nevermind*'s first single, on August 17 at the GMT Studios (stage 6) in Culver City, California. Filming began at 11:30 AM and lasted all day.

In this period of calm before the storm, two more compilations with Nirvana tracks were released. "Dive" appeared on the Sub Pop compilation *The Grunge Years*, released in June (with the jokey tag "Limited Edition of 500,000" on the cover). And another track from the *Dale Demo*, "Beeswax," was released on the compilation *Kill Rock Stars*, by the Olympia label of the same name, on August 21. The original issue of the album was limited to 1000, and came in a numbered, hand-screened cover. The record has since been issued on CD.

"Teen Spirit" was released September 10. The 7-inch and cassette were backed with "Even in His Youth"; a second cassette, 12-inch and CD added "Aneurysm," both from the January '91 Music Source session. The back cover featured a classic Charles Peterson shot from a show at the Commodore Ballroom in Vancouver, B.C., on March 8, showing Cobain apparently playing the guitar on his head. A promo CD single was released, with edited and full-length versions of the song; the edited version also appeared on a 12-inch promo on yellow vinyl. Another promo had a plastic bag around the case, filled with blue liquid.

In the U.K., the single was released in August on 7-inch and cassette (b/w "Drain You"), a black vinyl 12-inch featuring "Even in His Youth," a picture disc 12-inch featuring "Aneurysm," the CD featuring all four songs; the picture disc is the rarest version. A picture disc using different artwork was issued in Germany.

Finally, on September 24, *Nevermind* was released. An advance cassette was released, though no advance CDs were; CD promos were available after the album's release (the same would hold true for all of Nirvana's subsequent album releases). One CD promo was packaged in a "blue pack" the way "Teen Spirit" had been. The record was also released on vinyl. Though the cover listed 12 songs, *Nevermind* also had a "hidden" track, "Endless, Nameless," that came on some 10 minutes after the last listed track, "Something in the Way." It was accidentally left off the first pressing of the CD and cassette, but restored on later pressings. The album's back cover photo was by Cobain, credited as "Kurdt Kobain."

Mari Earl was impressed with "Teen Spirit," calling it "one of Kurt's best songs, lyrically and musically." Nonetheless, it was still something of a shock to see her nephew on TV. "When I first saw him on MTV I cried," she says, "because it was like, 'This is too much!' It was just like, wow, to know somebody that makes it big like that is really a very strange feeling. It was all these mixed emotions. I felt happy for him, I felt afraid for him, just a lot of different things 'cause I knew that he wasn't the most stable person in the world. But it wasn't like I consciously thought of that. I was just really excited for him and very happy for him in the beginning. But it was quite a lot for him, I really think. That was the big burst of their fame."

Earl also feels that Nirvana's sudden fame changed what music meant to Cobain. "Music was for Kurt, as it was for me at one time, an escape, a way to express what was inside himself," she says. "It was an understanding friend, predictable and comforting. When he became famous, music was no longer an escape for him, it was a nightmare of scheduled 'creativity' and harried performances. It was almost as if he became a caricature of himself and the whole grunge movement. Kurt's success only reinforced my suspicions of how the music business operates. By that, I mean the artist becomes a commodity, a can of beans, if you will, merely a saleable product. Can anything drain the human spirit more?"

Initially, neither the band or DGC had great expectations for the album; the first pressing was a modest 46,251 copies. The record release party was held September 13 at Re-bar, a hip dance club in Seattle. The club's manager says he still gets calls from Nirvana fans who think the band performed at the party, which they did not; only recorded music was played. The party was shut down when the band started a food fight, the club's owners not relishing a big clean-up job before admitting the evening's clientele.

The band's in-store appearance at Seattle record shop Beehive (now closed) on September 16, was less chaotic, if still enthusiastic. "The place was packed," remembers Charles Peterson. "It was just the rawest show I'd ever seen them do. It was so amazing. It was so raw and powerful." It was also the last time Nirvana would play to such a small crowd in Seattle. Little more than a month later, on Halloween, the group appeared Seattle's Paramount Theater, sharing a bill with Bikini Kill and Mudhoney. The show was recorded and filmed, and with the album rising in the charts, it was apparent Nirvana was taking off. "The whole thing was just such a scene," says Peterson. "And I couldn't figure out whether it was okay for me to photograph them or not!"

The fall tour also took the band to Chicago, where Butch Vig saw them at the Cabaret Metro. "The buzz in the air was unbelievable!" he says. "Kids were screaming and crying, and almost everyone already knew all the lyrics. I was thinking, 'Wow, I might eventually have a gold record,' and of course it went gold in a matter of weeks. A few months later, I talked to their manager John Silva and asked if there was any chance of *Nevermind* going #1. And he said, 'No way, not a chance.' The next week it was #1. After that, I had so many bands, labels, and managers approach me about getting the 'Nirvana sound,' it became a joke—there was and always will be only one Nirvana!"

Meanwhile, over in Europe, Jack Endino, on tour with Skin Yard, heard "Teen Spirit" for the first time. "That song followed us all over Europe," he says. "We started to get kind of freaked out; we couldn't get away from this damn Nirvana song!" Calls home kept the band up-to-date on *Nevermind*'s sales figures, and, like Mari Earl, Endino had a sense of trepidation. "It was obvious that this phenomenon was beginning to happen," he says. "And I sort of intuitively had a hunch that they weren't really psychologically prepared for success if it happened. Because they were just these nice guys from Aberdeen that seemed an awful long way from 'The Biz' and all the nasty stuff that goes on. And I didn't think they would enjoy that part of it particularly, if they ever got to see it. Which turned out to be true."

Endino also got to witness Nirvana's reaction to success first-hand, when Skin Yard opened for Nirvana at a November 14 show in Vienna (when the album was in the Top 40), and when Endino saw the band a few weeks later, November 25, in Amsterdam (when the album had reached the Top 10). "Kurt was okay in Vienna," he says. "They seemed to be having fun. In Amsterdam, he wasn't doing too good. It was a really weird show. Kurt was really pissed off; there were all these people with cameras and movie cameras on the stage, and he was a little out of tune and he was very angry at these cameras—'Get the hell off my stage!' And backstage he was really uneasy, he looked really pale. Everybody seemed to be really uneasy and very unhappy. Like suddenly the success was starting to bother them because people were starting to come at them. Suddenly people wouldn't leave them alone."

While in Europe, Nirvana made a number of interesting radio and television appearances. None of the radio appearances featured the group's current single, and one session didn't even include anything from *Nevermind*. The band's third session for John Peel included the as yet unrecorded "Dumb," "Drain You," and "Endless, Nameless." They also recorded a session for another British DJ, Mark Goodier, performing "Something in the Way," "Been a Son," "Aneurysm," and "New Wave Polly" (a fast, electric version of "Polly"). They also recorded a session for Holland radio station VARA, performing "Here She Comes Now," and "Where Did You Sleep Last Night?", the latter another song the band never officially recorded.

For their U.K. TV appearances, the band was locked into promoting "Teen Spirit," but found other ways to liven things up. After being introduced on "The Word," Cobain revealed the new love of his life, telling the audience, "I just want everyone in this room to know that Courtney Love, of the pop group Hole, is the best fuck in the world." On "Top of the Pops," Cobain adopted a booming baritone to deliver "Teen Spirit," and (along with the band) made no attempt to mime his instrument playing properly. When the host of *The Jonathan Ross Show* announced that the group would be performing "Lithium," they turned the tables and performed "Territorial Pissings" instead.

Back in the U.S., two more Nirvana-related recordings were being released. Earth's CD EP, *Bureaucratic Desire for Revenge,* was released in October, and featured guitar and background vocals by "Kurt Kobain," though Cobain and fellow backing vocalist Kelly Canary (formerly of Dickless and Teen Angel) were credited as "specialists." A video of the same name was released, packaged in a white case, in a limited run of 100 hand-numbered copies. The band, Cobain, and Canary do not appear in the video; the visuals are grainy "racy" films of people spanking each other interspersed with other found footage of such things as aircraft carriers. In November, *Teriyaki Asthma, Vols. 1–5* was released, compiling all five EPs in the series. The vinyl album was released in a limited run of 2000; it was also released on CD and cassette and is still in print. In Europe, the set was a double-album.

By January 1992, *Nevermind* had already gone platinum (it would eventually sell a total of 13.8 million copies worldwide, 7 million of that in the U.S.) and was on its way to topping the charts ("Teen Spirit" peaked at #6, while in the U.K., the album peaked at #13, "Teen Spirit" at #7). The weekend the album reached #1, Nirvana was in New York. On January 10, they taped a session for MTV, performing "Teen Spirit," "Drain You," "On a Plain," "Polly," and "Territorial Pissings." Alex Coletti, who worked on the shoot, told *Guitar World* that the band had performed five or six other songs that have never been aired, including "Molly's Lips" and "Stain." The next night, the band appeared on *Saturday Night Live,* performing "Teen Spirit" and "Territorial Pissings." Nirvanamania had arrived.

The next Nirvana recording to be issued was the *Hormoaning* promo, released to promote the band's February tour to Australia and Japan. *Hormoaning* contained six songs: "Aneurysm" and "Even in His Youth" from the "Teen Spirit" single, and "D-7," "Turnaround," "Son of a Gun," and "Molly's Lips" from the 1990 John Peel session. In Australia, the EP was released as a 12-inch record (on burgundy vinyl), a cassette, and CD (5000 copies of each format). In Japan, the release was CD only, and featured a different cover.

Another interesting promo CD released around at this time was *Nevermind, It's an Interview*. The CD featured interview segments intercut with song clips and complete tracks. Most of the complete tracks were taken from the band's Halloween '91 show in Seattle, and included "About a Girl," "Aneurysm," "Drain You," "On a Plain," "Molly's Lips," "School," along with the *Nevermind* versions of "Territorial Pissings" and "Teen Spirit." This promo is especially valuable as it contains material unavailable anywhere else.

"Drain You" was planned as *Nevermind*'s second single, and CD promos were released in late '91. But according to Jim Merlis, director of publicity at DGC, "It got kind of swamped by 'Teen Spirit' so it never really was played. 'Teen Spirit' had such a life of its own." As a result, there wasn't another single released until March 3, '92, when "Come As You Are" was issued. The 7-inch was b/w a live version of "Drain You," the cassette, 12-inch, and CD adding a live version of "School," both from the Halloween '91 show. The song was the only other single to reach the U.S. Top 40, peaking at #32. A CD promo and 12-inch promo were also released.

In the U.K., "Come As You Are" was again released in four formats; the 7-inch and cassette were b/w "Endless, Nameless," the 12-inch—both black vinyl and picture disc—added the live version of "School," and the CD added the live version of "Drain You." The song performed better in the U.K., reaching #14. In Germany, the 12-inch picture disc was b/w "Endless, Nameless" and the live version of "Drain You."

Though DGC was anxious to have Nirvana go back on the road, the group—specifically Cobain—demanded a break. The previous seven months touring had left them exhausted; "We'd be on an adventure," Novoselic told Michael Azerrad. "Now it's a circus." The unexpected success of *Nevermind* and the resulting media explosion added to the overall tension, leading to, among other arguments, a dispute over royalties. The band members had seemingly gone their seperate ways, Grohl to Virginia, Novoselic to his new home in Seattle, and Cobain, now married to Courtney Love, to Los Angeles.

One of Nirvana's few recording sessions of the year took place in April at Barrett Jones's Laundry Room studio, now relocated to Seattle. The move was precipitated by Jones's being kicked out of his home in Arlington. "I basically had two weeks to get out," he says. "And after spending some time trying to find another place to relocate my studio, I decided to move out here. And Dave had just moved out here and joined some band I'd never heard of called Nirvana. So I thought I'd move out here too!"

When Jones arrived in Seattle, in June '91, the Laundry Room was initially located in his house in West Seattle. "It was never really officially open there, but that is where I did the Nirvana stuff, and the King Buzzo record," he says, "King Buzzo" being Buzz Osborne (Grohl also appeared on the record). The April session, which Jones thinks took two days, was for the purpose of recording tracks for various singles and yet another tribute album: "Curmudgeon," "Oh, the Guilt," "Return of the Rat."

"All three songs had a place to go," Jones says. "I don't think they'd ever really played them before, but they figured them out pretty quick. They're all pretty easy. I think they were trying to be a little more punk rock about the whole thing. Trying to get away from the *Nevermind* glossiness. I think that was the purpose. They wanted to be as low budget as possible about it. I only had a little 8-track, and I wasn't even properly set up to record, but it came out great anyway." Jones doesn't think any outtakes or alternate versions were saved from the session.

During their stay in Seattle, Cobain and Love also dropped in on Seattle's Orpheum record store and confiscated what they claimed were unauthorized recordings being sold. Asked by the clerk to leave a note for the boss explaining the disappearance of the recordings, Love and Cobain duly complied writing the following explantion on the store's stationary: "i need for you not to make extra money off my husband so i can feed my children. Mrs. Cobain. Macaroni and cheese for all. love kurdt kobain."

In May '92, the first in a series of *Westwood One in Concert* releases featuring Nirvana was issued to radio stations; the double album also featured Led Zeppelin in concert. The following month, the first song from the April '92 sessions was released when "Return of the Rat" was featured as part of the box set *Eight Songs for Greg Sage and the Wipers,* released on the Portland indie label Tim/Kerr on June 20.

Thor Lindsay, one of T/K's founders, says the idea to do an album "paying tribute to the biggest alternative act to come out of Portland— until Everclear!" came from Sean Crogham (then in Crackerbash, now in Junior High) and Jim Talstra (then in the Dharma Bums, now in The

Maroons), who suggested it backstage during a show in 1991. Lindsay knew Cobain, and knew that he was a Wipers fan, and approached him to see if Nirvana would be interested in contributing. Cobain initially suggested Lindsay use the version of "D-7" they'd recorded for John Peel. Lindsay readily agreed; "It's one of the most phenomenal tracks I think Kurt ever did," he says.

But when "D-7" appeared on *Hormoaning,* licensing the song through Geffen became complicated. "And Kurt got pissed off and said, 'Fuck it, I'll record another track,'" Lindsay explains. "And basically a DAT turned up with 'Return of the Rat' on it. I was ecstatic. Kurt was into alternative labels and independent stuff."

The set, released in a limited edition of 10,000, contained four singles, and is now out of print. Colored vinyl was used on 4000 of the sets. "That turned out to be the biggest packaging nightmare of my life," says Lindsay, "because I didn't want it pirated or extra copies made of anything. So I actually had the 7-inches pressed at one plant, the picture sleeves at another plant, and the box sets made here in town. And we assembled them in my kitchen. It was literally out of control." Nor were the colored versions all the same. "Every 500 the color would change," Lindsay explains, "so there's a lot of variety there! Especially since the pressing plant screwed up on some of them; for example, there's only 200 of Hole's orange disc. And the aqua Nirvana is rare." Lindsay used a total of four translucent colors and four opaque colors. On March 15, 1993, the set was issued on CD with six additional tracks, necessitating a title change to *Fourteen Songs for Greg Sage and the Wipers.*

On July 21, Nirvana's next single, "Lithium," was released, the cassette, 12-inch, and CD b/w "Curmudgeon," and a live version of "Been a Son," also from the Halloween '91 show. The packaging was especially notable, featuring cover photography by Cobain, a sonogram of Cobain and Love's child, and all the lyrics to *Nevermind.* In the U.K., the 7-inch and cassette were b/w "Curmudgeon," the 12-inch picture disc added the live "Been a Son," and the CD added "D-7" from the Peel session. A promo CD single was also released; some were packaged in a special box that also featured *Nevermind, It's an Interview,* issued in a limited run of 100.

Nirvana hit the road again in June, touring in Ireland and Europe. Then in August, a profile of Love in *Vanity Fair*'s September issue (published in August) blew the lid off a subject that had been kept under wraps: the couple's drug use. Most damaging was the implication that Love had used heroin after she knew she was pregnant. When the story was published, Love maintained she'd stopped using drugs when she learned of her pregnancy. Cobain, however, had been using heroin regularly. He'd tried detoxing a number of times and was in the hospital detoxing again when Love gave birth to Frances Bean Cobain on August 18.

By the end of the month, rumors were flying about how Cobain's drug use was going to split the band, and that their August 30 appearance at the Reading Festival in Reading, England, would be their last show. Instead, they rallied, turning in one of the best performances of their career. Mocking the rumors, Cobain, wearing a hospital gown, had himself pushed onstage in a wheelchair, staggered to the mic, warbled the opening line of "The Rose," and collapsed. He then leaped up, and the band went on to play for nearly 90 minutes.

Charles Peterson, in one of the few times he photographed the band outside of the Northwest, was also at the show. "I was the only photographer that got to sit on the stage the whole time," he says. "Just to sit there and have Nirvana playing in front of you on this mammoth mammoth stage, and to my left was 50,000 people all singing along . . . it was unbelievable. It sent shivers up my spine the whole time. Sometimes I just had to drop the camera and just sort of take it all in."

The band's set spanned their entire career, from songs on the *Dale Demo* ("Spank Thru") to three numbers soon to be recorded on *In Utero,* "Dumb," "tourette's" (introduced as "The Eagle Has Landed") and "All Apologies" (dedicated to Love and Frances Bean). The band also joked about their supposed "demise." "This isn't our last show!" Novoselic said. "Yes it is," countered Cobain. "I would like to officially and publically announce that this is our last show." "Today!" said Novoselic. "Until we play on our November tour," continued Cobain. "Or do you want to record a record in November?" Portions of the show were also aired on radio.

Nirvana returned to the U.S. in triumph, their next victory winning Best Alternative Music Video (for "Teen Spirit") and Best New Artist in the *MTV Music Video Awards.* Cobain was at his most charming when accepting the latter award, smiling directly into the camera and saying, "You know, it's really hard to believe everything you read." The band had wanted to play "Rape Me," another song destined for *In Utero,* during their live spot, but caved in to pressure and played "Lithium"—but not before throwing in the opening measures of "Rape Me" as a tease.

Nirvana then performed in Portland, and, the following night, at the Coliseum in Seattle, their biggest show in the city to date. "It was really weird to see somebody that you know up on this huge stage," says Alice

Wheeler. "I felt really bad for Kurt. It seemed like he looked really lost up there." But weeks later, the group was back in a smaller setting when they appeared as the unannounced opening act for Mudhoney in two secret shows, October 3 at Western Washington University in Bellingham, and October 4 at the Crocodile Café in Seattle. At the latter show, the band was clearly relaxed, enjoying the chance to return to their roots, however fleetingly. For its part, the audience stood in awed appreciation, barely able to mosh.

Peterson attended both shows. "I was going to go up to Bellingham with Mudhoney anyway," he says. "And they were like, 'Oh, guess who else is playing?' 'Then I'm definitely coming up with you guys!' It was really good. My memory of it is there were all these student photographers down in the pit, and there was this one guy, he's got his camera, and he's dancing around, but he's right in front of where Kurt is. I'm like, 'If you're not going to take pictures, get out of the way.' And he was like, 'I've only got one shot left and I'm waiting for the destruction!'

"And the brilliant thing was, that night they didn't destroy their instruments!" Peterson continues. "These two seven year old kids came on stage and Kurt draped his guitar around one of them, and Chris draped his guitar around the other kid's neck. And everyone was like 'Smash it! Smash it!' And somehow this kid hauled Chris's bass over his head and smashed it onto the stage. And Alex, their tour manager, is just back there with his head in his hands, 'cause Chris never really smashed his basses. It was great. It was the perfect ending to it." These shows were the last live shows Peterson shot. Nirvana's final show of the month was a concert in Buenos Aires.

October also saw the release of another *Westwood One in Concert* double album, also featuring Roxy Blue. On November 30, "In Bloom" was released as a single in the U.K. only (though the U.S. did release the song as a CD promo). The 7-inch and cassette were b/w a live version of "Polly" from the band's December 28, '91 performance in Del Mar, California. The 12-inch picture disc and CD added a live version of "Sliver" from the same show. Portions of the show were also aired on radio. In November, Cobain also recorded a guitar track at the Laundry Room, for another side project, this one a single with William Burroughs that would be released on Tim/Kerr in 1993.

DGC had hoped to have new Nirvana album ready for the holiday season, but the band hadn't started recording demos until the fall. Instead, on December 15, they released *Incesticide*, a joint effort between the label and Sub Pop. Like their previous albums, *Incesticide* was released in CD, cassette, and vinyl formats, the record on blue vinyl. A sticker on the out-side read "Rare B-Sides, BBC Sessions, Original Demo Recordings, Outtakes, Stuff Never Before Available" (a total of six tracks were previously unreleased). The press release for the album contained Cobain's descriptions of the tracks (the same descriptions were also used in some ads), which included some errors ("Dive" was not recorded with Butch Vig in 1988, for example). Cobain also wrote the album's liner notes. The album didn't reach the Top 40, but did go platinum, selling a total of 3.2 million copies worldwide. There is a German CD promo packaged in a cardboard box. A video of "Sliver," largely filmed in Cobain's home, was made to promote the album.

The album's 15 tracks were culled from a variety of sources. "Hairspray Queen," and "Aero Zeppelin" were previously unreleased tracks from the *Dale Demo,* "Mexican Seafood" was the *Dale Demo* track that had appeared on *Teriyaki Asthma,* "Beeswax" was the *Dale Demo* track that had appeared on *Kill Rock Stars,* "Downer" was the *Dale Demo* track that had appeared on the *Bleach* CD, "Big Long Now" was a previously unreleased *Bleach* outtake, "Stain" had appeared on the *Blew* EP, "Sliver" and "Dive" were from the band's second single for Sub Pop (though the answering machine "epilogue" was excised from "Sliver"), "Turnaround," "Molly's Lips," and "Son of a Gun" were from the band's 1990 John Peel session and had appeared on *Hormoaning,* and "Been a Son," (New Wave) "Polly," and "Aneurysm" were previously unreleased tracks from the band's 1991 Mark Goodier session.

Neither "Hairspray Queen" or "Aero Zeppelin" were remixed for the album. "That's griped me for a while because I wish I'd had a chance to remix them," says Jack Endino. "Literally what they did is they took the tape from the first day I ever recorded them and mixed ten songs in one hour. And that's the tape that got put on *Incesticide.* It's always bummed me out. In any given afternoon I could've made a better mix of all those songs. But that's just the way it went."

As for the remaining *Dale Demo* tracks, Endino says "If You Must" is a track that Cobain didn't want released. "He hated that one almost immediately," he says. "And he never wanted anyone to ever hear it again. Which is one of the reasons it's not on *Incesticide.* He was embarrassed about it; it was too heavy. He was just like that sometimes. I think it's a great song."

Daniel House admits he was annoyed at losing his exclusivity with "Mexican Seafood." "The track was supposed to stay exclusive forever with *Teriyaki Asthma,*" he says. "Until years later I got a call from

Nirvana's attorney, informing me that I had never signed a contract with the band for the song, that a handshake was not adequate, and they were going to take the song and put it on *Incesticide* and I couldn't do a fucking thing about it, and if I tried to raise a finger they would sue me into oblivion. I just thought, 'What a strange way to introduce yourself!' But they let me keep the song on the CD. That was the final slap in the face that gee, a handshake's just not good anymore. And I was upset that we never got credit for it on the album."

And Steve Fisk says that other material was submitted for consideration on *Incesticide* as well. He thinks the 1987 session the band recorded at KAOS was "probably" submitted, and says that he also turned over the tape from his session with Nirvana in January '90. "The tape was allegedly missing at The Music Source for a while," he says. "And I knew that I'd seen it flying around the studio, because it was a Nirvana tape, and so people would take it out and play with it, mix it, juice it right up. And eventually I found it, and then I got it back to Sub Pop. And at one point, I made Sub Pop and Nirvana some mixes of what the other stuff sounded like to see if they wanted to finish it or anything. I did the best I could to pull to scratch voice into focus and make some mixes around that. But Kurt sings very quietly, so it wasn't useable."

DGC also released David Markey's *1991: The Year Punk Broke* on video during the year. The documentary was filmed during Sonic Youth's 1991 summer tour, when Nirvana was their opening act, and focused primarily on live footage of these two bands and others on the tour, including Babes in Toyland and Dinosaur Jr.

Another Nirvana-related release had come out with relatively little fanfare in 1992: Dave Grohl's first solo project. *Pocketwatch* was a 10-song cassette, released under the name *Late!* on the Arlington-based Simple Machines label. The material that Grohl had been regularly recording over the past years had come to the attention of Simple Machines' Jenny Toomey when she visited the Laundry Room. "I thought it was great," she says, "and I hassled him for a tape. About six months later, he gave me one when I was visiting in Olympia. My label was releasing a series of cassettes that focused on music that was either unfinished, imperfect or finished and perfect by bands that no longer played out, like Geek, My New Boyfriend, Saturnine. It made perfect sense to ask Dave to add his solo tape to the list, and he said yes."

Grohl plays all the instruments and provides all vocals on the tape, aside from backing vocals by Barrett Jones on "Petrol CB." But though the sleeve lists two recording dates for the project (December 23, '90 and

July 27, '91), Jones says the tape is really the product of a number of different sessions. The songs revealed Grohl's versatility as musician, singer, and songwriter; two of the songs would later turn up in Grohl's future projects.

Simple Machines still carries the tape, which is still duplicated from the second generation copy Grohl originally gave Toomey. "But it's sort of been a thorn in our side," she says. "Each mention of the cassette in *Rolling Stone* or wherever translates to piles of mail, and for the most part, these kids have never bought anything through the mail from an independent record company, so when they haven't received their tape in two weeks they write us nasty notes about how we've stolen their $5 and their mothers are going to sue us. The *Late!* tape has broken many an intern! But the one strange redeeming quality of the tape is the tape itself. Almost every time I listen to it—even now at this point of definite saturation—I still have to think it's a great record. It has a depth and vulnerability and crunch that you don't find on the Foo Fighters' record."

Toomey says there were plans to get an upgraded copy of the master and release the tape on CD, along with bonus tracks. "He went back and forth with the idea and then it fell off the face of the earth," she says. "I think he's worried about the quality. Which I can understand and appreciate, but his modesty is killing us! I know he also thinks it's cooler to have it this way. Which it definitely is. But it's been a mixed bag as our cassette masters degenerate. It's really only a matter of time until the cassette gets removed from the catalog." Until then, the tape is available for $5 from PO Box 10290, Arlington, VA 22210–1290—and please be patient.

The *Pocketwatch* material has also been bootlegged, and appears on such releases as *Dave Grohl Demos, Fighting the N Factor, Pocketwatch, Pocketwatch Demos, Reading '95 & Unreleased Demos,* and *Up Against!* Most of these releases contain additional live material from Grohl's next band, Foo Fighters.

Cobain started the new year by doing a photo session with Charles Peterson on January 1, 1993, at the Four Seasons Hotel in Seattle. The shoot was for an upcoming cover story in the national gay magazine *The Advocate.* "It was nice," remembers Peterson. "There were no publicity people, I didn't have an assistant, there was no hair and make-up. It was just in his bedroom at this hotel." Though Cobain, dressed in his pajamas, looked tired in the shots, the interview, which appeared in the magazine's February 9 issue, displayed his thoughtful, contemplative side. In a letter that ran in the January 24, 1994 issue, Cobain wrote, "Of all the gut-spilling and, uh, whining I did in 1993, I never felt more relaxed than with

The Advocate. What can I say? Thank you to the editors. I'll always be an advocate for fagdom."

Nirvana also performed two concerts in South America in January, where they also worked on demos for their next album. They had previously tried working on demos with Jack Endino at Seattle's Word of Mouth studio (as Reciprocal was now called), on October 26, '92. "They booked time several times and cancelled each time," he says. "Mainly because Courtney was having a baby. One of the sessions was literally supposed to be the weekend Courtney was having her baby. Finally, the band showed up one day, we set up the drums and bass, and then we waited all day for Kurt. He never showed up. But the next day he showed up, and they did six songs, exactly the same as they are on *In Utero.*"

The only songs Endino recalls from the session are "Heart-Shaped Box" and "tourette's." "And they ended up doing vocals on 'Rape Me,'" he adds. "No one ever wanted a cassette, so there's no cassettes out there being bootlegged. No one ever called back to finish them, to do the vocals, to mix it, to do anything. It was like someone talked them into going and doing these just so they would do demos. The band just had no interest in it."

The Word of Mouth sessions were the last time Endino worked with the band, and the atmosphere was very different to what it had been on previous occasions. "It was very tense," Endino says. "There was something dark in the air. Just the idea of Kurt showing up 12 hours late—it wasn't like a band. It was dysfunctional in some way. People were not communicating with each other. Kurt was sort of in a different reality from everybody else. It made me very uneasy. Everybody seemed to be very on edge. It just wasn't the same band it had been." The session was "enlivened" by the arrival of the police, due to a noise complaint—Grohl was playing his drums too loud. "His drumming was so loud, it was going right through the walls of the building," Endino says. "It was only the second noise complaint we'd ever had! It was kind of embarrassing. But they were almost done at that point."

"And that occasion of doing those demos was sufficiently uncomfortable that I couldn't imagine doing an album with them," he adds. "I thought, you know, whoever does the follow-up for *Nevermind* is going to get roasted. It won't be a commercial monster like *Nevermind* 'cause the band doesn't want to make that record. And so whoever does this next Nirvana record is going to be stuck between the major label and the band and it's going to be a very unpleasant place to be stuck.

"While they were recording the demos with me they happened to mention, 'Yeah, we were thinking of having Steve Albini do the record.' And

I was just like, wheeew! 'Steve, huh, yeah? That's a cool idea.' Just sort of thinking to myself, wow, they want to make a record with Albini! That's going to be amazing! But there's going to be some fireworks. Because all the major label people and a lot of fans were going to want to hear *Nevermind* Version 2. And Steve, of course, would have no interest in making *Nevermind* Version 2. And I thought this could be a really cool Nirvana record, but I didn't envy Steve at all. Steve is gonna get blamed, and shit is gonna fly, and that's exactly what happened. Fortunately, Steve dealt with it the way he usually does; by telling everybody to fuck off. And Nirvana pretty much stood by him, except for remixing two songs. And ultimately history will judge, but I think it's a good record."

Before the *In Utero* sessions began, another non-album track from the band was released, "Oh, the Guilt," on a split single with The Jesus Lizard, who contributed "Puss." The single was released on February 22, 1993, on the Touch and Go label, in a variety of formats: in the U.S. as a 7-inch, cassette single, and CD single, in the U.K. as a 7-inch (on blue vinyl, some including a poster) and CD single, and in Australia as a 7-inch picture disc and 12-inch. The worldwide run was 200,000, with the Australian picture disc limited to 1500.

The single had been in the works for a few years, inspired by the Sub Pop single that paired Mudhoney (covering Sonic Youth's "Halloween") and Sonic Youth (covering Mudhoney's "Touch Me I'm Sick"). "Then Nirvana became, like, the Beatles of the '90s," The Jesus Lizard's David Sims told *The Rocket*. "But they still wanted to do it, and we had to fig-ure out, well, do we want to do this and look like we're just riding on Nirvana's coattails, or we could just do it and not worry about it, which is what we ended up doing. . . . I think a lot of people who never would have bought a Jesus Lizard record went out and bought the Nirvana half of the single and got the bonus half, a Jesus Lizard song, and hopefully some of them liked that."

But despite the band's feelings about the project, DGC was reluctant to let yet another indie label have a new Nirvana track. At first, they sug-gested handling the manufacturing and distribution in the U.S. themselves, then asked to take care of all sales worldwide. But at Cobain's insistence, the record was released on Touch and Go exclusively.

The third week of February, Nirvana went to Pachyderm Studios Minnesota, to record their new album with Steve Albini. Albini had known of Nirvana since their emergence on the recording scene; as a member of Big Black, Albini had even recorded for Sub Pop before Nirvana (appearing on the compilation *Sub Pop 100*). He was also friends with Cory Rusk, head of Touch and Go. "Cory actually found out after Nirvana started putting records out on Sub Pop that they had originally wanted to be on Touch and Go," he says. "They had sent him demo tapes but he'd never seen them. So some of the millionaires on the planet would have different names if Cory had gotten that demo tape!"

It had been rumored that Albini was going to work on Nirvana's new album for some time. "I had heard that rumor for about six or eight months!" he says. "But no one had ever spoken to me from the band. I'd gotten so tired of that rumor I actually approached the magazine that printed it and sent them a fax saying, 'Look, if this is true, I don't know about it.'" Shortly after the item appeared, Albini was contacted by the band.

"To be honest, I really hadn't given their music that much attention," Albini admits. "It wasn't really the sort of stuff that appealed to me. But socially they were part of the same circle, so I kind of assumed, without really knowing, that they were basically like any of my other friends; music friends, guys in bands. And I talked to them pretty extensively before I agreed to do it, and we corresponded a little. They had liked all these other records I had done; Jesus Lizard records and The Pixies records and The Breeders records. And they seemed genuine in their interest and so I took them at their word."

Discussions between the two primarily revolved around how Nirvana wanted to go about making their record. "Their previous record had been a more labor intensive affair," Albini explains. "Very long strenuous recording sessions where things were done piecemeal. And I've never enjoyed working that way. I explained that I'd rather do things in a more straight-forward fashion, where things are recorded as they are, rather than trying to build things out of components. To try to record the band as a band. And they seemed ready for that, because while they enjoyed working with Butch, finishing the record off proved kind of difficult."

Before the band arrived, Albini received a cassette with demos they'd recorded in Rio; some tracks had vocals, "and I think one of those songs ended up being the 'secret track' on the album ['Gallons of Rubbing Alcohol Flow through the Strip']." Sessions were booked for 14 days, "but I think the total amount of time we spent on the record was 12 days," Albini says. "For what it's worth, we all had a great time. I really enjoyed doing it and I enjoyed meeting them and I enjoyed dealing with them. There was virtually no fiddling around. They were as prepared as any band that I've ever worked with."

At least eight of the 17 tracks recorded (including the "secret" track and songs that ended up on B-sides) had been part of the band's repertoire for some time, including "Dumb," "Pennyroyal Tea," "Rape Me," "tourette's," "All Apologies," and "Sappy," now renamed "Verse Chorus Verse." "Marigold," from Grohl's *Pocketwatch* tape, was also re-recorded. An early version of the album, which leaked out that summer, had the songs in the following order, in some cases with different names: "Rape Me," "Scentless Apprentice," "Heart-Shaped Box," "Milkmade" (renamed "Milk It"), "Dumb," "Four Month Media Blackout" (renamed "Radio Friendly Unit Shifter"), "Punky, New Wave Number" (renamed "Very Ape"), "Pennyroyal Tea," "Frances Farmer Will Have Her Revenge on Seattle," "Fineprint" (renamed "tourette's"), "Serve the Servants," "All Apologies," "Moist Vagina," "Marigold," "Verse Chorus Verse" and "Two Bass Kid" (renamed "I Hate Myself and Want to Die").

As far as additional material, Albini says "I'm sure some of that stuff exists as master tapes, but I really don't know. It's normal for some stuff to be generated that doesn't get followed up on." He adds that he doesn't think there were any outtakes from the sessions.

Though the album had been recorded quickly, it would be dogged by controversy over the next seven months. *Come As You Are* frankly states that DGC "hated" the album. According to Albini, "Gary Gersh [the band's A&R rep] called several different journalists, including Greg Cott, a journalist in Chicago, and told him that the album wasn't going to be released in its present form, that it wasn't fit to be released, and that it was all my fault. And so Greg Cott called me and said, 'What do you have to say about this?' And I said, 'It's a load of shit.' And Kurt had called me and said that the people at the label didn't like the record, and at that point he was still being fairly defensive and still trying to defend the choices they'd made. But the record company and Nirvana's management wasn't shy about trying to make the band feel that they'd made a mistake. And I think it contributed to the general psychotic frenzy that took over the final period of that record's completion."

As other media picked up the story, DGC denied that they didn't want to release the album, running a full-page ad in *Billboard,* and issuing a press release on May 11, headed "Nirvana's Kurt Cobain Debunks Rumors of Geffen Interference with New Album." In the release, Cobain was quoted as saying, "There has been no pressure from our record label to change the tracks we did with Albini. We have 100% control of our music!" Geffen's president, Ed Rosenblatt, added, "The simple truth is, as I have assured the members of Nirvana and their management all along, we will release whatever record the band delivers to us. . . . When the band has finished their album, to their satisfaction, they will turn it in and we'll give it a release date. It's that boring and straightforward."

Though Albini was not surprised by the label's reaction, he says, "I suspected that there would've been intervention earlier than there was. And because we got all the way through the recording and mixing process, without any intervention I thought we were in the clear. It was frustrating from my viewpoint because I felt like I was being used as a scapegoat and I felt like I was being used as a tool to try and put pressure on the band. And the people involved who were pressuring them didn't have the balls to say with a straight face, 'We want more control.' So what they said was, 'We're not happy with the results, and it's this guy's fault.'"

By this time, the band members themselves claimed they weren't happy with how the record had been mixed. "They did ask me to do remixes," Albini says. "But before I agreed to do it, I sat down and I played my copy of the master. And listening to it, I honestly felt like I couldn't do any better. If I had gone out there to remix this stuff, it would've been a compromise. Because it wouldn't have ended up sounding as good as it did already, and it would've been an indulgence. I felt like I would've been wasting their money in order to make a record that didn't sound as good. I just could not hear any room for improvement."

In the end, Nirvana decided to remix both "All Apologies" and "Heart-Shaped Box" (recording another guitar part and backing vocals for the latter song). The recording was done in Seattle's Bad Animals studio, partially owned by Ann and Nancy Wilson of Heart. The record was then remastered at Gateway Mastering in Portland, Maine. Albini explains how remastering effects the overall sound of an album: "In the mastering process, you can make changes in the sound quality, changes in the tonal quality, the stereo width, the dynamic range. When you're mixing a record, you're mixing one song at a time. When you're mastering an album, you're trying to make the album as a collection of those individual songs sound coherent. And owing to the sequencing of the songs and the fact that they're mixed at different times and different frames of mind, they can sound different one to the next. So the mastering is intended to make minor adjustments for those sorts of changes."

Albini remains critical of the final work done on *In Utero*. "The mastering session that was done took several days, at a studio where the mastering engineer is famous for being very manipulative of the material," he says. "A normal album mastering session is a couple of hours. So obviously they thought that they should butcher it in some way to try to satisfy these people and try to satisfy their own expectations. The dynamic range was narrowed, the stereo width was narrowed, there was a lot of mid-range boost EQ added, and the overall sound quality was softened. And the bass response was compromised to make it sound more consistent on radio and home speakers. But the way I would describe it in nontechnical terms is that they fucked it up. The end result, the record in the stores doesn't sound all that much like the record that was made. Though it's still them singing and playing their songs, and the musical quality of it still comes across.

"But they paid me to do a high quality recording of the band, and I don't feel like that's represented in the finished record," Albini concludes. "So it's impossible for me to feel proud of the end result. Although I very much enjoyed doing the record and I enjoyed the company of the band. And I have a lot of respect for them as people. I consider Dave and Chris friends. Dave approached me about working on a Foo Fighters record and changed his mind for whatever reason. But yeah, I consider them friends. I have a lot of respect for them. It's just all the pigs around them that sicken me."

Albini adds that the controversy over *In Utero* also had a negative impact on his career. "It was totally devasting to me from a business standpoint," he says. "The year following that Nirvana album I nearly went broke. Because it was officially regarded as inappropriate for bands to record with me on a mainstream level. Previously I'd been doing one or two big records a year. And after that Nirvana record there were two years that went by where I didn't do any. And it still rears its head. The Bush record that I just did went through a very similar record label fucking the record up after we'd finished it kind of thing."

Nirvana did three more shows prior to their fall tour. On April 9, they headlined a San Francisco benefit for the Tresnjevka Woman's Group, formed to aid rape survivors in Croatia; as a result of becoming more aware of the events in the former Yugoslavia, Novoselic went back to the original spelling of his name, Krist. On July 23, the band performed at Roseland, in New York City, as part of the New Music Seminar. Unreported at the time was the fact that Cobain suffered an overdose in his hotel hours before the show. On August 6, the group performed their last show as a trio, at Seattle's King Theater (a former movie house). The show was another benefit, raising money for the Mia Zapata Investigative Fund; Zapata, lead singer of Seattle band The Gits, had been found murdered the previous month.

Also prior to *In Utero*'s release, three more Nirvana-related recordings were issued. June saw the release of another Westwood One radio promo, this one a double CD set in their *Superstar Concert* series, which also featured Soul Asylum. In July, *Fumble,* another Scream album, was released on Dischord to coincide with a Scream reunion tour held over the summer, Grohl rejoining his former bandmates on the club circuit. July 1 also saw the release of Cobain's side-project, with author William S. Burroughs, the one-sided single "The 'Priest' They Called Him," released on Tim/Kerr.

The recording featured Burroughs reading one of his short stories to Cobain's guitar accompaniment. The project came about as T/K's Thor Lindsay knew Cobain was interested in Burroughs. "Me and Kurt had been talking beat books for a while, and trading them," he says. "I sent him a first edition, autographed edition of *Naked Lunch* with a dust jacket; that literally became his bible, pretty much is what he stated. Then he wanted to talk to Burroughs, so I gave him William's number. He told me, 'If there's any kind of idea about me and Burroughs . . .,' and I said, 'You should do a collaboration.' He said, 'I'd do it in a second!' So that's how 'Priest' came about."

The recording Cobain turned in to Lindsay contained "Twenty-seven minutes of true Kurt. And I sent that to William's assistant, and Burroughs read a chapter out of the 'The Priest.' Then they edited it to about 12 minutes. When the final package came out, Kurt was overwhelmed. It was just the way he wanted it. I was told that it was one of the last things he ever did in the studio. Those two Kurt records are pretty much the highlight of my career so far."

The single was issued as a CD and a 10-inch vinyl one-sided single, that had Cobain's and Burroughs's signatures etched on the other side. "I stole that idea from a Columbia promo I have, a 12-inch promo of Johnny Cash and Nick Lowe's 'Without Love,'" says Lindsay. "They had them inscribe their autographs on the B-side. So I had William Burroughs autograph a 10-inch square piece of cardboard. I tried to get Kurt to autograph it, and he wouldn't do it, and he wouldn't do it, so I went down to the [San Francisco] Cow Palace where they were doing the benefit, and I had him autograph it. And then I had it etched into the vinyl." 10,000 copies were issued on black vinyl, and there were also 10,000 picture discs; 5000 regular disc, and 5000 with yellow vinyl on the B-side; the discs were all hand-numbered. In yet another variation of his name spelling, the press release for the record referred to Cobain as "Kurtis Cohbaine."

At Nirvana's July show at the New Music Seminar, they'd added two musicians to their line-up; John Duncan on guitar—replaced by the Germs' Pat Smear in September for the band's final tours—and Lori

Goldston on cello. Goldston was a member of Seattle's Black Cat Orchestra, a moody, cabaret-styled ensemble. She was introduced to Nirvana through her work in a performance piece inspired by the recent events in Sarajevo. Novoselic had contacted the organizer of the piece to see if she knew of any available cellists, and Goldston was suggested. That summer, she started rehearsing with the group.

"I'd never laid eyes on anybody in Nirvana before I met them," she says. "I just went to rehearsal. It wasn't set up like an audition but it essentially was an audition. They were my favorite band, so I was flattered to be asked. And they're nice people. I thought they were great." Rehearsals were held three or four times a week, and Goldston found it easy to learn the parts. "Sometimes Kurt would just hum something," she says. "Or sometimes I would just pull the part off the record. Or sometimes I would come up with something. I'm pretty flexible that way. I can read music fine, but I'm also happy to improvise or work out a part or come up with something and have people change it a little bit."

It's been reported that during the band's show at Roseland, the audience booed during the "acoustic" part of the set. But listening to the show, it's hard to detect any booing at all. "I don't remember people booing," Goldston says. "People were kind of restless, but I don't remember anybody booing. But I was freaked out; I'd never played in front of that many people. I was pretty nervous."

Not long after, Charles Peterson did his final photo shoot with the group. "It was kind of disastrous for me," he admits. "I was really nervous because I didn't know what to do with them, and I hadn't photographed them posed in a long long time. Kurt was about an hour and a half late. It almost got to the point where Dave and Krist were like, 'Fuck this, let's leave.' And I was like, 'No, please, just wait!' And then Kurt showed up. They were all really nice; they cooperated well. But I wasn't thoroughly happy with my performance. In all these sessions, Kurt always hated having his picture taken, and he would let you know that. Then he'd go along with it. So you get the picture and go, I'm probably starting to over-reach myself—'Well, that's it.' And he'd be like, 'You sure you got enough?' In retrospect I should've done a lot more. But that's coming at it from a photographer's stand-point." Some of Peterson's photos from the session appeared on the cover of *Alternative Press* and *Musician*.

In August, the first single from *In Utero* was issued with the U.K. release of "Heart-Shaped Box." The 7-inch (initial copies on red vinyl) and cassette were b/w "Marigold," and the 12-inch and CD added "Milk It"; it reached #13. No singles from the album were released in the U.S.;

according to Mark Kates, an A&R rep at DGC, "Generally we don't release commercial singles because we feel it cannibalizes album sales." European singles are released, says Jim Merlis, because "Overseas there's a whole singles market. Generally the singles market in the United States is rap and Top 40 songs. It's a totally different market." Merlis adds that so many U.S. singles were released to promote *Nevermind* because "There was such a huge demand. 'Teen Spirit' was so huge and the album was so huge it took on a life of its own. You weren't even competing with yourself, because people were so hungry for Nirvana stuff."

But a CD promo of "Heart-Shaped Box" was released in the U.S. and reached the Top 10 in *Billboard*'s Modern Rock and Album Rock tracks. Another unique U.S. promo is a 12-inch record b/w *In Utero*'s European bonus track, "Gallons of Rubbing Alcohol Flow Through the Strip."

The same month, another track from the *In Utero* sessions was released when "Verse Chorus Verse" (which had been considered as an album title) appeared as an uncredited track on the AIDS benefit compilation *No Alternative*. An early run of CDs had a glitch in Bob Mould's track; these were recalled, but sent out as promos.

That year's *MTV Music Video Awards* saw the band winning another honor for the "In Bloom" video. September also saw the only public performance of Cobain and Love together at a Rock Against Rape benefit at the Club Lingerie in Hollywood. Love performed "Doll Parts" and "Miss World" (which would appear on Hole's next album, *Live Through This*), then introduced "my husband, Yoko." The two then played "Pennyroyal Tea" and "Where Did You Sleep Last Night?"

In Utero was released September 21 and entered the *Billboard* charts at #1 with first week sales of 180,000 copies (in the U.K., it peaked at #8). Again, a vinyl album was issued (on September 14), in a run of 25,000 copies, on clear vinyl. The album has sold 3.1 million copies in the U.S., and a total of 6.1 million worldwide. "Gallons of Rubbing Alcohol" is the "hidden" track on the European release of the CD (referred to on the cover as the "Devalued American Dollar Purchase Incentive Track"), which appears some 20 minutes after "All Apologies." The final unreleased track from the sessions, "I Hate Myself and Want to Die," also considered as *In Utero*'s title, appeared on the compilation *The Beavis and Butt-head Experience*, released in September on DGC.

September also saw the release of the Melvins' album *Houdini*, which featured Cobain as producer on seven tracks; he also played guitar on "Sky Pup." Cobain worked with the band in San Francisco, and called up Jack Endino for advice. "He called me up to ask me some questions about microphones," he says. "He just wanted to ask me some questions 'cause he was going to produce for the first time and he'd never done it before. And I talked to him a little bit and it was nice."

Immediately following *In Utero*'s release, Nirvana made a second appearance on "Saturday Night Live" on September 25 (rehearsals had been held the previous day), performing "Heart-Shaped Box" and "Rape Me." The U.S. tour began in mid-October and continued until January 8, 1994. For Goldston, who had previously played smaller clubs, it took a bit of time making the adjustment to large halls. "I got used to it, but it was freaky," she says. "It broke me from stage fright pretty permanently. In those first three or four shows, I just used up my lifetime supply of stage fright or something." There was also the matter of avoiding the various articles of clothing—particularly shoes—that people would toss on stage. "I got a ducking reflex going," says Goldston. "I'm sitting and I've got this expensive instrument; I can't afford another cello, you know? So I'd just duck!"

But the music remained a highlight. "The one thing that was amazing to me is that I heard all those songs every night for months and I never got sick of them," Goldston says. "The music was always really exciting to me. I would usually hang out at the side of the stage and listen, and I would totally enjoy hearing it every night." Goldston also remembers the band kicking around ideas for new songs and their next album. "I got the sense it would maybe be noticeably different in some way," she says. "But the idea of using oboes was the only concrete recurring theme on that subject!"

In the middle of the tour, Nirvana taped a performance for MTV's "Unplugged" series on November 18 at Sony Music Studios in New York. "I think having a cello [in the band] really tied in to 'Unplugged' happening," says Goldston. "Kurt wanted to have an oboe in there too, which I thought was great. That's an instrument you hear even less in pop music than a cello! And basically 'Unplugged' was an assignment—someone tells you, 'Come up with a whole acoustic set.' And it's a nice thing 'cause it gets you thinking about stuff you wouldn't necessarily be thinking about."

Nirvana arrived in New York earlier that week to play two shows, November 14 at the Coliseum, and November 15 at Roseland. Rehearsals for "Unplugged" were held the same week at an SST rehearsal studio in New Jersey. The set was an eclectic mix of songs from every Nirvana album along with six covers. Goldston remembers a few other songs were rehearsed but cut from the final set, including "Molly's Lips." "I was sorry to see that go," she says. "It's a really fun song to play. I think 'Been a Son' was also talked about at some point."

There was a final rehearsal the day of the taping. That evening, Goldston admits to another bout of stage fright. "I was pretty nervous," she says. "I think everybody was nervous. It's always hard to tell how things are turning out when you're playing them; it's really hard to have any kind of perspective. But when I hear it now, I think it sounds really good and it does sound relaxed. But at the time I never would've guessed that. Because I thought everybody was probably too nervous to play very well and it was a little stiff. I was totally wrong. It sounds a little bit like we're just playing in somebody's living room. Which is I think ideal.

"I hated those cameras though," she adds. "'cause they were flying around; it's MTV so the camera's moving around all the time and it's right next to you. It's hard if you're playing music 'cause if you're playing music and it's going really good, you want to just be out of your body and then this camera's just right next to you pulling you back into it."

A total of 14 songs were performed: "About a Girl," "Come As You Are," "Jesus Doesn't Want Me for a Sunbeam," "The Man Who Sold the World," "Pennyroyal Tea," "Dumb," "Polly," "On a Plain," "Something in the Way," "Plateau," "Oh Me," "Lake of Fire," "All Apologies," and "Where Did You Sleep Last Night?" The Meat Puppets, then touring with Nirvana, sat in on "Plateau," "Oh, Me," and "Lake of Fire." Both "Oh Me" and "Something in the Way" were cut when the show was broadcast on December 16 (the show was also simulcast on radio).

If the band was nervous, as Goldston says, it didn't show during the taping. The band discussed what numbers to play next as if just deciding the setlist; after playing "Dumb," and prior to playing "Polly," Cobain told the audience, "The reason we didn't want to play these two songs in a row is because they're exactly the same song!" In the break before playing "Where Did You Sleep . . . ," the crowd tossed out various requests, including "Rape Me" ("I don't think MTV would let us play that!" Cobain cracked). Finally, Cobain dismissed everyone's suggestions with a jocular, "Fuck you all, this is the last song of the evening!" Unusually for an "Unplugged," none of the songs were taped again; all were first takes. "I would've expected them to do some again," says Goldston, "but everybody liked it. I was surprised. I was glad it was over, that's all I remember! I still get nervous if I see the show."

Less than a month later, Nirvana was again in front of MTV's cameras, taping an appearance for the station's "Live and Loud" New Year's Eve broadcast. The taping was held December 13 at Seattle's Pier 48, a terminal for ferries going to Victoria, B.C. The original line-up was to be The Breeders, Cypress Hill, Pearl Jam, and Nirvana, but Pearl Jam cancelled on the day of the taping, ostensibly because of Eddie Vedder's illness (the remaining members of Pearl Jam had rehearsed at the venue the day before).

Nirvana rehearsed the morning of December 13. Goldston remembers the experience as being "so strange. It was in this huge building and it was freezing cold. And we were hanging out in these little ratty trailers inside the building. The sound was actually kind of rough. It was a little bit difficult for us technically. Everybody's stuff was set up on this tiny stage and it was all kind of crammed in. But it was enough fun that nobody cared that much."

The band turned in a powerful set, and, because of Pearl Jam's cancellation, was able to play longer than originally scheduled. Starting at 7 PM, the band's set included "Radio Friendly Unit Shifter," "Drain You," "Breed," "Serve the Servants," "Rape Me" (finally, MTV did let them play the song), "Sliver," "Pennyroyal Tea," "Scentless Apprentice," "All Apologies," "Heart-Shaped Box," "Blew," "The Man Who Sold the World," "School," "Come As You Are," "Lithium," "About a Girl," and a final jam, during which the band destroyed their instruments, and Cobain beckoned the moshers to join him onstage. But the MTV broadcast cut the set down to 10 songs, concentrating on tracks from *Nevermind* and *In Utero*: "Radio Friendly . . .," "Drain You," "Breed," "Serve the Servants," "Rape Me," "Heart-Shaped Box," "Pennyroyal Tea," "Scentless Apprentice," "Lithium," and the final jam.

Alice Wheeler made it backstage with Lori Goldston. "I was just hanging out, and then I saw Kurt," she says. "I was like, 'Hey, Kurt, what's going on?' He's like, 'Who is that?' 'Me, Alice.' 'Oh! What are you doing? Do you have your camera? Take my picture!' Every time I saw him, he always demanded I take his picture." Wheeler took a number of pictures of Cobain wearing sunglasses and colored tinfoil leis.

December also saw the release of a second single in the U.K., "All Apologies." The 7-inch and cassette were b/w "Rape Me," the 12-inch and CD adding "mv" (as "Moist Vagina" had been renamed). 1993 also saw the release of a Sonic Youth promo CD that featured Cobain's artwork. *Whore's Moaning* (an obvious play on Nirvana's own *Hormoaning* promo) is a five-track CD released to coincide with Sonic Youth's tour of Australia that year. The black cover features a photocopy of one of Cobain's dolls on the front, and a drawing by Cobain on the back. In light of subsequent events, the back cover took on disturbing overtones—the drawing showed a woman pointing a gun in her mouth.

Nirvana played their final U.S. dates January 7–8, '94, in Seattle. The venue was on the grounds of the Seattle Center, site of the 1962 World's

Fair, and where Nirvana had last played at the Coliseum in 1992. The Arena is now called the "Mercer Arena" to distinguish it from the rebuilt Coliseum, now called the "Key Arena." Goldston remembers that the group was tired and ill by this point; "Everybody had just been sick—everybody'd gotten some horrible flu," she says. Goldston did not tour with the band when the tour continued in Europe in February '94; Melora Craeger was hired to play cello. Goldston returned to the Black Cat Orchestra, and the group issued their first self-titled CD in the fall of 1996.

Immediately prior to their European tour, Nirvana entered the studio for what would be the last time. The band had heard good things about Robert Lang Studios in North Seattle, and scheduled three days of recording January 28–30. "The first two days Krist and Dave did tracking on a couple songs," says Lang (Smear was not at the sessions). "And then they did some other tunes. One song was totally completed with Kurt's vocals on it; Kurt came in Sunday in the afternoon and did some vocals. Then they did some guitar tracks and then we went and had dinner. They were so happy; the way the tracks sounded, how quick it went down; the whole vibe was really good. They actually had some time scheduled in here when they were going to get back from their European tour. And of course that never came to be."

Nirvana's final leg of touring began with two television appearances; February 4 on *Nulle Part A*, taped in Paris, where the band performed "Rape Me," "Pennyroyal Tea," and "Drain You," and February 23 on *The Tunnel*, taped in Rome, where the band performed "Serve the Servants" and "Dumb."

On March 29, *In Utero* was reissued in the U.S. with a new back cover. The change had been made due to the Wal-Mart and K Mart chains' refusal to carry the album, ostensibly because of lack of customer demand, but really because the chains objected to the back cover artwork, which featured a Cobain-designed collage of flowers, bones, and fetuses. A "non-offensive" section of the collage was blown-up to fill the entire back cover, and the song "Rape Me" was changed to "Waif Me." A remixed version of "Pennyroyal Tea," originally planned as a single release in the U.K., was also reportedly used on this reissue.

Questions were raised in the press about Nirvana's caving in to pressure to "censor" their album cover, but the band was dealing with a far more serious issue at the time. In contrast to some of the memorable dates on the fall tour, the European tour had not gone well, with Cobain getting progressively sicker throughout the month. After a final show March 1 in Munich, the tour was cancelled. Novoselic returned to Seattle; Grohl remained in Germany to work on a video for the upcoming Backbeat film (he played on the film's soundtrack); and Cobain flew to Rome, where he checked into suite 541 at the Hotel Excelsior. Love joined Cobain on March 3.

In the early hours of March 4, Love awoke and discovered Cobain on the floor. He was rushed to the hospital in a coma. Though Gold Mountain claimed the incident was the result of an accidental overdose of rohypnol (a tranquilizer) and champagne ("He wanted to celebrate after not seeing Courtney for so long"), it later emerged that Cobain had actually taken as many as 50 pills in an attempt to kill himself; he also left a suicide note. Few outside the band's inner circle—including some of the band's friends—were aware of the true nature of the event.

Cobain recovered, and within the week was sent home. By now, it was clear to those close to him was that Cobain was desperately unhappy with his situation. As Nirvana's success had accelerated, so had Cobain's drug use. Unfortunately, drugs then gave Cobain another problem—addiction—while exacerbating the situation he was trying to escape from—the pressures the band's success had generated.

As far as the general public knew, Cobain spent the month of March recovering from his "accidental overdose." In reality, his life was spinning out of control. On March 18, Love called police to the couple's new home in Seattle's exclusive Madrona neighborhood (R.E.M.'s Peter Buck and Stephanie Dorgan, owner of the Crocodile Café, live in a house a block away). According to Love, Cobain had locked himself in a room and threatened to kill himself. When the police arrived, Cobain insisted he did not want to kill himself, and had simply been trying to get away from Love. Because of the "volatile situation with the threat of suicide" (in the words of the police report), the police confiscated four guns, 25 boxes of ammunition, and a bottle of assorted pills, but no charges were filed.

In an attempt to get Cobain to deal with drug habit (which he'd resumed on returning from Rome), Love then called an intervention, which took place on March 25. Cobain initially agreed to go to a rehab clinic in California with Love, but later refused to board the plane. Hoping that he would follow her, Love went on without him. Shortly after, Cobain again agreed to go to a clinic. Strangely, it was arranged for him to check into Exodus, a clinic he'd been at two years previously and walked out of, saying of the place, "It was disgusting."

In an interview with Barbara Walters, Love later speculated that the intervention may have been a mistake. "[Cobain] was ganged-up upon," she said. "I don't think that intervention works on certain people of a certain age. . . . I shouldn't have called for an intervention. I just panicked." In any case, drugs were only part of Cobain's problem; the larger issue was his unhappiness with his life. On March 30, Cobain and Dylan Carlson went to Stan Baker Sports in Seattle and purchased a Remington MII shotgun. Cobain asked Carlson to purchase the gun, fearing that the recent confiscation of his other weapons by the Seattle police somehow made him ineligible to purchase new weapons. Cobain then flew to California and checked into Exodus. Two days later, on Friday, Good Friday and April Fool's Day, Cobain climbed the facility's wall and flew back to Seattle.

The next day, Cobain purchased shells for his new shotgun, and after sporadic communication with a few friends, seemingly disappeared. A missing person's report was filed, and private investigators staked out the house and other locations. But no one found Cobain until the morning of April 8, when an electrician discovered his body on the second floor of the property's detached garage. At 9:40 AM, Seattle radio station KXRX broke the news that the body of an "unidentified white male in his 20s" had been found at the Cobain residence. By noon, unofficial reports confirmed the body was Cobain's. The King County Medical Examiner's Office determined that the cause of death was a self-inflicted shotgun wound, and that the estimated date of death was April 5.

The response to Cobain's death was immediate and intense. Journalists from around the world descended upon the city, and fans made pilgrimages to Cobain's house, called radio stations to express their feelings, and headed to the record stores to buy Nirvana's albums—over the next two weeks, 185,000 Nirvana records were sold. On Sunday, April 10, a public memorial service was held at the Seattle Center Flag Plaza. The service was emceed by DJs from three local stations, and opened with a short speech from Rev. Steve Towles, who then headed over to the nearby Unity Church where a private service was being held. A poet, Michael Swails, read a poem, and Marco Collins, Program Director at KNDD, read a letter from one of Cobain's uncles.

The most emotional moments came when tape recordings with Love's and Novoselic's statements were played. Love read from Cobain's suicide note, interjecting her own comments as if in a final, desperate attempt to have an argument with him. Novoselic's statement was briefer and less emotionally fraught; both Love and Novoselic delivered essentially the same statements at the private service. The public memorial ended with comments from a counselor at the Seattle Crisis Clinic. Attendees then swarmed over a nearby fountain, singing along to tapes of Nirvana's music and venting their frustrations.

Cobain's death led to Mari Earl putting together a presentation about his life, which features a brief video and a performance of her own original song, "It's Worth It." "The day that Kurt died I cried and cried and cried," she explains. "I went through a lot of grief. And as I grieved for him I began to think about the kids that were his followers. Very young kids. And I was worried. I thought there would be more suicides because of his suicide. And so that was what the original spark was. I have a lot of faith in God, and I just cried out and I said, 'God, if there's anything I can do to help these young people that he left behind, please let me do it. I can't do anything for Kurt now. Let me help others.' So that's where it started." Earl's presentation has primarily been done in schools.

Though the members of Nirvana went into seclusion, various Nirvana-related releases were already scheduled to appear over the next few months. A remix of "Pennyroyal Tea" was planned as Nirvana's next U.K. single, but the release was cancelled after Cobain's death. But a promo CD for the single was released in the U.K. in May, featuring the remix, "I Hate Myself and Want to Die" and "Where Did You Sleep Last Night" from "Unplugged."

Grohl turned up as drummer on *Backbeat: Music from the Motion Picture,* released in late March; there were also advance cassettes. The film focused on the early days of the Beatles, and had an alternative "supergroup" playing rock 'n' roll classics like "Long Tall Sally" and "Twist and Shout." In the U.K., the tracks "Money," "Rock 'n' Roll Music," and "Please Mr. Postman" were released as singles, with at least one promo single released of the latter track. Two different soundtracks were released, one with the alternative "supergroup," and the other, similarly titled *Backbeat: Music from the Original Motion Picture Soundtrack,* featuring jazz instrumentals. In addition to the different titles, the soundtrack with Grohl has a collage with scenes from the movie on the cover; the other soundtrack has a painting by the film's subject, Stuart Sutcliffe.

In May, Nirvana turned up on Westwood One's *On the Edge* radio CD promo, which featured music and interviews; in June, the *Westwood One in Concert* CD promo featured one of the band's 1991 BBC sessions. On July 5, the first new Nirvana track to be released since Cobain's death appeared on the compilation *DGC Rarities Vol. 1.* The track "Pay to Play" was taken from the band's 1990 session at Smart Studios. Its inclusion on the compilation had been decided on before Cobain had died, meaning it was not considered a tribute release.

On July 12, Novoselic and Grohl made their first live performance after Cobain's death as part of the Stinky Puffs, a band led by Simon

Timony, then 10 years old. Timony had previously released a four-song EP, which he'd sent to Cobain, who acknowledged the gift in the liner notes of *Incesticide*. Timony later met the band members when his then-stepfather's band, Half Japanese, opened for Nirvana during the band's fall '93 tour. Timony himself joined the band onstage during their November 15 performance at Roseland.

The July 12 performance was the opening night of the Yo Yo A Go Go Festival, held in Olympia (Yoyo being another Olympia label). Sheenah Fair, Timony's mother and the Stinky Puffs' drummer, asked Novoselic to sit in with the band. "Krist wrote the most beautiful letter back to us," she says. "And it was 'I can't believe you asked me to do this. Should I do this? I think I should do this. I'm gonna do this. Should I do this? This would be a good thing.'" On the night of the show, Grohl was also on hand with DGC's Mark Kates. "I saw Dave checking out Krist just about to go on," Fair says. "And I said, 'Dude, get a drum set. Come on, come on with us. This'll be good, it'll be good for you.' He's like, 'I'm gonna fuck it up—I don't even know your music!'" Eventually, Grohl did agree to go on, and though their appearance was unannounced, the media on hand for opening night of the festival insured instant coverage of the event. "One journalist said that Simon had peformed a mass healing," says Fair. "And that's really how it felt." The set, which included a song for Cobain, "I Love You Anyway," was recorded and released the following year.

On August 23, a press release from DGC announced the next full-length Nirvana recordings planned for release. *Verse Chorus Verse*, set for release in November, was to be a double album, including live performances from 1989 to 1994, and the band's entire "Unplugged" set. "It was going to be a sort of yin and yang of Nirvana," says Jim Merlis. Merlis adds the releases were planned due to high demand for new Nirvana recordings—and the fact that the band's "Unplugged" set was already being widely bootlegged.

But the following week, on September 1, DGC issued another press release saying the live performance part of the set was being postponed, as Novoselic and Grohl had found it too difficult to work on; "The emotional aspect of it all threw us for a loop," said Novoselic. "'Unplugged' didn't take much work, production-wise," Merlis explains. "It was done. And the live record was done, but when they went in to mix, Krist and Dave just couldn't do it. It was just too hard."

The press release gave some the impression that work on the live set had not progressed very far. In fact, the album had been completed except for mixing, which Merlis confirms. "It was a whole cohesive album. And it's different from the one that came out later [*Wishkah*]. They went back and started at square one with this because they gained a little perspective on it." A very small number of copies of the original album set, in its unmixed state, were made for DGC staff; Merlis thinks about four copies.

MTV Unplugged in New York was released on November 1, and despite MTV's continuous airing of the program since Cobain's death, the album easily entered the charts at #1 with first week sales of 310,500 (it reached #2 in the U.K.). "Something in the Way" and "Oh Me," cut from the original broadcast, were added to the album. Advance cassettes were released, and promo CDs were also available; for the album, for the songs "About a Girl," "The Man Who Sold the World," and one with both the *Unplugged* and *In Utero* versions of "All Apologies." In Holland and Australia the CD single "About a Girl"/"Something in the Way" was released.

The band's set had been a haunting one at the time it was first aired; now, in the wake of Cobain's death, it had taken on an additional poignancy. "That record in particular gave Nirvana a whole new audience," says Merlis. "I think it showed another side of Nirvana that a lot of people, maybe some of the older people, didn't realize. And it was really nice to see what was in their minds, what influenced them." *Unplugged* would go on to win a Grammy for Best Alternative Music Performance. Nirvana won another MTV Music Video Award in 1994, for "Heart-Shaped Box."

The same month, the band's first full-length video, *Live! Tonight! Sold Out!*, was released on November 15. The video primarily covered Nirvana's break-through into the mainstream, compiling live performances from their fall '91 tour, through their January 16, 1993 performance in Sao Paulo, Brazil. "*Live! Tonight!* was actually supposed to come out in '93," says Jim Merlis, "but it wasn't completed; they were touring and they didn't have time to work on it anymore. And it's so Kurt-like, it's incredible. It has his stamp all over it. You really get the sense of things going haywire; this local band from Seattle who just wanted to make a living playing music all of a sudden becoming this huge phenomenon, which they never anticipated. I think that's what Kurt is trying to show in that whole thing, especially that last montage of all that press stuff, 'MTV News' and whatnot, that's very Kurt."

The tape came with a cover sticker that read "Includes Never-Before-Seen Live Footage, Backstage Tomfoolery and Interviews from the Days of *Nevermind*." There was also a paper insert listing the shows the performances were drawn from (and illustrated primarily with Charles Peterson's photographs). There are a number of mistakes on the insert: the performances of "Breed" and "Polly," said to be from a Seattle '92 performance, are actually from the band's Halloween '91 show in Seattle (footage from the '92 performance does appear in the closing "destruction jam"); the band's appearance in Japan took place in 1992, not 1991; nor did the band play in Tacoma in 1992—their last appearance in that city was in 1990. Advance tapes were also available for the press.

As a document of the band's "break-through" period *Live! Tonight!* was in many ways more compelling than the band's next live album. The performances were strong, the interview segments clearly illustrated the band's sense of humor, and the overall feel provided fans with a welcome reminder of why they liked the band in the first place. *Live! Tonight!* has sold over 100,000 copies in the U.S. to date, and has remained in *Billboard*'s Video Sales chart for over two years.

While both *Unplugged* and *Live! Tonight!* were receiving good reviews, Novoselic and Grohl were slowly returning to live performance. In early fall, Novoselic made an appearance at the Garlic Festival in Arlington, Washington, performing in a make-shift band that included Nirvana guitar tech Earnie Bailey, with a surprise guest appearance by Eddie Vedder. On November 19, Grohl drummed for Tom Petty when Petty appeared on *Saturday Night Live;* he also contemplated joining Petty's band on a permanent basis.

1995 was the first year in seven years that no Nirvana songs were issued. But the former band members kept busy with a variety of projects. The first one the public heard of was Grohl's new band, Foo Fighters, Air Force slang for U.F.O.'s. Grohl had sifted through the material he'd recorded over the years, and entered Seattle's Robert Lang Studios in October '94 with the intention of launching a new musical endeavor. He again played all the instruments and sang all the vocals on the 15 tracks he recorded, with the exception of "X-Static," which featured the Afghan Whigs' Greg Dulli on guitar. And naturally, Barrett Jones was on hand.

"I was just there to make him sound good, help him out," says Jones. "He made all the decisions. I always knew that he'd put something out on his own. He'd been kicking the idea around, and his songs are too good not to. I know he's sort of made it sound like he wasn't planning on putting it out, but I always expected that it would get put out. I always knew it would be huge and great! I mean, I've known him for so long and I've always known how talented he is. He never had as much confidence in himself as I did!"

The songs were recorded October 17–24. "We've always worked really fast together," Jones says. "There weren't any different takes of things.

He'd just get the songs down. I personally don't like to work with lots of choices; it's either right or it's wrong. And he pretty much does things correctly the first time. Most everything's the first take on there."

The songs had all been written over a period of several years. An earlier version of "Winnebago" had appeared on *Pocketwatch.* "Alone and Easy Target," "Floaty," "Good Grief," and "Exhausted" were initially recorded in '92. "Weenie Beenie," "Podunk" and "For All the Cows" were written in '93 ("as were lots of other songs I sure hope no one ever hears," Grohl said later). Other songs on the tape included "This Is a Call," "I'll Stick Around," "Big Me," "Oh, George," "X-Static," "Wattershed," and "Butterflies." "Butterflies" is the only track from the tape not yet officially released.

Copies of the tape soon leaked out. Two songs were "officially" previewed on January 8, '95, as part of Pearl Jam's *Self-Pollution Radio* broadcast, and KNDD and Los Angeles station KROQ later began airing songs from the tape, until they were hit with a "cease-and-desist" order. Excitement about Grohl's hooky, power pop quickly built, and soon labels were approaching him with deals. He finally signed with Capitol, where Gary Gersh, the former DGC A&R rep, was now president. Twelve songs from Grohl's tape were chosen to be issued on Grohl's own Roswell Records label, with distribution handled through Capitol.

But Grohl had no intention of keeping Foo Fighters a solo project, and had passed out copies of the tape to other musicians, including Pat Smear, who quickly agreed to be in the new band. Grohl also brought in bassist Nate Mendel and drummer William Goldsmith, from Seattle's Sunny Day Real Estate, who had recently broken up. On March 3, '95, Foo Fighters made their large-scale public debut at the Satyricon Club in Portland, Oregon, playing the next night at the all ages venue The Velvet Elvis in Seattle (the group's first performance was at a party shortly before the Portland gig).

That same month, Novoselic debuted his new band, Sweet 75, which included Bobbie Lurie on drums, and Yva Las Vegas on vocals; Las Vegas and Novoselic swapped guitar and bass. The band's first appearance was as a surprise opening act for TAD at a St. Patrick's Day show at RKCNDY in Seattle, directly across the street from where the Motor Sports International Garage had been. The band's second performance April 20 at the Seattle club Moe, was a fundraiser for Artists for a Hate Free America. By that summer, Lurie had been replaced by Bill Rieflin (formerly of Ministry). Though rooted in a crunchy pop vein, the band's music has an edge to it, largely due to Las Vegas's strong, compelling vocals.

Getting Sweet 75 off the ground proved to be a little more problematic. Endino was approached by the band to produce their debut album, but DGC, the band's label, was reluctant to use him. "Krist was like, 'They won't let us work with you because they don't want it to sound like *Bleach*,'" says Endino. "I wouldn't either, but it doesn't do me any good!" When the label's choice of producer, Ric Ocasek, turned the project down, Endino again expressed his interest. "I was like, 'Well, I'd love to do it, and if you want me to do it, call me. But I understand the position you're in.' And Krist was very apologetic about the whole thing."

The band had already made a complete album length demo at Robert Lang Studios, and has recorded material at at least one other Seattle studio, Soundhouse. Their album was recorded at A&M Studios in California, with Paul Fox producing. Rieflin, who recorded with the group, has since left, as he was uninterested in touring.

That spring saw the release of Mike Watt's solo album, *Ball-Hog Or Tugboat?*, on Columbia. Every track was embellished by guest appearances, including not only Grohl and Novoselic (Grohl on "Big Train" and Grohl and Novoselic on "Against the 70's") and Pat Smear (on "Forever—One Reporter's Opinion"), but also Eddie Vedder, Mark Lanegan, Thurston Moore, and an answer-machine message from Kathleen Hanna (the Grohl and Novoselic tracks were also recorded at Robert Lang Studios). In addition to being released on CD and cassette, the album was released as a double vinyl set, and in a limited edition CD package, a 10-inch by five-and-a-half inch folder. Watt went on a spring tour to promote the record, with Foo Fighters as one of the opening acts.

In June, Foo Fighters released their first single, in the U.K. (a U.S. single would not be released until 1996). "Exhausted" was released in three formats; as a 7-inch b/w "Winnebago," an outtake from the original Foo Fighters tape (on both black and red vinyl), and the 12-inch (a limited pressing of 1000 on glow in the dark vinyl) and CD adding "Podunk," another outtake from the tape. In the U.S., a promo 12-inch of "Exhausted"/"Winnebago" was released.

That summer also saw the release of the Stinky Puffs' *A Little Tiny Smelly Bit of Something Smells Funny in Here* on Elemental, on CD only. The album features both studio and live versions of the same four songs ("Buddies Aren't Butts," "Menendez' Killed Their Parents," "I'll Love You Anyway," and "I Am Gross!/No You're Not!") the live tracks being the versions recorded at the 1994 Yo Yo A Go Go Festival (the ninth track, "Pizza Break," is another studio track). Another version of "I'll Love You Anyway" appears on the Stinky Puffs' latest release, *Songs and Advice for*

Kids Who Have Been Left Behind. Though no Nirvana members appear on the record, it does feature a picture of Cobain on the cover, and is dedicated to Frances Bean Cobain.

The self-titled *Foo Fighters* album was finally released on July 4; photos on the inside sleeve were all taken from the band's first public gigs, in Portland (Grohl wearing the dark t-shirt) and Seattle (Grohl wearing the wool t-shirt). Promo CDs of the album were available, along with a promo CD of "This Is a Call." The album reached #23 in the *Billboard* charts. The Australian version of the album has six extra tracks; the Japanese version has two.

In August, Foo Fighters' second single, "I'll Stick Around," was released in the U.K.; the bonus tracks were taken from another Laundry Room session. The 7-inch (on red vinyl) was b/w "How I Miss You," and the 12-inch and CD added "Ozone."

In October, Charles Peterson's first book, *Screaming Life: A Chronicle of the Seattle Music Scene* was published. Though Peterson's photos had appeared in a number of publications (as well as *Come As You Are*), *Screaming Life* was a more comprehensive look at the Northwest rock scene, with photos of a number of different acts. The book featured photos from nearly every session Peterson did with Nirvana. Initial copies of the book also included a nine-track CD, which included Nirvana's "Negative Creep."

In November, the third Foo Fighters single, "For All the Cows," was released, the bonus tracks taken from the band's performance at the 1995 Reading Festival [England]. The 7-inch was b/w "Watershed," and the 12-inch and CD added "For All the Cows." That same month, a box set of Nirvana's U.K. singles was released, including "Smells Like Teen Spirit," "Come As You Are," "Lithium," "In Bloom," "Heart-Shaped Box," and "All Apologies."

1996 would see the official release of a number of live Nirvana tracks, beginning with a version of "Radio Friendly Unit Shifter" included on the benefit compilation *Home Alive: The Art of Self-Defense*, released in January on Epic. The album took its name from the Seattle-based group Home Alive, formed in the wake of Mia Zapata's murder. Home Alive regularly offers self-defense courses, and has attracted national attention due to the involvement of Seattle rock musicians like 7 Year Bitch. "Radio Friendly Unit Shifter," was taken from a performance from February 18, 1994 in Grenoble, France.

In March, *Nevermind* was released as a gold CD and on high quality vinyl by Mobile Fidelity Sound Lab; the fact that gold, and not aluminum is used in the CDs is supposed to make them more resistant to decomposition, and Mobile Fidelity's mastering technique also enhances the sound. Ironically, the catalog number for this disc ended up being "UDCD 666." "That's exactly where it fell!" says Karen Thomas, a publicist for Mobile Fidelity. "I went into the mastering department, the guys who give the releases the numbers, and I went, 'You guys, come on!' And they just looked at me completely straight and said, 'That's where it fell.'"

More curious was the typo that appeared on the album cover. "All of the copy came from Geffen, on a disc, and we just put it in the computer so we didn't have to retype anything,'" says Thomas. "The CD booklet came out fine. And then here comes the LP, and on one part of it it says 'Produced by Butch Vig and 'Virvana.' When somebody called us saying 'Were you guys playing a joke? Did you know this mistake was on here?' we didn't have a clue! Because we didn't even retype anything. Is that bizarre! It was spooky." Though not noted on the cover, the CD does have "Endless, Nameless." *In Utero* was released by Mobile Fidelity in January '97; if not available in store, you can find Mobile Fidelity products at their website, http://www.mofi.com.

March saw the release of another Foo Fighters single, "Big Me," this time released in the U.S. and U.K. In the U.S., the CD featured all the bonus tracks that had appeared on the Foo Fighters previous U.K. singles: "Winnebago," "How I Miss You," "Podunk," "Ozone," and live versions of "For All the Cows" and "Wattershed" (these six tracks also appeared on their own on an Australian EP). In the U.K., the bonus tracks were drawn from a radio session recorded for the B.B.C. on November 23; "Floaty," "Gas Chamber," and "Alone and Easy Target."

The video for "Big Me," a take-off on commercials for Mentos mints, would go on to win three awards at the *18th Annual Billboard Music Video Awards*: Clip of the Year, Best New Artist (alternative/modern rock), and the Maximum Vision Award, and an award at last year's *MTV Music Videos Awards*. Foo Fighters' cover of Gary Numan's "Down in the Park" turned up on a compilation released the same month, *Songs in the Key of X: The X-Files Soundtrack,* on Warner Bros. Another soundtrack, featuring instrumentals, was released at the same time: *The Truth and the Light: Music for the X-Files.* Only the former disc has the Foo Fighters track.

In May, an alternate version of Hole's "Live Through This" surfaced on KNDD. The take features Cobain singing during the track, and was recorded during the "Live Through This" sessions. A DGC rep confirmed that Cobain sang "on a couple of songs" during the sessions, but denies that his involvement went any further than that. KNDD obtained the tape from a source close to the band; other stations around the country taped it from KNDD and began airing it themselves.

This past summer [1996], *Yo Yo A Go Go,* a compilation of live tracks from the 1994 festival, was released on Yoyo, including the Stinky Puffs' "I Love You Anyway" with Grohl and Novoselic. Finally, on October 1, 1996, came the long-awaited live Nirvana album, *From the Muddy Banks of the Wishkah.* Advance cassettes were released, with CD promos available along with a promo CD single of "Aneurysm." The album became the third Nirvana release to enter the *Billboard* charts at #1, with first week sales of 158,000 copies. Novoselic wrote the liner notes, and the album was also released as a double vinyl set (packaged in a single sleeve), the fourth side consisting of banter with the audiences.

The majority of the 17 tracks were taken from the *Nevermind* tour of 1991, though there were two tracks from '89, one from '92, three from '93, and one from '94. The latter date is incorrectly identified as being from the Seattle Center Arena, January 5, 1994; the band's shows were January 7 and 8. Though it might have served the group better to present a complete live show, *Wishkah* did offer a good look at Nirvana's more raucous side.

October also saw the release of *Hype!,* the soundtrack for the film of the same name, on Sub Pop; Nirvana's track was "Negative Creep." On November 5, the soundtrack was released as a vinyl box set, with four singles and a poster. The Nirvana track appears on a green disc, also with the Wipers' "Return of the Rat" and a live version of Mudhoney's "Touch Me I'm Sick."

Hype!, which received limited release in October, was a documentary about the evolution of the "Seattle Scene." One of the most electrifying moments in the film is Nirvana's performance of "Teen Spirit" at the O.K. Hotel in Seattle in April '90. Its inclusion was a coup for the film's director, Doug Pray, as he hadn't been able to get an interview with Nirvana. "Krist met with me about a year into the project, and he looked at footage," he says. "I think he didn't know what to do. Because I think honestly Kurt wanted nothing to do with this documentary. I can't speak for him, it's just my theory that at that point, why would he want anything? It doesn't matter if it's cool or wrong or good or bad, it's just nothing. He didn't want anything like that. But believe me, I sent plenty of letters and sneaking notes through friends and friends of friends and tapes and everything I could! I just wanted to know that they'd at least seen what I was trying to do and understood the spirit of it. And then if they said no, that's totally fine."

The "Teen Spirit" footage was finally acquired through a local film-maker who had filmed the show. "It's really cool that there is that video footage because Kurt's so alive and that's cool," says Pray. "And without it, before we had that Nirvana footage, it was a little sad because we only had black and white shots of people talking about him and people mourning his loss, his death. It's cool, I think, to have something, even a minute or two, which is all it is, of him just playing."[1]

One video that did come out at the end of the year [1996] was *Teen Spirit: The Tribute to Kurt Cobain,* on PolyGram Video. The hour-long documentary combines footage of Aberdeen and Seattle with interviews from journalists, associates, and fans. There is no live Nirvana footage, though there are interviews with the band. Though haphazardly edited, *Teen Spirit* does offer an interesting, if brief, overview of its subject. The cover features some of Charles Peterson's shots from the January '93 *Advocate* shoot.

December saw the release of another Grohl-related project, dating back to 1990—*Harlingtox Angel Divine* (a.k.a. Harlingtox A.D.). "Harlingtox A.D. basically was me and Dave and this guy Tos Nieuwenhuizen who's a friend of ours; he used to be in a band called God," says Barrett Jones. "The three of us basically in two days [in April '90] just came up with some music and recorded it at one of my studios, the last one I had in Arlington. And then a week or two later, we ran into this friend of ours, Bruce Merkle, he played in this band called 9353, downtown at a club. And sort of as an afterthought we said, 'Hey, we just recorded some music. Do you want to sing on it?' So we gave him a tape and he took a while and figured out the lyrics. Then we put it on. And that's pretty much how it came about.

"We never played all four of us at the same time, ever," Jones continues. "Never been a band, never did anything else except record this one tape. I always thought it was so great that it needed to get out somehow at some point. And I waited for the right time until I had the means and the time and the money to do it. It's an interesting little novelty item." The self-titled EP consists of five songs, and was released on Jones's new label, the appropriately named Laundry Room Records. One track from the EP, "Recycled Children Never to Be Grown," was also included on a promo CD.

"I've been involved in just about every single aspect there is in the music business," Jones explains. "Officially I'm not really running the

---

1. *Hype!* Played the college circuit in late '96, and was released on video in September '97.—*Ed.*

label; Justin's [Goldberg, formerly a Sony A&R rep] doing all the business things that I don't want to deal with. I didn't expect it to expand as quickly as it is right now. The whole philosophy is to not go overboard with things and just get the bands involved as much as possible and teach them as much as possible 'cause really in this world of music that we're in, there's really no support for young bands who are learning."

As 1997 begins, there are already a number of Nirvana-related projects on the horizon. Sweet 75's album will probably be released in the spring, along with Foo Fighters' second album (recorded at Bear Creek Studio in Woodinville, one of Seattle's neighboring towns). Grohl may also appear on the soundtrack for the upcoming film *First Love Last Rites*. But the release of *Wishkah* has many speculating that the album will be the final Nirvana release. In fact, there are any number of tracks in the vaults to be considered for future release, but Jim Merlis says there are no plans for any Nirvana releases at the moment, adding, "You just want to make sure there's good quality in what you do. You don't want to scrape the barrel. You don't want to put stuff out that the band never meant for anyone to hear, like rough demos. There's a legacy of the band and you don't want to ruin that."

Of course, collectors have already been plundering the realm of demos and live releases for many years, and this interest extends to non-music items as well. This past September, the Executive Collectibles Gallery "Rock & Reel '96" auction not only featured such items as Nirvana autographs and backstage passes, but such ephemera as a "Publishers Clearinghouse" sweepstakes entry form sent to Cobain's house (the name misspelled "Covain"), a medical bill, an empty hair dye bottle, and an empty prescription bottle (for Ampicillin). All the items sold.

With a market so eager to snap up anything related to Nirvana, it's safe to assume some kind of official release will be forthcoming (a collection of the band's videos, embellished by their various television appearances, could be an obvious choice). And with both Grohl and Novoselic still active musicians, we're guaranteed a variety of releases in the years to come.

Leadbelly had his throat cut in a Texas juke joint and survived, but with an ugly scar that ran almost from ear to ear.

—Robert Palmer, *Deep Blues*

Leadbelly survived many violent attacks upon his person, including incarceration in some of America's toughest prisons. But his ears remained and so did the music. He not only survived, he also sang his way out of prison. While serving a thirty-year sentence for murder in Texas—he was notorious for a quick temper that often landed him in the hands of the law—Leadbelly avoided most of the rougher work details by playing guitar and singing for the other prisoners and prison officials. Leadbelly took the next step and sang a song about freedom for the governor of Texas, who granted him a pardon. Five years later, however, he was back in jail.

Leadbelly was born Huddie Ledbetter on January 21, 1888, the child of poor sharecroppers. As a young man he wandered around his native Louisiana playing folk music on various instruments until fate stepped in and placed Blind Lemon Jefferson in his path. This meeting—most music historians place the date in 1915—changed American music. Jefferson taught Leadbelly the blues, and they traveled and played music together. Leadbelly's music became a powerful mixture of folk and the blues, and he concentrated on the twelve-string guitar. A handful of his songs became the foundation of modern blues and rock 'n' roll. It was during his second prison sentence that his music became known to the rest of America.

The king of the twelve-string guitar was serving a sentence for assault in Louisiana when John and Alan Lomax discovered him. The Lomaxes were at the prison to record folk and prison songs. They were immediately astounded by Leadbelly's musical ability and his encyclopedic knowledge of African-American folk music. Realizing that he was a national treasure, the Lomaxes secured another pardon for Leadbelly, and he went north to play his music. He never became wealthy or even financially secure from his performances but he influenced a generation of folk singers including Woody Guthrie and Pete Seeger. He died in 1949; a year later the Weavers covered his signature tune "Good Night Irene," and it quickly became the number-one song in the country. Leadbelly was inducted into the Rock 'n' Roll Hall of Fame in 1988.

It was in 1988 that Kurt Cobain discovered the album called *Leadbelly's Last Sessions*. From that moment Leadbelly had a powerful influence on his music. It can be felt in Nirvana's surprising turn of rhythms and the dry, pointed use of lyrics throughout their songs from "About a Girl" to "Dumb." The first recording done of a Leadbelly number by the members of Nirvana occurred when Cobain played guitar and Novoselic played bass on Mark Lanegan's version of Leadbelly's "Where Did You Sleep Last Night?" for Lanegan's 1990 release *The Winding Sheet.* In 1993, Nirvana ended the *MTV Unplugged* performance with "Where Did You Sleep Last Night?" but not before Cobain remarked that Leadbelly was his "favorite performer." In one song, Nirvana traced the entire history of American music and ended it in front of a television camera.

Leadbelly sang to get out of jail and ended up imprisoned in the Smithsonian and the Rock 'n' Roll Hall of Fame. He also ended up in the sound of Nirvana.

DAVID FRICKE
BLOOD ON THE TRACKS

Melody Maker, October 29, 1994

It's been a year, almost to the day, since I interviewed Kurt Cobain. We were in Chicago and Nirvana had just played—by Cobain's own admission—one of the most abominable shows, a start-to-finish disaster at the Aragon Ballroom fraught with monitor problems, an acoustic interlude all but drowned out by the roar of the moshpit and, by set's end, Cobain's own visible, emotional surrender.

He couldn't even get it up for a ritualistic guitar-smashing—just a shrug, then a shuffle to the wings. It was a lousy gig, the first major bummer of the two-week-old *In Utero* tour and Cobain knew it.

But, up in his publicist's hotel room, Cobain drew on a succession of cigarettes, a hazy wreath of smoke rising about his head like a gauzy halo, and insisted that life was good and getting better. He insisted that "I Hate Myself and I Want to Die," a two minute rumblefuck of asthmatic howling and caustic distortion, yanked from *In Utero* at the eleventh hour, was nothing more than a joke, a dig at the boohounds who dismissed him, as Cobain tartly puts it, as "a pissy, complaining, freaked-out schizophrenic who wants to kill himself all the time."

And he said—with a straight face and a sober, even tone in his voice—that "I've never been happier in my life . . . I'm a much happier guy than a lot of people think I am."

I believed him. And printed it in *Rolling Stone*. Six months later, Cobain made a liar out of me. Our conversation in Chicago, a four-hour session that ran until near sun-up, was the last major interview Cobain ever gave.

But there was a lot of truth in what he said that night—about his marriage, his child and especially about his music (the fear of formula), the punk rock *cul de sac* ("Even to put 'About a Girl' on *Bleach* was a risk") and the shaky future of Nirvana.

"That's what I've been kind of hinting at in this whole interview. That we're almost exhausted," Cobain admitted flatly. "We've gone to the point where things are becoming repetitious. There's not something you can move up toward, there's not something you can look forward to."

Cobain had not given up entirely. Over the next few weeks, he put a great deal of thought, effort and feeling into what he knew could be a turning point, a major statement of aesthetics and purpose—an hour-long acoustic concert by Nirvana on *MTV Unplugged*. The chamber-strum segments that Nirvana had been performing on the *In Utero* tour were more than a broad hint at Cobain's sense of imprisonment in the bullroaring power trio format.

Unplugged was a chance to make music of nuance and cut his songwriting right to the ivory-white bone—a chance to be *heard,* not just applauded.

That show, taped on a brisk November evening at a cavernous soundstage on Manhattan's West Side, became not a turning point, but a swansong. Listening back to my advance cassette of *Unplugged*—as I have over and over again these past couple of weeks—I can't help thinking of this music as a lost opportunity, a glimpse of daylight that for whatever reasons and demons soon went dark again.

I was at the taping, felt something very strong, warm and desperate coming from that stage—and I miss it now. To this day, I have not watched Nirvana's *Unplugged* on television, chopped up by commercials and jump-cut edits, refracted through the illusory melodrama of subsequent events.

I prefer to remember that show the way I saw it—with my own eyes and ears.

That's probably the way Cobain would have preferred it. According to the street buzz at the time, he literally agonized over the *Unplugged* project. He cherrypicked songs for the set lists, deliberately eliminating obvious crowd-pleasers ("Smells Like Teen Spirit," "Lithium") in favour of material that better suited the medium and the mood.

With the same generosity that he applied to selecting opening acts on tour, Cobain wanted to devote serious airtime to cover versions, pumping up some volume for a few of his undersung heroes. And he rehearsed the band rigorously, trying to establish a vibrant balance between delicate formality and raw emotion.

Courtney Love recently told me that she tried to get her husband to relax a little. Hey, this is television, you can always call a retake. But the perfectionist in him didn't buy it.

The night of the taping, Cobain and Nirvana—Krist Novoselic on acoustic bass and Squeezebox, Dave Grohl on light-limbed percussion, Pat Smear on sweet-and-sour guitar flourishes, Lori Goldston on heartbreaking cello moan—did the impossible. Fourteen songs, one take each.

When the last strains of "Where Did You Sleep Last Night?" finally died away, Cobain shyly acknowledged the eruption of cheers and applause, shambled over to the mixing desk for a brief word with someone in technical authority and then evaporated backstage.

To appreciate the enormity of that achievement, consider the *very long* night I spent with Neil Young at an *Unplugged* taping a year earlier.

Given his reputation as someone who has scrapped entire albums on the eve of release because of some microscopic flaw, Young was in typical form—putting his ad hoc band through as many as four takes per tune. After three hours of arduous repetition and technical re-adjustments, Young raised the White Flag. He sent the band packing and, as a consolation prize for the rest of us, performed a searing solo version of "Last Train to Tulsa" that was better than anything else played that night.

A few weeks later, Young re-taped the entire show and "Last Train to Tulsa" stayed in the can.

Cobain, on the other hand, was in and out of that studio inside an hour. He performed not for the cameras but for the crowd. He gave us his best—and left.

I remember a lot of things from that night. Like feeling embarrassed when a helpful Geffen publicist hustled me to the front of the guest-list line—and then feeling damn lucky when I got in early and nabbed a wonderful perch on a riser near the stage, with a tight-focus view of Cobain hunched over his guitar, screwing his face as he intently savoured, and spit out, every word into the microphone.

There were the candles and garlands cast across the stage, giving the event an air of almost religious sobriety—or, in retrospect, requiem. And there was the glint of challenge in Cobain's gravely voice as he started the show with "About A Girl," the rough diamond on *Bleach* that prefigured the pride-stripped-bare melancholia of "All Apologies" and "Something in the Way": "This is off our first record. Most people don't know it."

There was enough knowing applause to call his bluff. Oddly, the one song that was greeted by a disquieting hush was actually the best-known cover in the set, David Bowie's "The Man Who Sold the World." It was, and still is on the *Unplugged* record, a performance of passing-shadow revelation, its ironic take on snake oil celebrity and false promise grimly amplified by the sidewinder creep of the fuzztoned guitar hook and the ambiguous menace in Cobain's singing: *"I thought you died alone / A long, long time ago / Oh, no, not me / We never lost control."*

Today, there's an eerie after-resonance to almost every song that Cobain wrote for Nirvana; he borrowed this one but made it his own nonetheless.

The historic and emotional baggage attached to the posthumous release of *Unplugged* threatens to eclipse the humanity and wry humour that was also a great part of the night. Like the brief moments of comic, nervous indecision as Cobain turned to the band, with the camera still rolling, and asked, "Am I going to do this by myself?" Pause. Strum. "Do it yourself," Krist Novoselic replied.

"I think I'll try it in a different key," Cobain announced with droll derring-do. "I'll try it in a normal key. And, if it sounds bad, these people will just have to wait." Thin, crooked grin. Collective crowd giggle. At which point, Cobain invested everything he had in a solo version—just skeletal strumming and voice—of "Pennyroyal Tea," fraught with so much black energy and heart-stopping portent it still gives me shivers. The coda: after he's finished, someone behind Cobain on the bandstand says, "That sounded good." Cobain's response: a brusque, impish "Shut up!"

Then there was the crack about trying to get David Geffen to front Cobain half a million bucks so he could buy one of Leadbelly's original guitars. And the three-song segment devoted to the Meat Puppets (only two numbers made the cut in the original broadcast) was a warm, unexpected joy.

Cobain had long been a fan and advocate for the Meat Puppets, a first generation SST band that had stubbornly outlived labelmates like Hüsker Dü and The Minutemen, but had never enjoyed their just deserts. The Puppet songs Cobain picked for the show were all from *Meat Puppets II*, first released in 1983—back when Cobain was still living in Aberdeen, Washington, besotted with a local misfit band called the Melvins.

Yet "Plateau," "Oh Me," and "Lake of Fire" remain among the finest of Curt and Cris Kirkwood's early desert-voodoo cocktails of rickety campfire balladry, bent-pop melodicism and spitfire psychedelia, and the impact, however indirect, of the brothers' punky expeditions into Arizona gothic on Cobain's own writing later could be heard quite plainly in the acoustic recasting of Cobain's songs for *Unplugged.*

Tonight, he returned that favour by sharing his stage with the Kirkwoods, who lent major hippie hair presence to the evening and strummed with aplomb (those are Curt's rubbery acoustic riffs in the judgment-day blues "Lake of Fire")—a gesture that was of inestimable help in getting the Meat Puppet's next album, *Too High To Die,* in the American Top 40.

The signoff, "Where Did You Sleep Last Night?," a traditional folk lament long associated with Leadbelly and first recorded by Cobain with Mark Lanegan of Screaming Trees on a Lanegan solo album, was no surprise. Nirvana had been encoring with the song, unplugged, onstage every night.

Except, this time, you could hear the subtleties, the icepick stabs of hurt and accusation, with dramatic, disturbing clarity—like a wiretap into someone's war-torn bedroom. On a television programme frequently co-opted by name acts as a promotional vehicle for bogus fireside sensitivity (not to mention dressed-down re-runs of old hits for future CD release), Cobain finished the show with a fearless display of fresh blood and exposed nerves. The audience filed out, buzzing with admiration, but a little quieter and more pensive than usual.

In addition to the weight of circumstances that sits heavily on *Unplugged,* there is a burden of expectation that awaits it on release day— the hunger for easy answers to uneasy questions.

Is this what Cobain wanted to do with his songs—with or without Nirvana? Would Cobain's aborted plans to work with Michael Stipe bear similar folk-pop fruit?

Is rock 'n' roll such a lost cause in its middle age that even someone like Cobain—who found his voice in the music's most abrasive, vengeful-adolescent extremes—could so completely lose the faith?

That he never lost faith in music—as a healing force and as a vent of frustration and expression—was evident even in his last days, when he cut those last few Nirvana demos with Pat Smear and made those ill-fated plans to work with Stipe.

That he was coming to the end of his rope with the verse-chorus-scream cycle of fuzz-punk pop was no secret. "We have failed in showing the lighter, more dynamic side of our band," he told me during that *Rolling Stone* interview. "The big guitar sound is what the kids want to hear."

And Stipe himself has gone on record in recent *Monster* interviews as saying that what he and Cobain had talked about was a step or two beyond mere unplugging. Somewhere, he's mentioned Dylan's *Blood On The Tracks* album, and that there would have been Hammond organs in the mix—maybe.

But it's all conjecture. Wasted speculation. In blind desperation, immune even to his own native instincts, Kurt Cobain violently and deliberately ended his own life. If you really want to be cold about it, he abruptly altered the course of rock by removing himself from the gameboard. The stakes had gotten too high, the options too complicated, the rewards too suffocating.

The most consoling thing about the outpouring of grief and argument over Cobain's death—troubled young man or selfish bastard?—is that it has brought one of rock's unspoken dilemmas out into the open.

Who lives the bigger lie in rock stardom, the adored or the adoring? We treat celebrities as if they were to the manner born, not manufactured, holding them to higher standards of humanity, glamour and debauchery (occasionally all at the same time). They relish in the illusion, then complain about the responsibilities that come with reward.

Cobain got caught in a vice between the glory and the lie. He enjoyed the rush of blasting through the castle walls of the Eighties pop brahmin (Jackson, Springsteen, Madonna, Prince), then discovered the hidden costs of what he'd achieved. Ultimately, by his own skewed emotional arithmetic, he was compelled to pay up with his own life.

Who will replace Cobain in that space he made for himself in the music? I don't know—and don't care. A loss like this, and the tragic means to it, are not so casually quantifiable. And I would be an unforgivable cheat on Cobain's legacy to place absurd bets on surreal prospects: Eddie Vedder, the widow Courtney, the bigmouth singer in Oasis, that bouncy bassist in Green Day. Give it a rest. Now. Rock 'n' roll has been damn near crippled for the past 25 years by the endless and hopeless search for the Next Big Thing: the new Beatles/Stones/Dylan/Smiths/add-the-obsession-of-your-choice-here.

We spend too much time spinning out wheels in the past tense, consumed with hunger for the familiar. Sure, Cobain had his loves and idols: the Beatles, AC/DC, Daniel Johnson, the Raincoats, to name just a handful. But he was never a slave to them. And he'd be really pissed if everything he gave—and gave up—was reduced to a cheap sentiment like the New Nirvana or the Next Kurt Cobain.

His music and memory deserve better.

We owe him that much.

EVERETT TRUE

LOVE HANGOVER

Melody Maker, August 13, 1994

J C Dobbs, Philadelphia 1994

Life gets you like that sometimes.

I'm with Luscious Jackson, feeling real fine. Maybe this job ain't so bad after all. The band's just had their first decent meal in weeks, courtesy of the *Maker*: they're on a rare day off from Lollapolooza's traveling freakshow. We're cruising the main strip, checking out a sighting of Kim and Kelley Deal made six hours previously. We wander into the local rock club—coincidentally the last small club I ever saw Nirvana play—and suddenly life hits a major hiccup. Courtney Love is inside, readying herself to play onstage.

(In my heat-racked sleep, I hear Courtney walking up the stairs— loud, real loud—screaming my name, getting closer and closer. Someone is pounding on my hotel door. I wake in a cold sweat, expecting to find a dead body outside my room. Someone offers me a Rohypnol and I freak. This is not a dream.)

So, Courtney is about to play a live show and she looks good. Real good. But she also looks wasted. Real wasted. Over at the back, Kim Deal is holding court; falling over, a carton of cigarettes under her arm. She sees me and smiles conspiratorially. To one side, some Goats hang. To another, Tibetan monks are shooting pinball. Luscious Jackson looks a bit bewildered. A cool feminist poet buys Courtney a drink. Billy Corgan is also in the vicinity. Courtney tries to get him and me to make up: "But Everett, you'd *like* him. You're both scapegoats, you're both my closest friends. And he's so much like Kurt."

She forces us to touch hands. We both run. Literally.

(And, in my sweat-drenched sleep, I'm floundering. Famous rock stars queue up to make out with me and I'm helpless to resist. Kim Deal screams at me for half an hour, is real, real mean to me, and tears flow

down my face like blood. Someone calls my name and it's Thurston and Kim, holding court with their new-born baby outside CBGB's like visiting royalty. Someone offers me another shot of champagne and I freak. This has got to be a dream. Hasn't it? Please?)

So, Billy's onstage now and he looks pretty darn near wasted, too. He's giving some long rambling speech about his dark side, his misogynist side, and I suspect that in his own fumbling way he's attempting irony and it's mostly aimed in my direction. So I sound self-important? I'm so fucking sorry. It's the way I get treated, okay? Billy's telling the scummy audience about the time some girl-fan came up to his hotel room and asked him to sign her breasts and he refused (accepted?) and threw her half-naked out of the place. And then he laughs self-consciously and asks us to make way for Courtney Love, widow to the stars.

I blanch, and see if I can't get some industry scumbag to order me a double whiskey. No dice. No one knows who I am. When did I start to suffer from such terrifyingly real visions? And why?

(And in my darkest nightmare, people who really should know better are asking me whether I think Kurt would still be alive if he hadn't met Courtney. What, you mean if I hadn't introduced them that night back in L.A.? Fuck you. Just fucking fuck you. But these are only nightmares, right? Nothing to do with reality.)

And then Courtney is getting onstage, and she's giving a long preamble about . . . okay, about me and Billy Corgan, actually, and how we should make up and be friends, and also asking how many of the audience are Pisces like Kurt was and how she'll fuck them all afterwards, and we all laugh and clap and smile 'cos you can't help but admire Courtney—her strength, her humour, even through the darkest period of her life. Dont'cha all love a survivor? Ain't they so fucking cute?

(And in my nightmares, I see a totally wasted Courtney Love strap on a guitar in front of a crowd of disinterested people and I find myself unable to reach her, unable to help her. Why is she up there? Why is she putting herself through this? Does she want people to crucify her? Love her? Idolise her? Respect her? Maybe she just wants to prove to herself even someone who can make the front cover of People *magazine can still be real, still have soul. It doesn't seem like her life can be very real now. Except for the pain. Maybe the only place she has left to be real is on the stage, but she doesn't even have a band left to lend her music the dignity and support it deserves.)*

So, Courtney begins her three-song set with "Doll Parts" and it sounds like the first fucking time she ever played that song to me—down a Cricklewood phoneline at 4AM, alone in the kitchen at a party. Shambling, amateurish, absolutely painful to listen to, inward-turned, oblivious to what the outside world might care or think. *"I am / Doll parts / Doll face / Doll heart"* . . . it's as fine an example of bitter self-mockery as I have ever wanted to come close to. I can't fucking bring myself to watch her. I hide underneath plumes of cigarette smoke, silent tears creasing my face. People clap and cheer, dutifully. Wow! It's just like being in some crazy movie!

(And, in my darkest nightmare, it's May and I'm traveling with Hole bassist Kristen Pfaff through Europe, talking about what makes life vital and music worthwhile, laughing even through all the pain and I have a premonition that I'll never see her again. It's a nightmare. I ignore it. I'm still clearly freaked out by that guy Cobain's death.)

Courtney introduces her next song, "Penny Royaltea," the one she co-wrote with Kurt, with a long preamble about how former *Maker* Reviews Editor Jim Arundel once called it the worst song Nirvana ever played and simultaneously Hole's finest moment. The insult is implicit. But actually, Courtney, this is kinda true—mainly 'cos your version was so much more vicious than Kurt's. He treated the song almost as a throwaway; you completely tore it apart. Hole never were Nirvana. Period. Ever. And why the fuck would people—especially you, Courtney—want to compare the two bands? Tonight, "Penny Royaltea" sounds truly appalling—painful to listen to on any number of levels, not least for what it represents and the vast emptiness which is left in Courtney's life, which she will never fill, even if she were allowed to. It seems to last an eternity, what with all the false chords and false starts and Courtney's almost sobbing whisper of a scream dragging through painful evocations. Why is it her throaty, powerful roar of a voice still sounds so chilling?

(And through my pain, I see myself punching walls in Minneapolis, talking death with cool indie rock stars from Louisville, getting blasted on New York sidewalks, tears streaming down my face in planes going nowhere, listening to songs which can never hope to mirror the way I feel inside. A refrain from a Hole song keeps spiraling crazily inside my head, "Live through this with me / And I swear that I will die for you." I swear I don't even know what those words mean any more.)

I have a tape recorder in my bag, halfway through all this, it occurs to me I should switch it on. But why bother? This is not real. This is just some crazy fucked-up dream. And I can't begin to capture on tape what isn't there.

Courtney starts to leave, but decides one more will suffice: the single, "Miss World." A friend from one of the bands playing later tonight stands by, to lend support and add vocals where previously Kristen would've done. Her friend has her work cut out, that's for sure. Courtney is almost incoherent by now, staring at the ceiling, not even caring which chords or which notes she hits. *"I am a girl, so sick I cannot try."* For fuck's sake, Courtney. Please.

(And, in my dreams, I'm quoting lines from Blondie's "Atomic" to my best friend Courtney and telling her how her hair looks beautiful tonight. You looked fuckin' great tonight, Courtney. Really.)

Chronology

Have you not done tormenting me with your accursed time! It's abominable! When! When!

—Samuel Beckett, *Waiting for Godot*

Nirvana	The World
1959	William S. Burroughs publishes *Naked Lunch*.
1965 Krist Novoselic is born.	The Beatles release *Rubber Soul*.
1966	The Beatles release *Revolver*. After John Lennon quips, "We are more popular than Jesus now," people all across America burn Beatles albums.
1967 Kurt Cobain is born.	The war in Vietnam escalates as do the protests against it. The Beatles release *Sergeant Pepper's Lonely Hearts Club Band*.
1968	The Beatles release *The White Album*. Martin Luther King, Jr. and Robert Kennedy are assassinated.
1969 Dave Grohl is born.	The Beatles release *Abbey Road*. Jack Kerouac and Ho Chi Minh die. The first U.S. troops are withdrawn from Vietnam, and President Richard Nixon begins secretly bombing Cambodia. The Stooges release their first album. The Manson murders occur.

1970		The Beatles break up. Jimi Hendrix and Janis Joplin die. National guardsmen kill four students at Kent State University. The Stooges release *Fun House*.
1971		Jim Morrison is found dead in Paris.
1973		Pablo Picasso dies. His last words are reportedly, "Painting remains to be invented."
1974		Facing impeachment, President Nixon resigns. President Gerald Ford pardons him.
1975		The war in Vietnam is declared "finished" as Communist forces capture Saigon.
1976		Jimmy Carter elected president. The Ramones release their first album.
1977		The Sex Pistols release *Never Mind the Bollocks: Here's the Sex Pistols*. A year later they perform their last show in San Francisco.
1980		John Lennon is shot to death in New York. Ronald Reagan is elected president. Hostages held in Iran are released.
1981		John Hinckley attempts to assassinate President Reagan in Washington. Reagan recovers and several months later fires striking air traffic controllers.
1983		U.S. forces invade Grenada. The Meat Puppets release *Meat Puppets II*.
1984		Nicaragua files a suit against the United States in the World Court over the CIA's covert operations.
1985	Kurt meets Krist and they begin to play music together.	Mikhail Gorbachev is elected the new leader of the Soviet Union. Sonic Youth release *Bad Moon Rising*.
1986		The space shuttle *Challenger* explodes after takeoff. The nuclear power plant at Chernobyl, Ukraine,

also explodes. First reports of the Iran-Contra affair are released, and at the end of the year Reagan says that he made a "mistake" in agreeing to trade arms for hostages. Sonic Youth release *EVOL*.

1987   The first lineup of Nirvana is formed with Aaron Burckhard on drums.

A fourteen-year-old girl is abducted as she leaves a punk show. She is raped and tortured by a man named Gerald Friend. (Kurt Cobain later writes "Polly" based on the incident.) Sonic Youth release *Sister*.

1988   Nirvana—with Dale Crover on drums—records a demo with Jack Endino. The Sub Pop label hears the tape and offers to record Nirvana's first single.

George Bush is elected president. Sonic Youth release the aptly titled *Daydream Nation*. The Pixies release *Surfer Rosa*.

1989   Nirvana releases *Bleach*. The band embarks on their first European tour with Tad.

A massive demonstration in Tiananmen Square is crushed by Chinese troops. The Berlin Wall falls on Nov. 9. Near the end of the year, U.S. forces invade Panama. Soundgarden release *Louder Than Love*. Samuel Beckett dies.

1990   Dave Grohl joins Nirvana.

In Yugoslavia, the first elections are held since the death of Tito. Nelson Mandela is freed. Sonic Youth release *Goo*.

1991   Nirvana signs with Geffen/DGC and tours Europe with Sonic Youth. *Nevermind* is released in September and by October the record is certified gold. MTV starts to air "Smells Like Teen Spirit" continuously.

The Persian Gulf War begins and lasts a little over a month. Croatia and Slovenia declare their independence from Yugoslavia. Fighting erupts, but a precarious peace agreement is reached.

1992   On Jan. 11, *Nevermind* knocks everybody out of the way and takes the #1 spot on the U.S. *Billboard* charts. It soon becomes the #1 album in Belgium, France, Ireland, Israel, Spain, Sweden, and Canada. In February, Kurt Cobain and Courtney Love are married. In April, the band appears on the cover of *Rolling Stone*. The band tours Australia, Japan, and Europe. Frances Bean Cobain is born. The

The fragile peace in what used to be Yugoslavia is shattered and civil war ensues. Rumors of "ethnic cleansing" quickly spread. In Los Angeles, riots erupt after a not-guilty verdict is delivered in the Rodney King case. Bill Clinton is elected president.

band plays the *MTV Video Music Awards*. *Incesticide* is released in December.

1993 Nirvana plays a benefit for Bosnian rape victims at the Cow Palace in San Francisco. In September, *In Utero* is released. Later in the year Nirvana tours the U.S. with Pat Smear in the lineup. The band performs on *MTV Unplugged*.

The Melvins release *Houdini*, an album coproduced by Kurt Cobain.

1994 Kurt Cobain is found dead, the result of a self-inflicted gunshot wound. *MTV Unplugged in New York* is released.

Guy Debord shoots himself in the heart. Hole releases *Live Through This*. Charles Bukowski dies.

1995

Sonic Youth release *Washing Machine*.

1996 *From the Muddy Banks of the Wishkah* is released.

1997

Soundgarden break up. Allen Ginsberg and William S. Burroughs die.

Selected Discography

The following is a list of U.S. singles, EPs, and albums. For more detailed documentation of Nirvana's recordings, see Gillian G. Gaar's "Verse Chorus Verse: The Recording History of Nirvana" on page 164.

Singles and EPs

Love Buzz/Big Cheese (Sub Pop, 1988)

Blew (Tupelo, 1989)

Mexican Seafood, on the compilation *Teriyaki Asthma Vol. 1* (C/Z, 1989)

Sliver/Dive (Sub Pop, 1990)

Molly's Lips/Candy by The Fluid (Sub Pop, 1991)

Here She Comes Now/Venus in Furs, by the Melvins (Communion, 1991)

Smells Like Teen Spirit/Even in His Youth/Aneurysm (Geffen/DGC, 1991)

Come As You Are/School/Drain You (Geffen/DGC, 1992)

Lithium/Been a Son/Curmudgeon (Geffen/DGC, 1992)

Oh, the Guilt/Puss, by the Jesus Lizard (Touch and Go, 1993)

Albums

Bleach (Sub Pop, 1989)

Nevermind (Geffen/DGC, 1991)

Incesticide (Geffen/DGC, 1992)

In Utero (Geffen/DGC, 1993)

MTV Unplugged in New York (Geffen/DGC, 1994)

From the Muddy Banks of the Wishkah (Geffen/DGC, 1996)

Other Important Recordings

Spank Thru, on *Sub Pop 200* (Sub Pop, 1988)

Where Did You Sleep Last Night? on Mark Lanegan's *The Winding Sheet* (Sub Pop, 1990) (Cobain on guitar, Novoselic on bass)

Beeswax, on *Kill Rock Stars* (Kill Rock Stars, 1991)

Verse Chorus Verse, on *No Alternative* (Arista, 1993)

I Hate Myself and I Want to Die, on *The Beavis and Butt-head Experience* (Geffen, 1993)

The "Priest" They Called Him, by William S. Burroughs (Tim Kerr, 1993) (Cobain on guitar)

Pay to Play, on *DGC Rarities Vol. 1* (Geffen/DGC, 1994)

Essential Films

1991: The Year That Punk Broke (Geffen Video)

Hype! (Republic Video)

Live! Tonight! Sold Out! (Geffen Video)

Selected Bibliography

Arnold, Gina. *Kiss This: Punk in the Present Tense*. New York: St. Martin's Press, 1997.

———. *Route 666: The Road to Nirvana*. New York: St. Martin's Press, 1993.

Artaud, Antonin. *The Theater and Its Double*. Translated by Mary Caroline Richards. New York: Grove Weidenfeld, 1958.

Azerrad, Michael. *Come As You Are: The Story of Nirvana*. New York: Doubleday, 1994.

Bangs, Lester. *Psychotic Reactions and Carburetor Dung*. Edited by Greil Marcus. New York: Vintage Books, 1988.

———. "In Which Another Pompous Blowhard Purports to Possess the True Meaning of Punk Rock." In *The Penguin Book of Rock 'n' Roll Writing*, edited by Clinton Heylin. New York: Penguin, 1992.

Bayley, Roberta, et al. *Blank Generation Revisited: The Early Days of Punk Rock*. New York: Schirmer Books, 1997.

Baudrillard, Jean. *America*. Translated by Chris Turner. London and New York: Verso, 1988.

———. *Simulations*. Translated by Paul Foss, Paul Patton, and Philip Beitchman. New York: Semiotext(e), 1983.

Beckett, Samuel. *Collected Shorter Plays*. New York: Grove Press, 1984.

———. *The Complete Short Prose 1929–1989*. New York: Grove Press, 1995.

———. *Endgame*. New York: Grove Press, 1958.

———. *Molloy, Malone Dies, and The Unnameable.* New York: Grove Press, 1958.

———. *Waiting for Godot.* New York: Grove Press, 1954.

Bracken, Len. *Guy Debord—Revolutionary.* Venice, Calif.: Feral House, 1997.

Bockris, Victor, and Gerard Malanga. *Up-Tight: The Story of the Velvet Underground.* New York: Omnibus Press, 1986.

Bockris, Victor. *With William Burroughs: A Report from the Bunker.* New York: St. Martin's/Griffen, 1996.

Bukowski, Charles. *Erections, Ejaculations, Exhibitions and General Tales of Ordinary Madness.* Edited by Gail Chiarrello. San Francisco: City Lights, 1967.

———. *Notes of a Dirty Old Man.* Santa Rosa, Calif.: Black Sparrow Press, 1969.

———. *Poems Written before Jumping out of an 8 Story Window.* Santa Rosa, Calif.: Black Sparrow Press, 1968.

———. *Septuagenarian Stew: Stories and Poems.* Santa Rosa, Calif.: Black Sparrow Press, 1990.

Burroughs, William S. *The Exterminator.* New York: Grove Press, 1973.

———. *Junky.* New York: Grove Press, 1953.

———. *The Last Words of Dutch Schultz.* New York: Arcade, 1973.

———. *Naked Lunch.* New York: Grove Press, 1959.

———. *Nova Express.* New York: Grove Press, 1964.

———. *My Education: A Book of Dreams.* New York: Penguin, 1995.

———. *The Soft Machine.* New York: Grove Press, 1966.

———. *The Ticket That Exploded.* New York: Grove Press, 1966.

Crisafulli, Chuck. *Teen Spirit: The Stories behind Every Nirvana Song.* New York: Simon and Schuster, 1996.

Dalton, David. *El Sid: Saint Vicious.* New York: St. Martin's Press, 1997.

Davies, Hunter. *The Beatles: The Authorized Biography.* New York: McGraw-Hill, 1978.

Debord, Guy. *The Society of the Spectacle.* Translated by Donald Nicholson-Smith. New York: Zone Books, 1994.

Ferguson, Sarah. "The Comfort of Being Sad." *Utne Reader* (July/August 1994): 60–62.

Foege, Alec. *Confusion is Next: The Sonic Youth Story.* New York: St. Martin's Press, 1994.

Fricke, David. "Radio Friendly Unit Shifters." *Melody Maker,* July 31, 1993, 6–7.

Ginsberg, Allen. *Collected Poems: 1947–1980.* New York: Harper and Row, 1984.

Gordon, Kim. "American Prayers." *Artforum* 23, no. 8 (April 1985): 73–77.

———. "I'm Really Scared When I Kill in My Dreams." *Artforum* 21, no. 5 (January 1983): 54–57.

Heylin, Clinton. *From the Velvets to the Voidoids: A Pre-Punk History for a Post-Punk World.* New York: Penguin, 1993.

———, ed. *The Penguin Book of Rock 'n' Roll Writing.* New York: Penguin, 1992.

Humphrey, Clark. *Loser: The Real Seattle Music Story.* Portland: Feral House, 1995.

Kant, Immanuel. *On History.* Translated by Lewis White Beck, Robert E. Anchor, and Emil L. Fackenheim. Indianapolis: Bobbs Merrill, 1963.

Kellner, Douglas. *The Persian Gulf TV War.* Boulder and Oxford: Westview Press, 1992.

Kerouac, Jack. *On the Road.* New York: Signet, 1957.

Kierkegaard, Søren. *A Kierkegaard Anthology.* Edited by Robert Bretall. Princeton University Press, 1969.

Lydon, John. *Rotten: No Irish, No Blacks, No Dogs.* New York: St. Martin's Press, 1994.

Marcus, Greil. *Lipstick Traces: A Secret History of the Twentieth Century.* Cambridge: Harvard University Press, 1989.

———. *Mystery Train: Images of America in Rock 'n' Roll Music.* New York: E. P. Dutton, 1975.

———. *Ranters and Crowd Pleasers: Punk in Pop Music, 1977–1992.* New York: Doubleday, 1993.

Marx, Karl. *Civil War in France: The Paris Commune.* New York: International Publishers, 1940.

————. *Early Writings.* Translated by Rodney Livingstone and Gregor Benton. London: Penguin, 1974.

————. *The 18th Brumarie of Louis Bonaparte.* New York: International Publishers, 1963.

McNeil, Legs and Gillian McCain. *Please Kill Me: The Uncensored Oral History of Punk.* New York: Penguin, 1996.

Moore, Thurston. "Stabb's Hand Touched Me and I Slept." In *The Penguin Book of Rock 'n' Roll Writing,* edited by Clinton Heylin. New York: Penguin, 1992

Morrell, Brad. *Nirvana and the Sound of Seattle.* London: Omnibus Press, 1993.

Palmer, Robert. *Deep Blues.* New York: Penguin, 1991.

————. *Rock 'n' Roll: An Unruly History.* New York: Harmony Books, 1995.

Pater, Walter. *The Renaissance.* New York: Oxford University Press, 1986.

Pop, Iggy, and Anne Wehrer. *I Need More.* Los Angeles: 2.13.61 Publications, Inc., 1982.

The editors of *Rolling Stone. Cobain.* New York: Rolling Stone Press, 1994.

Sanford, Christopher. *Kurt Cobain.* New York: Carroll and Graf Publishers, Inc., 1995.

Savage, Jon. *England's Dreaming: Anarchy, Sex Pistols, Punk Rock, and Beyond.* New York: St. Martin's Press, 1992.

Süskind, Patrick. *Perfume.* Translated by John E. Woods. New York: Pocket Books, 1986.

Thompson, Dave. *Never Fade Away: The Kurt Cobain Story.* New York: St. Martin's Press, 1994.

Thompson, Elizabeth and David Gutman. *The John Lennon Companion.* New York: Schirmer Books, 1996.

True, Everett. "Sleepless in Seattle." *Melody Maker,* December 25, 1993, 66–68.

Tytell, John. *Naked Angels: The Lives and Literature of the Beat Generation.* New York: Grove Press, 1976.

Wiener, John. *Come Together: John Lennon in His Time.* Urbana and Chicago: University of Illinois Press, 1984.

Zak, Albin III. *The Velvet Underground Companion.* New York: Schirmer Books, 1997.

About the Contributors

Kevin Allman writes for *The Advocate*.

Dawn Anderson is one of the few people to have actually been born in Seattle. She was the editor of *Backlash,* an all-local Seattle rock 'zine, from 1987 to 1991. She has also written about rock music for *The Rocket, The Seattle Times, The Seattle Weekly,* and others.

Gina Arnold is the author of *Route 666: The Road to Nirvana* and *Kiss This: Punk in the Present Tense.*

William S. Burroughs changed literature several times. His life and work also inspired the punk movement. (You can see him in Gus Van Sant's film *Drugstore Cowboy.*) His books include *Junky, Naked Lunch, The Ticket That Exploded, Cities of the Red Night, Queer,* and *My Education: A Book of Dreams.* He died in 1997.

David Fricke is a senior editor at *Rolling Stone.* He joined the magazine in 1985. He has also written for *Melody Maker, Musician, Mojo, People,* and *The New York Times.* He is the author of *Animal Instinct,* a biography of Def Leppard, and he has written liner notes for major CD reissues by the Byrds, Moby Grape, the Velvet Underground, John Prine, and Led Zeppelin.

Gillian G. Gaar has been writing about music, film, and popular culture for over eighteen years and has written for *Rolling Stone, Q, Pulse, Option,* and *Goldmine,* among other publications. Her book, *She's a*

Rebel: The History of Women in Rock, was published in 1992. She has also contributed to several books: *A Survey of American Culture, Scribner's American Biography, The Scribner Encyclopedia of American Lives, Music Central '96* (a CD-ROM) and *Trouble Girls: The Rolling Stone Book of Women in Rock.* Gaar worked at *The Rocket,* Seattle's music biweekly, where she was Senior Editor; her review of *From the Muddy Banks of the Wishkah* in that publication won a Music Journalism Award in 1997 in the "Regional Periodicals, Criticism or Review" category. She lives in Seattle.

Joe Gore writes for *Guitar Player Magazine.*

L. A. Kanter writes for *Guitar Player Magazine.*

Patrick MacDonald writes for *The Seattle Times.*

Jon Pareles is one of America's most respected music critics. He currently writes about music for the *New York Times.*

Craig Rosen writes for *Billboard.*

Deborah Russell writes for *Billboard.*

Darcey Steinke writes for *Spin.* She has also written two marvelous novels: *Suicide Blonde* and *Jesus Saves.*

Everett True supplied the following bio for himself:

Born: 1961
Starsign: Taurus
Personality: bullish
Hobbies: playing piano, collecting toys, attending rock concerts
Favourite colour: yellow
Favourite food: cheese
Favourite drink: tea
Favourite animal: cat
Favourite sport: Mario Kart Racing
Favourite musician: Nina Simone
Favourite album: Dexy's Midnight Runners' Don't Stand Me Down
Favourite song: Irma Thomas's "Coming from Behind"
Favourite film: Breakfast at Tiffany's

Carreer to Date:

1981–89   Silkscreen painter (Robert Seabright's)

1984–88   Freelance writer (NME)

1988–1992   Staff writer (Melody Maker)

1992–1997   Assistant Editor (Melody Maker)

1997   Editor (Vox)

Highlight of career (to date):   Huggy Bear interview

Ambition: not to be lonely

Permissions

Index

About the Editors

John Rocco t   lished
articles in the   *rnity,*
and *High Ti*   ooks,
1997) and is   *of the*
Grateful Dea

Brian Rocco